M. TULLI CICERONIS

PRO ARCHIA
POETA ORATIO

ANNOTATED COLLECTION

Cicero: *Pro Archia Poeta Oratio*, Third Edition (2014)
Horace: Selected *Odes* and *Satire* 1.9, Second Edition Revised (2014)
Ovid: *Amores, Metamorphoses* Selections, Third Edition (2013)
Writing Passion: A Catullus Reader, Second Edition (2013)
Writing Passion Plus: A Catullus Reader Supplement (2013)

Forthcoming
Cicero: *De Amicitia*, Second Edition
Cicero: *Pro Caelio*, Fourth Edition

CICERO

Pro Archia Poeta Oratio

3rd edition

Introduction
Text
Vocabulary
and
Commentary

by

Steven M. Cerutti

With a Foreword By
Lawrence Richardson, jr

Bolchazy-Carducci Publishers, Inc.
Mundelein, Illinois USA

General Editor: Gaby Huebner

Contributing Editors: Aaron Baker, Laurie Haight Keenan, Bridget Dean, Laurel Draper

Cover Design: Adam Phillip Velez

Cover Illustrations: This denarius, minted in Rome ca. 66 BCE by Q. Pomponius Musa, is one of a series of nine types, each depicting on its reverse one of the nine muses. Shown here is Calliope, the Muse of epic poetry, playing the lyre while resting it on a column. (Photograph courtesy of the American Numismatic Society); Background illustration of Modern-day Arpinum © 2006 Patricia Lynn Miller

AP is a registered trademark of the College Entrance Examination Board, which was not involved in the production of, and does not endorse, this product.

Cicero: Pro Archia Poeta Oratio
Third Edition

Steven M. Cerutti

Bolchazy-Carducci Publishers, Inc.
1570 Baskin Road
Mundelein, Illinois 60060
www.bolchazy.com

Printed in the United States of America
2014
by United Graphics

ISBN 978-0-86516-805-3

Library of Congress Cataloging-in-Publication Data

Cicero, Marcus Tullius, author.
  [Pro Archia]
  Pro Archia poeta : oratio / Cicero ; introduction, text, vocabulary and commentary by Steven M. Cerutti ; with a foreword by Lawrence Richardson, Jr. -- 3rd edition.
      pages cm
  Includes bibliographical references and index.
  ISBN 978-0-86516-805-3 (pbk. : alk. paper) 1. Cicero, Marcus Tullius. Pro Archia. I. Cerutti, Steven M. II. Title.
  PA6279.A9C47 2014
  875'.01--dc23

                                                                    2014016421

For Larry and Em

CONTENTS

FOREWORD

No other speech of Cicero's, possibly no selection of Latin prose, better repays close reading than the defense of the poet Archias. It is the epitome of what Latin at its very best can be, almost every sentence a jewel shaped and polished to perfection, elegant, lucid, a delight to the ear and the understanding. It is a brief speech, spare in its presentation of the legal aspects of the case, clearly structured, graceful in its handling of its appeal to the jury. But the *Pro Archia* goes beyond the necessity of defending a beloved and admired teacher in a lawsuit intended by the prosecution to embarrass rather his patrons and supporters than the defendant himself. It opens up the larger question of the value of literature, its endurance and humanizing quality, its rich appeal to the finer side of man's nature. As an introduction to Cicero as a humanist and the breadth of his approach it is unequaled, and it shows him at his best as a successful pleader, as a literary stylist, and as a dedicated humanist.

This speech was for many years a staple in the Latin curriculum of the schools; one usually read it immediately after the Catilinarians. More recently it has been neglected; changes in language instruction and the lack of a suitable edition squeezed it out of common use. But it deserves better; it makes a perfect introduction not only to Cicero but to Latin as a literary language. Students coming to Latin older and more sophisticated than used to be the case will find it a many-faceted delight: historically fascinating, linguistically exquisite, rhetorically compelling, a richly informative experience. It is to serve that purpose that the present edition has been put together and is offered, designed to be read as soon as a student has mastered the rudiments of Latin grammar and syntax, and therefore provided with facing vocabulary lists and an especially full apparatus of notes on grammatical and rhetorical features.

L. RICHARDSON, JR
James B. Duke Professor of Latin
Duke University

PREFACE TO THE THIRD EDITION

I ncorporated into this new edition of Cicero's *Pro Archia Poeta Oratio* are eight passages from Quintilian's *Institutio Oratoria*, each chosen for its relevance to a specific section of the speech and interleaved into the text. By including these excerpts from Quintilian's famous exposition of his theory of educating Rome's privileged sons in the art of forensic oratory, it is my hope and aim to enhance students' appreciation for Cicero's rhetorical artistry as the leading advocate and legal mind of his time. Of no less importance is the keen insight that Quintilian brings to the practice and methodology of the art of Cicero's oratory, which he holds up as the model, the example, the standard, to be followed by all serious students of forensic rhetoric. I am confident that these selections from the *Institutio Oratoria* will provide an excellent complement to Cicero's *Pro Archia*, not just because Quintilian's work shares with Cicero's the theme of the importance of a liberal arts education, but also because it informs so well on the principles and practices of oratory and advocacy in the true Ciceronian tradition. Furthermore, because Quintilian modeled his own prose style so faithfully on that of Cicero, these eight new passages will prove not only instructive, but also a joy to read. Indeed, if one had to sum up Quintilian in a word, that word would be "Ciceronian."

Students who go on to read Latin at the upper levels are taught that as the Latin language evolved from the republic of Caesar and Cicero, to the empire of Statius and Seneca, later Latin literature (referred to by many scholars, unfortunately, by the pejorative sobriquet "Silver Latin") became more compressed, its sentences more elliptical and epigrammatic. While this is arguably the case, there are the exceptions that prove the rule. Just as Seneca's philosophical dialogues, like those of Cicero, are wonderfully accessible to the intermediate student for their simplicity of language and clarity of thought, so too is the case with Quintilian's Latinity, for its observance of the periodic style that students of Cicero come to embrace as one of his most enduring and endearing trademarks. Indeed, one could say that Quintilian, in holding Cicero up as his own stylistic *praeceptor*, was following his advice to his young and rising readership of Rome's future orators:

...oratorem sibi aliquem, quod apud maiores fieri solebat, deligat, quem sequatur, quem imitetur.

Let the student choose for himself a particular orator—a practice that used to happen among our ancestors—a man whom he will follow, a man whom he will imitate. (*Inst.* 10.5.19)

Each passage is complete with facing vocabulary and its own apparatus of notes on grammatical and rhetorical features.

Steven M. Cerutti
New Year's Day, 2014

PREFACE

USING THIS BOOK

This commentary was produced with one simple, albeit ambitious goal in mind: to make Cicero's *Pro Archia* accessible to students as early as the second year of their study of Latin in high schools, colleges, and universities. Because it is more than likely, therefore, that this speech will be a student's first encounter with a complete, unabridged Latin text, the notes were designed to facilitate translation by identifying noun cases and verb forms and explaining grammatical constructions and syntactical peculiarities. But because it is impossible to master the complexity of Latin grammar without also having a basic understanding of the rhetorical elements that are an integral part of the fabric and structure of the Latin language, this commentary also attempts to introduce the student to the rhetorical devices that are basic to the composition of formal Latin prose, particularly those that are trademarks of Cicero's oratory.

Vocabulary is always a major obstacle to the neophyte at Latin; therefore, this edition also contains a running vocabulary list that corresponds to the text and appears on facing pages. Included in this list are all but the most basic Latin words, glossed in standard, dictionary format. The second time a word occurs, it is marked with an asterisk; the third time, two asterisks; the fourth time, three asterisks, and thereafter it is dropped from the list. The purpose behind this is simple: Cicero tends to use a rich, but not unlimited vocabulary, and like every author (or politician, for that matter) he has his favorite words and expressions, and these recur with some regularity. Since the *Pro Archia* is one of Cicero's shortest speeches, it is likely that the student, after seeing a word glossed four times, will, on the fifth encounter with the word, be able to recognize it and, in context, recall its meaning.

Several other features of this edition will also prove useful to both student and teacher alike. Appendix I contains a glossary of proper names and places, so that space in the commentary need not be taken up with long explanations of the numerous historical figures and geographical locations to which Cicero alludes in the course of the speech. Moreover, whenever a rhetorical device, figure of speech, or political office is treated in the commentary, its name appears in small capitals (e.g., HENDIADYS, CHIASMUS, CONSUL, PRAETOR, etc.), indicating that a definition of the term can be found in the glossary of Appendix II. Those figures of speech required for the Advanced Placement Test are indicated by a dagger (†). Finally, a complete Latin lexicon for the speech is supplied at the end of the volume.

The Text

As is the case for all surviving works of Latin literature, the *Pro Archia* did not pass into our hands without certain problems arising from the transmission and compilation of the manuscripts through which it was preserved over the centuries. Fortunately, the text of the speech as we have it today is for the most part sound. For those few passages where textual emendation was needed, I generally employed the suggestions of editors in which the sense was easiest to follow. Because a commentary designed for students of Latin at the intermediate level should not burden its readers with cumbersome, detailed explanations of textual matters, I have kept discussion of these to a minimum. The text of the speech that follows, therefore, while it is based on A. C. Clark's 1911 Oxford text and is numbered according to its thirty-two consecutive sections, is unique to this edition: capitalization and punctuation are my own, and in order to facilitate the correspondence between text, notes, and running vocabulary, consecutive line numbering (1–397) has been used throughout.

Acknowledgments

For her careful attention to the writing and the content of the commentary, I would like to express most sincere gratitude to Linda Fabrizio, without whose oversight this second edition, designed to prepare students for the Advanced Placement examination, would not have been possible. Furthermore, I will forever remain in debt to Lawrence Richardson, jr, Brian Hook, and Joseph J. Hughes, friends and colleagues, for reading early drafts of this manuscript, testing them in their classrooms, and thus saving me, as always, from many embarrassing errors and oversights.

    I must especially thank Alex Cuff, Deanya Lattimore, and John Scott, students in my *Age of Cicero* seminar, who suffered through an early draft of this commentary and kept honed the edge of my didactic resolve. I feel I speak for them, and for all future students of Cicero for whom this commentary was written, when I finally acknowledge Ladislaus Bolchazy, whose personal commitment to the formidable task of keeping Classics alive and lively in the classroom made this edition, and others like it, possible.

STEVEN M. CERUTTI
New Year's Day, 2006

INTRODUCTION

LIFE OF CICERO

Marcus Tullius Cicero was born on 3 January, 106 B.C., in Arpinum, a small town in the Volscian hills about seventy miles southeast of Rome; he died on 7 December, 43 B.C., one of the first victims of the proscriptions carried out by Mark Antony and Octavian following the appointment of the Second Triumvirate. Had Cicero survived another twenty-four days, he would have lived a full sixty-four years, the better part of what would be the last century of the Roman republic. Despite his death at the hands of Antony's soldiers, Cicero's career as Rome's consummate statesman transcends that of any of his contemporaries, and the orations, philosophical dialogues, and letters that survive him continue to speak their volumes to us—enduring beyond, and seemingly independent of, the historical period in which he wrote them.

It would be impossible here to present anything like a complete biography of Cicero, a man who dedicated his life to public service and the defense of his friends; who survived three civil wars and periods of undeserved exile from the fatherland he loved. For our purposes, it must be enough to provide a brief sketch of Cicero's life and career leading up to his delivery of the *Pro Archia* in 62 B.C.; for those interested in further reading on this subject, biographical studies abound, and several good ones are included in the bibliography.

It was expected of all young men with political aspirations to begin their careers with military service. Cicero, however, seemed to find army life distasteful, and so carried out as brief a military tour as he could. He served first under Cn. Pompeius Strabo from 90 to 89 B.C., and in the following year under L. Cornelius Sulla in the Social War, a civil conflict in which the Italian allied towns (*municipia*), which had long been seeking the franchise of Roman citizenship, rose up in arms against Rome. Although Rome emerged victorious, the complicated political arrangement that would be reached in the settlement gave the Italian allies most of what they had been after in the first place. Cicero, no doubt relieved to see his military service at an end, returned to his education, the focus of which, as for most young Romans on the fast track to a career in the public courts, was rhetoric. At some point during this period, probably in his late teens or early twenties, Cicero wrote his first major work, the *De Inventione Rhetorica*, a treatise—some would say a textbook—on rhetorical composition. It was the first of many books on the theory and practice of oratory that Cicero would produce in his lifetime.

Cicero's career as a lawyer (*patronus*) began to take shape in 81 B.C. with his defense of P. Quinctius, a relatively insignificant private suit. Cicero was twenty-six years old. We can assume he won, as the speech survives, and also because in the following year, during the dictatorship of Sulla, Cicero landed an important, high-profile case: the defense of Sex. Roscius of Ameria on a trumped-up charge of having murdered his father (*parricidium*) in order to inherit the family estate. As it was the first murder trial to be held under the jurisdiction of Sulla's newly-established *quaestio de sicariis et veneficiis*, a court reserved exclusively for cases involving murder, it must have been somewhat of a sensation. So, when Cicero won acquittal for his client by exposing a key member of Sulla's staff as the true culprit, he was well on his way, at the young age of twenty-seven, to establishing himself as Rome's leading *patronus*. Furthermore, that he had managed not to implicate the dictator Sulla in the misdeeds of his henchman showed Cicero's political savvy.

But it was impossible to build a successful legal career without also mounting the CURSUS HONORUM, Rome's political ladder. Therefore Cicero, at the minimum legal age of thirty, successfully stood for election to the office of QUAESTOR for the year 75 B.C., the first magistracy in the series of one-year elective offices (*honores*) culminating, for the lucky few, in the highest magistracy of state, the consulship. Cicero served his quaestorship under Sex. Peducaeus, who was then serving his second year as governor of western Sicily, one of Rome's richest provinces. Upon returning to Rome Cicero spent the next few years once again pursuing his career before the bar when in 70 B.C., C. Verres, governor of Sicily from 73–70 B.C., was accused of corruption in the management of his province. Cicero was chosen to conduct the prosecution, and he carried the case to a brilliant victory. But for Cicero, even more significant than winning the conviction of a man such as Verres, who had far more social and political connections than he, was the fact that the man defending Verres was none other than Q. Hortensius Hortalus, a seasoned statesman and Rome's leading *patronus* at the time. This victory firmly established Cicero as, if not yet Rome's premier *patronus*, then certainly a serious contender for the title. Moreover, the gratitude of the Sicilian envoys that came to Rome for the trial ensured that the rest of Cicero's political career would be generously bankrolled.

In the same year that he prosecuted Verres, Cicero stood for election to the office of AEDILE. As with the quaestorship, Cicero reached this next office on the CURSUS HONORUM at the minimum legal age: thirty-six. Next, in 67 B.C., he was elected to the office of PRAETOR, again at the minimum age: thirty-nine. Finally, in 63 B.C., at the minimum age of forty-three, he held Rome's highest honor: the office of CONSUL.

63 B.C. was a banner year for Cicero. Not only was he a *novus homo* ("new man")—that is, the first member of his *gens* ("family") to attain Rome's highest office—but that year marked his highest service to the state. In the consular elections of the previous year, one of the candidates Cicero had defeated was L. Sergius Catilina (generally referred to as "Catiline"), a Roman of the noblest birth, but also a demagogue of dangerous potential. Presenting himself a second time in July of 63 B.C. for the consulship of 62 B.C., Catiline failed once again to be elected; and so, having run himself into debt in the course of two failed attempts at winning the consulship, he hatched a conspiracy to overthrow the government. Thanks to informants among Catiline's household slaves, Cicero got wind of the plot and, in his famous four "Catilinarian Orations," delivered toward the end of 63 B.C., Cicero exposed Catiline's plans to the senate and urged them to pass a *senatus consultum ultimum*, a virtual declaration of martial law that empowered the two CONSULS to take whatever steps necessary to ensure the safety of the state. Catiline himself fled Rome even before Cicero could deliver the last of his four Catilinarian orations, but in his haste to leave the city he left behind him several key conspirators whom Cicero, acting on the advice of the senate, had executed on the 5th of December. Cicero would later argue that the gravity of the situation and the seriousness of the conspirators' crimes had given him the authority to do this, but, as he had failed to grant the conspirators a trial or appeal to the Roman people, he was on dubious legal ground at best. The fact that all five conspirators, among whom was the PRAETOR P. Cornelius Lentulus Sura, were from notable Roman aristocratic families, would also come back to haunt him.

Some five years after the execution of the conspirators Cicero paid a heavy price for his actions. P. Clodius Pulcher, a young and reckless aristocrat, had harbored a grudge against Cicero because Cicero had publicly testified in court against him in the trial following the *Bona*

Dea scandal of 61 B.C. In 58 B.C., Clodius passed a bill into law stating
that anyone who had executed a Roman citizen without a trial before
the people should be banished from Rome. As if to remove any doubt
that this bill was aimed at Cicero, Clodius passed a second bill naming
him specifically. Though this second bill was most certainly unconsti-
tutional, as it was aimed at a single individual, Cicero left Rome for
Thessalonica in Macedonia, where he would spend the better part of a
year in miserable exile.

Cicero would be recalled from exile by popular demand in the following year; but the Rome to which he returned had changed. That
a demagogue such as Clodius could have used the Roman constitu-
tion—the very institution that Cicero had spent so much of his life
serving—against him carried a message: the final days of the republic
were in sight.

LIFE OF ARCHIAS AND THE PRO ARCHIA

What little we know of Archias' life we learn from the *Pro Archia*, the
speech Cicero delivered in 62 B.C. in defense of Archias' claim to Roman
citizenship. A. Licinius Archias, a Greek born in Antioch around 120
B.C., was already an accomplished poet when he arrived in Rome shortly
before 100 B.C. It was a propitious time indeed, as it presented him with
the opportunity to memorialize through his poetry the military exploits of L. Lucullus, one of Rome's leading generals and an influential
politician. For this service, Lucullus became Archias' literary patron.
In 93 B.C., Lucullus helped him obtain citizenship of the *municipium* of
Heraclea, the principal town of Lucania in Magna Graecia, a region of
southern Italy originally settled by Greek colonists. Lucullus probably
planned this as an intermediate step to securing for Archias full Rome
citizenship by setting him up with a permanent residence in the city. At
some point Archias did move to Rome, for according to Cicero the poet
was one of the principal mentors of his early education as an orator.

Along with powerful friends, however, came powerful enemies, and
there is reason to believe that it was Archias' close association with
Lucullus that led to the prosecution of the poet in 62 B.C. on the charge
of having obtained Roman citizenship illegally. If the trial was the work
of Lucullus' political rivals—and of this we will never be certain—the
man behind the prosecution was probably Cn. Pompeius Magnus (generally known as "Pompey"). By prosecuting Archias, Pompey could

indirectly, but nonetheless effectively, strike a blow against his enemy Lucullus. Had he been convicted, Archias would have lost his citizenship and would have been forced to leave Rome. Thus he would bring public disgrace on both himself and his patron Lucullus. But fortunately for Archias, Lucullus was not without influential friends as well, among whom was Cicero, who championed Archias' defense with his delivery of what we have today as the *Pro Archia Poeta Oratio*.

The two laws under which Archias was eligible for Roman citizenship were: (1) the *Lex Iulia de Civitate Latinis Danda* of 90 B.C., which granted Roman citizenship to the citizens of all Italian *municipia*, provided they had not taken sides against Rome in the Social War; and (2) the *Lex Plautia Papiria de Civitate Sociis Danda* of the following year (89 B.C.), which stated that an individual was eligible for citizenship, provided he met three conditions: (a) that he was a citizen of a city allied to Rome; (b) that he maintained a permanent residence in Rome; and (c) that he presented himself to a PRAETOR within sixty days of the passing of the law.

It was probably on a charge of violating the *Lex Papia de Peregrinis*, a law passed in 65 B.C. that challenged false claims to citizenship and called for the expulsion from Rome of all foreigners, that Archias was prosecuted. The case against him was based on four technicalities: (1) there is no official record of Archias' having been enrolled as a citizen in the *municipium* of Heraclea; (2) he did not maintain a permanent residence in Rome; (3) the records of the PRAETORS of 89 B.C., in which Archias' name appears, are unreliable; and, (4) there is no record of his name in the census rolls taken at Rome during the period during which Archias claims to have lived there.

In response, Cicero argues: (1) of course there is no documentation of his citizenship at Heraclea because, as everyone knows already, the *tabularium*, or records office, of Heraclea had been burned during the Social War (but he also produces representatives from Heraclea as eyewitnesses to testify that Archias had indeed been a citizen of the town); (2) Archias certainly did have a residence at Rome (although he does not expound upon this); (3) with the exception of the records of the PRAETORS Appius and Gabinius, those of Metellus, in which Archias' name does appear, are extremely reliable; and (4) the absence of Archias' name from the census records at Rome is due to the fact that Archias was away from Rome (on campaign with Lucullus) on each occasion that the census had been taken.

The Structure of the Pro Archia

The audience of Cicero's day would expect a forensic speech to follow a certain pattern and contain, in some form or other, the following elements: (1) an *exordium*, or opening statement; (2) a *narratio*, or statement of the facts of the case; (3) a *refutatio*, or attempt to disprove the allegations of the opposition; (4) a *confirmatio*, or the orator's version of events; and (5) a *peroratio*, or closing statement. The following outline shows how Cicero follows this structure in the *Pro Archia*:

I.   EXORDIUM (1–41): the primary purpose of the opening statement was to win the *benevolentia* ("good will") of the audience, particularly the *iudices*, who would decide the outcome of the case. To achieve this, Cicero takes care to introduce himself and his client in terms that will win the sympathy and support of the court while preparing them for the kind of defense that he is going to present.

II.   NARRATIO (42–89): in this section of the speech, where the orator usually presents the facts of the case, such as they are, Cicero recounts Archias' life, starting from his birth at Antioch and early career as a poet, to his arrival in Rome in 102 B.C.

III.   REFUTATIO (90–143): in his rebuttal, or counter-argument, Cicero addresses the three legal issues raised by the prosecution: (1) the lack of any written proof of Archias' citizenship at Heraclea; (2) the question of whether he maintained a domicile at Rome in compliance with the *Lex Plautia Papiria*; and (3) his alleged failure to register with the PRAETOR within the prescribed sixty-day period.

IV.   CONFIRMATIO (144–375): here Cicero presents his case in support of Archias' citizenship. Having already responded to the legal arguments of the prosecution in the preceding REFUTATIO, Cicero takes this opportunity to deliver an eloquent disquisition on the important role that the liberal arts, and poets such as Archias who devote their lives to their study and cultivation, play in a civilized society.

V.   PERORATIO (376–397): in his brief closing statement, Cicero concludes his defense with an emotional appeal to the *iudices* for the restoration of his client.

In his defense of Archias Cicero is careful to address each of the legal arguments raised by the prosecution; but as the speech progresses, it soon becomes clear that Cicero must have realized that his strongest case lay not in the law but in the *persona* ("character") of his client. Cicero's *Pro Archia* is not so much the defense of an individual poet, as it is a disquisition on the importance of the liberal arts (*artes liberales*), or fine arts (*artes bonae* or *optimae*), and those who cultivate them.

Because this theme is the heart of Cicero's defense, he cleverly reveals it in the EXORDIUM of the oration. Although the brief opening statement runs only forty-one lines and contains just seven sentences—some of which are admittedly among the longest and most complex of the entire oration—it has as its centerpiece (20–22) the following declaration:

> *Etenim omnes artes quae ad humanitatem pertinent habent quoddam commune vinclum et quasi cognatione quadam inter se continentur.*

> To be sure, all the arts that are relevant to civilized culture share a certain common bond, and are connected, one to another, by a sort of, as it were, blood relationship.

By strategically placing this sentence at the center of the EXORDIUM, Cicero prepares his audience for what will be the heart of his defense: poets, by the very nature of their craft and dedication to the *artes optimae*, are an indispensable and inseparable part of the fabric of the *humanitas Romana*. Cicero makes this point clear in the final sentence of the EXORDIUM (38–41):

> *...perficiam profecto ut hunc A. Licinium non modo non segregandum, cum sit civis, a numero civium verum etiam, si non esset, putetis asciscendum fuisse.*

> ...I shall bring it about, without question, that you should consider that my client Aulus Licinius [Archias] not only ought not to be excluded from the ranks of the citizens, since he already is a citizen, but even if he were not, that he must be enrolled.

In the EXORDIUM Cicero also announces to his audience that he is going to use a "different style of speaking" (*novum genus dicendi*) in the presentation of his defense—one that may seem alien to a court of law, but is in this case appropriate due to the character of his client. It is perhaps for this reason that the *Pro Archia* stands out from all of Cicero's orations as one of the finest examples of the rhetorical potential of the Latin language. Every sentence of the oration is a polished masterpiece, a study in the elegance of classical rhetoric and rhetorical composition expressed through the simple symmetry that characterizes golden Latin artistry.

We do not know if Cicero's defense of Archias was successful. In a letter to his close friend Atticus, dated 61 B.C., however, Cicero refers to Archias as though he were still living in Rome and for this reason alone, it seems safe to assume the trial ended in acquittal. That Cicero's brother, Quintus, was the PRAETOR who presided at the trial, probably did not prove a disadvantage to the defense.

LIFE OF QUINTILIAN

In order to understand the life of Quintilian and the purpose behind his *Institutio Oratoria* one needs first to understand the politically charged world in which Quintilian lived, and the audience for whom he wrote. Quintilian followed his father into a career as an advocate and teacher of rhetoric in a society for which the art of oratory and the practice of legal advocacy had for generations been held up as the highest calling and most honorable profession to which a man could aspire. Unfortunately, by the end of the first century after Christ, it was also a society for which oratory would be on the decline, a trend that was first documented by Publius Cornelius Tacitus, annalist and former student of Quintilian. For the moment, in the world in which Quintilian was born and raised, the mastery of oratory and forensic rhetoric still assured a gainful career before the bar of the many standing courts of Rome, and held the promise of swift and successful advancement into a political career of limitless prospect.

While the government of the republic of Cicero's day operated with more transparency as regards the appointment of magistrates than the administrations that came and crumbled under the regimes of the Caesars, the offices of the original *cursus honorum*, Rome's traditional political ladder, were largely, if sometimes albeit ceremoniously, still intact and relevant during the first century after Christ (the office of consul, for example, persisted in the Western Roman Empire until the year 534).

Chasing a career in politics remained—in 68 A.D. as it had in 68 B.C.—still
the best game in town. Successful progress through the *cursus honorum*
continued to purchase the political swag and sway necessary to carve
for oneself the highly lucrative, and dangerously powerful, military position of provincial governor (indeed, it was the revolt of several provincial governors, both before and after the suicide of Nero, that spawned
the turmoil of 69 A.D., the notorious "year of the four emperors"). Furthermore, the successful administration of one's *provincia*, especially if
accomplished against a tableau of all that death and danger dare, could
result in the conferring upon the *imperator* that most coveted of honors, the triumph: a days-long jamboree awarded by formal decree of the
senate that climaxed in a full-dress military parade through the streets,
circuses, and celebratory arches of Rome. In this way, too, the traditions
of the old republic still obtained: martial ambition was a proven path to
political greatness trodden by the sandals of Roman generals and self-
appointed pooh-bahs generations before Julius Caesar ever buckled on
a cuirass, and would continue to be for generations to follow. But the
incentive to embark upon a career in politics was seductive for other
more practical, if not personal reasons: not least among them was the
fact that winning public office, even by grasping the lowest rung of the
cursus honorum, entitled a man to a life steeped in senatorial cachet even
if his flagged ambitions would urge him no farther up that ladder.

Marcus Fabius Quintilianus was born in the western Roman province of Spain in the town of Calagurris (modern-day Calahorra). What
piecemeal evidence the historical record has left us points to his birth occurring most likely in or around the year 35 A.D., and his death certainly
no later than 100. At some point in his late teens, probably during the
early reign of Nero, his family moved to Rome. There his father established a successful practice as a rhetorician and was known to Seneca,
Nero's boyhood tutor and sometime political advisor, who also hailed
from Spain (as did other contemporary literary notables such as Lucan,
Columella, and Martial). It was during this time in Rome that Quintilian completed his education, and among his teachers would count, if
the unnamed scholiast of Juvenal's sixth Satire can be trusted, the *gram-
maticus Remmius Palaemon*, and the well-known *rhetor Domitius Afer*.

In his early twenties Quintilian returned to his native Spain, no
doubt with the intention of making a gift of his experience as a rhetorician and advocate to the people of his provincial Spanish homeland. He
would return to Rome in August of 68 to bear witness and wassail to the

auspicious auguries of the January inauguration of Servius Sulpicius Galba (Spain's former provincial governor) as the new Caesar Augustus and consul for the year 69 A.D. Among fellow well-wishers was Marcus Salvius Otho, governor of nearby Lusitania and one of the first to support Galba's grab for power in the vacuum created by Nero's suicide. But Otho's well-wishing would soon be revealed as less than well intentioned: just two weeks later, on the fifteenth of January, Otho would see Galba's head bobble on the end of a *pilum*. After secretly maneuvering a coup d'état with the backing of Galba's own Praetorian Guard, Otho turned the barracks loose on the man whom only two weeks earlier they had sworn to protect and serve. A pack of centurions descended on the *Forum Romanum* and overtook Galba's litter as it passed before the Temple of Vesta (the emperor was returning from performing his duties as Pontifex Maximus at the altar of the Temple of Palatine Apollo). Progress of the royal train was overtaken and the royal chair overturned, sending the septuagenarian Caesar sprawling onto the pavers of the *Via Sacra* where, like the sacrificial victim over which he had presided moments earlier up on the hill where Romulus first pitched his hut, Galba's throat was cut. Rome's sixth emperor staggered several feet before bleeding out on the steps of the Temple of Divine Julius Caesar, its first.

When Galba was first hailed as Caesar by the Sixth Legion at Cartagena, following the suppression of the revolt of Vindex in April of 68, Nero was still fiddling his way through famine in Rome (he would not throw himself on his sword until June). Before his ascension, Galba had served as governor of Hispania Citerior for eight years. Now, in late August, we find Quintilian among the entourage that accompanied the man who would be emperor for a fortnight to the capital to receive the endorsement and ratification of the senate. If Quintilian had any knowledge of or played any part in the conspiracy to assassinate Galba, no source mentions it. Indeed, if anything, Quintilian's loyalties would have leaned the other way, for along with Galba's death perished any hope the young rhetorician might have embraced for living comfortably as speechwriter-in-chief to the newly installed Caesar.

Or did it? Quintilian survived the bloodshed of that tumultuous year that saw three emperors—Galba, Otho, and Vitellius—violently throned only to be even more violently overthrown, and lived to flourish under the reformation of the Flavians. Over the next twenty years, Quintilian became a powerful, well-respected, and well-paid rhetorician and advocate who had the ear of the emperor Vespasian, if at the price of having to kiss the ring of Domitian, his younger and more troubled son. For his loyal service to the royal court he became Rome's first rhetorician to be awarded a handsome annual salary paid out of the senate's fiscal coffers. In his retirement, the job of tutoring Domitian's two adopted heirs to the throne fell to him, even as Domitian fell from the grace of his most trusted inner circle thanks to his mounting paranoia and morally questionable judgment and practices. But proud as he may have been to be tapped for the job, Quintilian would not hold the position very long. The father of the two young princes (the grandson of Vespasian's brother), Flavius Clemens, would soon be charged with *maiestas* (treason), allegedly for sympathizing with the Jewish cause, and dispatched along with his wife, Domitilla (Domitian's niece). The fate of the two boys is not known, nor are they mentioned again.

Quintilian retired in 88, a watershed year in Domitian's reign that culminated in the revolt of L. Antonius Saturninus and marked the beginning of an end that perhaps even Quintilian could see coming. In fact, it would have been hard to miss. Botched plots, palace intrigues, and hugger-mugger conspiracies darkened and consumed the last years of Domitian's ever increasingly brutal reign, though none managed to topple the tyrant. Then, on 18 September, 96 A.D., in the fifteenth year of his reign, an incongruous collusion between Domitian's praetorian prefects and the emperor's wife, Domitia Longina (with his named successor Nerva no doubt tacitly in league), accomplished the successful coup-d'état. Domitian was caught unattended and unarmed in his palatine bedroom and stabbed to death (according to Suetonius, as the blows rained down he reached for the dagger he kept under his pillow only to find it had been inconveniently removed). As for Quintilian, he could boast that he had retired not only as Rome's most famous teacher (Pliny the Younger was among his pupils, as were Tacitus, Suetonius, and Juvenal), but also quite arguably its wealthiest. After nearly thirty years of practicing and teaching rhetoric and advocacy, Quintilian retired in large part to write what would become the *Institutio Oratoria*. In his didactic opus dedicated to *bonae mentis iuventutes* Quintilian laid out in twelve books all that he had learned, practiced, and taught over his long and distinguished career.

Quintilian may have died a wealthy man, but he also died heartbroken and alone. Shortly before retiring and already in his late fifties, Quintilian married a young girl of pubescent teenage years, as was the Roman custom. But his young bride would fall ill and die before her nineteenth birthday, leaving behind two young sons whose education Rome's greatest teacher would never have the opportunity to provide: one child died shortly after the mother at the age of five, the other reaching only nine. Quintilian himself must have been gravely ill by then as well, for from his own words one can clearly understand that the purpose behind his writing the *Institutio Oratoria* was to produce a work through which his sole remaining son could educate himself should death take the father first. But sick as he may have been, sadly, such was not the gods' will. Even as Quintilian desperately toiled to finish the *Institutio Oratoria* before his own death, the boy died instead. He writes:

> ...*hanc optimam partem relicturus hereditatis videbatur, ut si me, quod aequum et optabile fuit, fata intercepissent, praeceptore tamen patre uteretur.*

> I was seeing myself as ready to leave this as the best part of his inheritance, so that if the fates had taken me from his side—a thing that was right and devoutly to be wished— nevertheless my son would still be able to have his father for a teacher. (*Inst.* 6. Pr. 1.8–11)

Quintilian is also the author of two other works on the subject of rhetoric, the first titled *De Causis Corruptae Eloquentiae*, and the second *Duo Libri Artis Rhetoricae*; at least one of his speeches, the *Pro Naevio Arpiniano*, was also published. These are lost to us. His *Institutio Oratoria* is his only surviving work.

A NOTE ON SPECIALIZED TERMINOLOGY IN LATIN TEXTBOOK COMMENTARIES

You may notice as you consult the notes in this book that specialized terminology is used. This terminology makes it possible to discuss the Latin language succinctly and exactly, using a sort of "meta-language" of terms with which everyone who studies the language at some time needs to become familiar.

Although some of these terms may be new to you, learning what they mean is a simple enough task. The meaning of many of them can be gleaned from the context. For more technical terms, APPENDIX II provides definitions. If you are uncertain how to pronounce these terms, consult a standard English dictionary.

ABBREVIATIONS

A. General

abl.	ablative		leg.	legal
acc.	accusative		m.	masculine
adj.	adjective		n.	neuter
adv.	adverb		pass.	passive
B.	Bennett, *A New Latin Grammar*		pl.	plural
			prep.	preposition
cf.	*confer* ("compare")		pron.	pronoun
comp.	comparative		q.v.	*quod vide* ("which see")
conj.	conjunction		refl.	reflexive
correl.	correlative		rel.	relative
dat.	dative		sc.	*scilicet* ("supply from context")
e.g.	*exempli gratia* ("for example")			
			sing.	singular
encl.	enclitic		spec.	specifically
esp.	especially		subj.	subjunctive
f.	feminine		subst.	substantive
gen.	genitive		superl.	superlative
i.e.	*id est* ("that is")		s.v.	*sub voce* ("under the heading")
impers.	impersonal			
indecl.	indeclinable		usu.	usually
indic.	indicative		w.	with
inf.	infinitive		<	derives from
interrog.	interrogative			

B. Praenomina

A.	Aulus		L.	Lucius		Ser.	Servius
Ap(p).	Appius		M.	Marcus		Sex.	Sextus
C.	Gaius		M'.	Manius		Sp.	Spurius
Cn.	Gnaeus		P.	Publius		T.	Titus
D.	Decimus		Q.	Quintus		Ti.	Tiberius

M. TULLI CICERONIS

PRO ARCHIA
POETA ORATIO

EXORDIUM
(1–41)

For Cicero, the primary purpose of the EXORDIUM, *or opening statement, was to win the* benevolentia *(good will) of his audience, particularly the* iudices, *whose judgment would decide the fate of his client. Cicero begins by introducing himself in terms of three essential qualities that define him as an orator — ingenium (natural talent), exercitatio (experience), and ratio (strategy for the particular case at hand). Always the humble servant, however, Cicero is careful, as he is quick, to temper his acknowledgment of each of these qualities with a modest disclaimer before attributing to his client and former teacher, A. Licinius Archias, whatever success he has achieved as an orator. He concludes the* EXORDIUM *by asking his audience to indulge him if he uses in his defense a new style of speaking* (novum genus dicendi), *one suited more to the nature of his client, a poet, than to a court of law.*

1. **ingenium, ~i,** *n.,* natural ability, talent.
   iudex, iudicis, *m.,* one appointed to decide a case, a juror.
   sentio, sentire, sensi, sensus, to realize, perceive.
2. **exiguus, ~a, ~um,** small, scanty, slight, insignificant.
   exercitatio, exercitationis, *f.,* practice, experience.
3. **infitior, infitiari, infitiatus,** to deny.
   mediocriter, *(adv.)* somewhat, to a moderate extent, moderately.
   verso, ~are, ~avi, ~atus, to turn *(pass.:* to be engaged in).
4. **ratio, rationis,** *f., (w. gen.)* a methodology, strategy, or system; a professional ethic directing one's actions.
   ars, artis, *f.,* art, skill; *(pl.)* cultural pursuits, liberal studies.
   studium, ~i, *n., (w. gen.)* study *(of something);* intellectual pursuit.
   disciplina, ~ae, *f.,* formal instruction, training.
5. **proficiscor, proficisci, profectus,** to set forth, derive *(from a source, etc.).*
   confiteor, confiteri, confessus, to confess, admit.
   aetas, aetatis, *f.,* the span of one's life; a lifetime.
6. **abhorreo, abhorrere, abhorrui,** to be adverse to *(w.* **a** + *abl.).*
7. **fructus, ~us,** *m.,* profit, benefit, reward.
   repeto, repetere, repetivi (~ii), repetitus, to seek in return.
   prope, *(adv.)* almost, nearly, all but.
   ius, iuris, *n., (w. poss. adj.)* one's right, what one is entitled to.
   debeo, debere, debui, debitus, *(w. inf.)* to be under obligation *(to do something).*

M. Tulli Ciceronis
Pro Archia Poeta Oratio

1. Si quid est in me ingeni, iudices, quod sentio quam sit exiguum, aut si qua exercitatio dicendi, in qua me non infitior mediocriter esse versatum, aut si huiusce rei ratio aliqua ab optimarum artium studiis ac disciplina
5   profecta, a qua ego nullum confiteor aetatis meae tempus abhorruisse, earum rerum omnium vel in primis hic A. Licinius fructum a me repetere prope suo iure debet. Nam

---

1–7. **Si...debet:** a compound condition with three PROTASES, each followed by a relative clause introduced by a relative pronoun whose antecedent is in the PROTASIS that precedes it (*ingeni* ⇒ *quod* :: *exercitatio* ⇒ *in qua* :: *ratio* ⇒ *a qua*), B 302. See note on *a qua* (4–5) below.

1. **Si...est in me:** "if there is in me," i.e., "if I have..." **quid:** = *aliquid* after *si*, as also *nisi, num,* and *ne* (cf. *qua* for *aliqua* in the second PROTASIS), B 91.5. **ingeni:** partitive genitive with *quid*, "anything of talent," i.e., "any talent." **iudices:** vocative plural, "members of the jury."

1–2. **quod...exiguum:** "which I realize how slight it is." While *quod* is the subject of the *quam* clause, an indirect question dependent on *sentio*, it has been attracted into the governing clause as the direct object of *sentio*, an example of the rhetorical figure PROLEPSIS.

2–4. **qua exercitatio dicendi:** sc. *est in me.* **qua:** = *aliqua* (see note on 1 above). **me... esse versatum:** indirect statement with *infitior*, B 331.1. **huiusce rei ratio aliqua:** sc. *est in me:* "if I have any strategy..." **-ce:** the enclitic particle emphasizes the pronoun *huius:* "of this case before us."

4–5. **ratio...profecta:** note how the "bookend" placement of the nominative *ratio* (=A) and its modifier *profecta* (=A) BRACKETS the two prepositional phrases, *ab...studiis* (= B) *ac disciplina* (= B), creating CHIASMUS (A B :: B A), B 350.11c. **nullum...tempus:** accusative, subject of *abhorruisse*, indirect statement with *confiteor*. **a qua:** the antecedent is *ratio*, ANTICIPATED by *aliqua* (as the preceding *quid* [*ingeni*] anticipates the *quod* clause, and *qua* [*exercitatio*] anticipates the *in qua* clause).

6–7. **hic:** i.e., Archias. Cicero uses *hic* (in other grammatical cases) in the following examples to refer to Archias: *hunc* (10), *huius* (12), *huic* (15) *in hoc* (17). **earum... debet:** the APODOSIS, or main clause, of the condition. **rerum omnium:** i.e., *ingenium, exercitatio,* and *ratio.* **vel:** intensifies *in primis*, "first and foremost," B 240.3. **hic A(ulus) Licinius:** Cicero properly uses Archias' Roman *praenomen* and *nomen* to recommend him to the Roman audience. **hic:** i.e., Archias. **prope suo iure:** "nearly by his own right."

8.   **quoad,** (*interrog. and rel. adv.*) as far as.

     mens, mentis, *f.,* the mind.

     respicio, respicere, respexi, respectus, to look back on.

     spatium, ~i, *n.,* a period, interval.

9.   **praeteritus, ~a, ~um,** past, bygone, former.

     pueritia, ~ae, *f.,* childhood.

     recordor, recordari, recordatus, to call to mind, recall.

10.   * **repeto, repetere, repetivi (~ii), repetitus,** to trace, search for.

     princeps, principis, first in time, earliest; most important.

11.   **suscipio, suscipere, suscepi, susceptus,** to undertake.

     ingredior, ingredi, ingressus, to begin, embark.

     * **ratio, rationis,** *f.,* (*w. gen.*) course, curriculum (*of study, etc*).

12.   * **studium, ~i,** *n.,* study, intellectual pursuit.

     exsto, exstare, exstiti, to emerge, stand out, exist (*in a given manner or capacity*).

     hortatus, ~us, *m.,* encouragement.

13.   **praeceptum, ~i,** *n.,* instruction, precept.

     conformo, ~are, ~avi, ~atus, to train, shape, mold.

     aliquando, (*adv.*) occasionally, at some time; from time to time.

     salus, salutis, *f.,* a means of deliverance (*usu. judicial*); security.

14.   **accipio, accipere, accepi, acceptus,** to take, receive.

     opitulor, opitulari, opitulatus, (*w. dat.*) to give help (*to*).

     servo, ~are, ~avi, ~atus, to defend (*esp. in court*).

15.   **profecto,** (*adv.*) surely, certainly.

     quantum, (*interrog. and rel. adv.*) to what extent, to the extent to which (< the neuter accusative singular of the interrogative and relative pronoun **quantus, ~a, ~um**).

     situs, ~a, ~um, placed or lying in one's control or power.

16.   **ops, opis,** *f.,* aid, assistance.

     fero, ferre, tuli, latus, to convey, bestow; to bear, endure.

     * **debeo, debere, debui, debitus,** (*w. inf.*) to be under obligation (*to do something*).

quoad longissime potest mens mea respicere spatium
praeteriti temporis et pueritiae memoriam recordari
10 ultimam, inde usque repetens hunc video mihi principem
et ad suscipiendam et ad ingrediendam rationem horum
studiorum exstitisse. Quod si haec vox huius hortatu
praeceptisque conformata non nullis aliquando saluti fuit,
a quo id accepimus quo ceteris opitulari et alios servare
15 possemus, huic profecto ipsi, quantum est situm in nobis,
et opem et salutem ferre debemus. 2 Ac ne quis a nobis hoc

8–10. **longissime:** construe with *respicere*, "to look back as far (into the past) as possible..." *B* 293.2. **respicere...recordari:** (deponent) are both complementary infinitives with *potest*. Each has its own direct object (*spatium...memoriam*) with a genitive modifier (*temporis...pueritiae*). The position of a genitive modifier can come before or after the noun to which it is attached. In this one sentence, Cicero gives us an example of each position. **spatium...memoriam:** note the CHIASMUS (acc. gen. :: gen. acc.). **praeteriti temporis:** "the passage of time gone by." **memoriam...ultimam:** "earliest memory." **inde usque:** construe with *repetens* (sc. *memoriam*), "searching my memory from that point on..." **hunc video:** the *hunc* is accusative subject of the infinitives. Notice how Cicero has placed the subject accusative in front of the main verb of the head, *video* (as he just did in 2, *me* is subject of *esse versatum*). *principem* is accusative in apposition to *hunc*. **hunc...principem:** i.e., Archias; *hunc* = accusative subject of *exstitisse*, an indirect statement dependent on *video* with *principem* in apposition to it: "I see that this man has stood out as foremost (*principem*) for me (*mihi*)..."

11. **ad suscipiendam...ingrediendam rationem:** *ad* + the accusative of the gerundive expresses purpose, *B* 338.

12–13. **Quod si:** "But if..." an adverbial use of the accusative of the relative pronoun, *B* 185.2. **vox...non nullis...saluti fuit:** the "double dative" construction, "my voice was for some a means of deliverance." *Non nullis* is a dative of reference, *saluti* a dative of purpose, *B* 191.2.b. **non nullis:** LITOTES, "not none" = some. **vox...conformata:** note how the separation of *vox* and *conformata* (called HYPERBATON) BRACKETS the ablatives *hortatu praeceptisque*, creating CHIASMUS. **huius:** i.e., Archias.

14–16. **a quo:** i.e., Archias; the relative clause precedes its antecedent (*huic...ipsi*). **accepimus, possemus, in nobis...debemus:** Cicero often uses the first person plural for the first person singular. Compare the use of the royal/editorial "we" (*B* 242.3). **quo...possemus:** "by which we (= I) are able..." a result clause (antecedent = *id* [i.e., oratory]), *B* 284.2. **ceteris:** dative object of *opitulari*. **huic...ipsi:** i.e., Archias, dative indirect object of *ferre* (16) below.

15–16. **quantum...in nobis:** an adverbial (*quantum*) clause of extent; take with *ferre*: "as much as (to what extent) is in our power." **opem et salutem:** note how the two nouns echo the meanings of the previous (line 14) infinitives, *opitulari (opem) et...servare (salutem)*, emphasizing Cicero's role as Archias' legal defender.

17. **ita,** (*adv.*) so, thus, in this way; as follows.

   forte, (*adv.*) perhaps, by chance.

   miror, ~ari, ~atus, to wonder.

   facultas, facultatis, *f.,* ability, skill.

18. * **ingenium, ~i,** *n.,* natural talent, ability.

   ** **ratio, rationis,** *f.,* (*w. gen.*) a methodology, strategy, or system; a professional ethic directing one's actions.

   * **disciplina, ~ae,** *f.,* formal instruction, training.

19. **quidem,** (*particle*) indeed, certainly, to be sure (*usu. emphasizes the word it immediately follows*); **ne...quidem,** not even (*always brackets the word or phrase it emphasizes*).

   ** **studium, ~i,** *n.,* study or pursuit.

   penitus, (*adv.*) completely, thoroughly.

   umquam, (*adv.*) at any time, ever.

   dedo, dedere dedidi, deditum, (*refl. w.* **se** + *dat.*) to devote oneself (*to something*); (*pass.*) to be devoted (*to something*).

20. **etenim,** (*conj.*) for; and indeed; the fact is.

   * **ars, artis,** *f.,* art, skill; (*pl.*) cultural pursuits, liberal studies.

   humanitas, humanitatis, *f.,* civilization, culture.

   pertineo, pertinere, pertinui, to pertain, relate to.

21. **communis, ~e,** common, shared jointly by two parties.

   vinculum, ~i, *n.,* a bond.

   quasi, (*adv.*) as it were, in a manner of speaking.

   cognatio, cognationis, *f.,* a blood relationship, kinship.

22. **contineo, continere, continui, contentus,** to hold together (*by bonds of relationship, common interests*).

   mirus, ~a, ~um, extraordinary, remarkable, strange.

23. **quaestio, quaestionis,** *f.,* a judicial investigation, trial.

   legitimus, ~a, ~um, of or concerned with the law.

   iudicium, ~i, *n.,* a legal proceeding, a trial.

   publicus, ~a, ~um, public (*i.e., before the* **populus Romanus**).

ita dici forte miretur, quod alia quaedam in hoc facultas sit ingeni neque haec dicendi ratio aut disciplina, ne nos quidem huic uni studio penitus umquam dediti fuimus.

20 Etenim omnes artes quae ad humanitatem pertinent habent quoddam commune vinculum et quasi cognatione quadam inter se continentur. 3 Sed ne cui vestrum mirum esse videatur, me in quaestione legitima et in iudicio publico,

---

16–17. **Ac ne quis a nobis hoc** (p. 5) **ita dici forte miretur:** a negative purpose clause (B 282.1), governed loosely by the main clause (*ne nos quidem...dediti fuimus*, 19–20): "and in order that no one wonder that this case (*hoc*) is being presented (*dici*) by me in this fashion (*ita*)... [let me assure you that] not even I have devoted all my time to this one single pursuit (i.e., oratory)." **miretur:** subjunctive in the negative purpose clause. It also introduces an indirect statement. **ne quis** = *ne aliquis* (see note on 1 above). **a nobis:** (= *a me*) ablative of agent with the passive infinitive of a 3rd conjugation verb, *dici* ("is spoken"). **hoc:** "this case" (accusative subject in an indirect statement). **quod:** "the fact that." The whole clause (*quod...sit*) explains, in apposition, the preceding *hoc* (B 299.V.a): "namely that there is..." **in hoc:** i.e., Archias ("in this man").

17–19. **alia quaedam...facultas...ingeni:** Cicero contrasts the talents of Archias in poetry against his own in oratory (*neque* = "and not"). **dicendi ratio:** i.e., oratory, Cicero's domain. **ne...quidem:** the construction emphasizes the word it surrounds, "not even we (= I)." **huic uni studio:** i.e., oratory, dative with *dediti fuimus*. **dediti fuimus:** sometimes *fui, fuisti,* etc., are used instead of *sum, es,* etc., in forming the perfect indicative, B 102 n.1.

21–22. **quasi cognatione quadam:** "as it were by a kind of kindred relationship." Cicero qualifies *cognatione* with both *quasi* and *quadam* because he is using the term, which technically describes a familial, blood-relationship, metaphorically (cf. *quoddam commune* above; also *quasi divino quodam spiritu*, 233–234 below). **inter se continentur:** "are connected, one to another."

22–37. **Sed...dicendi:** the skeleton of this long sentence is: *Sed ne...mirum esse videatur, me...hoc uti genere...quod...abhorreat, quaeso a vobis ut...detis hanc veniam...ut me...patiamini...loqui...et...uti...genere dicendi.*

22–23. **Sed ne cui:** *cui* (= *alicui*, see note on 1 above), dative with *videatur* ("it seems"). **videatur:** subjunctive in a negative purpose clause (B 282.1) dependent on *quaeso* (see line 28 below), the main verb of the sentence (note: *mirum esse* = subjective infinitive of *videatur*). **vestrum:** (< *vos*) partitive genitive with *cui*, "to anyone of you." **me...hoc uti genere dicendi** (line 26): indirect statement introduced by *mirum esse*. **me:** subject accusatve of *uti* (present infinitive < *utor*), an accusative + infinitive clause functioning as the subject of *mirum esse* (see note on 26–28 below). **in quaestione legitima et in iudicio publico:** a court (*quaestio*) concerned with the law (*lex*), convened before a judge (*iudex*) or jury (*iudices*); it could be either a civil or criminal case (as this one was), but was distinct from a private suit.

24.   **apud,** (*prep. w. acc. denoting position or relationship*) at (*the house of*); in (*the army of*); before, in the presence of (*a magistrate, etc.*).

   praetor, praetoris, *m.,* the magistrate immediate to the consul, who usually presided over a public court.

   populus, populi, *m.,* people, population (*usu.* the Roman people).

   lectus, ~a, ~um, excellent, special, worthy of choice.

25.   **vir, viri,** *m.,* a man; hero; husband.

   severus, ~a, ~um, strict, old-fashioned.

   * **iudex, iudicis,** *m.,* one appointed to decide a case, a juror.

   conventus, ~us, *m.,* an assembly, a court of law.

26.   **utor, uti, usus,** (*w. abl.*) to use, employ.

   genus, generis, *n.,* type, style.

27.   **consuetudo, consuetudinis,** *f.,* practice, one's customary manner.

   * **iudicium, ~i,** *n.,* a legal proceeding, or trial.

   forensis, ~e, of, or connected to, the law courts.

28.   **sermo, sermonis,** *m.,* a way or style of speaking.

   * **abhorreo, abhorrere, abhorrui,** (*w.* a + *abl.*) to be averse or opposed (*to something or someone*).

   quaeso, quaesere, quaesivi, quaesitus, (< **quaero**) to ask.

   causa, ~ae, *f.,* cause, trial.

29.   **venia, ~ae,** *f.,* indulgence, favor.

   accommodo, ~are, ~avi, ~atus, to suit, accommodate; (*pass.*) to be appropriate (*to or for something*).

   reus, ~i, *m.,* a defendant.

30.   **quemadmodum,** (*interrog. and rel. adv.*) as, in the manner in which (= **ad quem modum**).

   spero, ~are, ~avi, ~atus, to hope.

   molestus, ~a, ~um, annoying, tiresome, tedious.

31.   **eruditus, ~a, ~um,** learned, accomplished.

   concursus, ~us, *m.,* a crowd, assembly.

32.   **litteratus, ~a, ~um,** well-read, cultured.

   * **humanitas, humanitatis,** *f.,* civilization, culture.

33.   **denique,** (*adv.*) finally, at length, at last.

   * **praetor, praetoris,** *m.,* the Roman magistrate, immediate to the consul, who usually presided over a public court.

   exerceo, exercere, exercui, exercitus, (*w.* **iudicium**) to preside.

   ** **iudicium, ~i,** *n.,* a legal proceeding, a trial.

   patior, pati, passus, (*w. inf.*) to allow.

   *** **studium, ~i,** *n.,* study or pursuit.

cum res agatur apud praetorem populi Romani, lectissimum
25 virum, et apud severissimos iudices, tanto conventu hominum ac frequentia, hoc uti genere dicendi, quod non
modo a consuetudine iudiciorum, verum etiam a forensi sermone abhorreat, quaeso a vobis ut in hac causa
mihi detis hanc veniam accommodatam huic reo, vobis,
30 quemadmodum spero, non molestam, ut me pro summo
poeta atque eruditissimo homine dicentem hoc concursu
hominum litteratissimorum, hac vestra humanitate, hoc
denique praetore exercente iudicium, patiamini de studiis

24–25. **cum res agatur:** a temporal clause, "when the case is being conducted,"
B 289. **apud praetorem:** the PRAETOR was a magistrate second only to the CONSUL;
during this period of the republic there were eight PRAETORS whose duties included
presiding over the *quaestiones perpetuae* (full-time standing courts). **lectissimum virum:** in APPOSITION to *praetorem:* "a first-choice man." Cicero's brother, Quintus, who
presided at Archias' trial, was elected PRAETOR in 62 B.C. first in the polls, hence the
superlative.

25–26. **tanto conventu hominum ac frequentia:** ablative absolute (without a
present participle, here expressing attendant circumstance, *B* 227). The phrase also
contains an example of HENDIADYS, a rhetorical device whereby two nouns (*conventu...ac frequentia*) are joined to convey a single idea: "with so great a throng and
crowd of men" = "with so numerous a throng of men," *B* 374.4.

26–28. **hoc...genere:** ablative with *uti* (< *utor*), subjective infinitive of *mirum esse*
(see note on 22–23 above), *B* 218.1. **dicendi:** genitive of the gerund, modifying *genere.* **quod...abhorreat:** antecedent = *genere.* **non modo...verum etiam:** "not only...
but also," a favorite construction for Cicero.

28–30. **quaeso:** the main verb of the sentence. **ut...detis:** indirect command with
quaeso, B 295.1 (*detis* = 2nd person plural present subjunctive < *do, dare*). **accommodatam...non molestam:** read *non molestam* after *accommodatam* and construe respectively with the datives *reo* and *vobis* (note the CHIASTIC word order: *accommodatam...
reo :: vobis...non molestam*). **huic reo:** i.e., Archias. **quemadmodum spero:** a parenthetical aside, "as I hope."

30–33. **ut...patiamini:** an indirect command dependent on *detis veniam.* **me:** accusative subject of *loqui* (34) and *uti* (36), objective infinitives of *patiamini* (33), *B* 328.
dicentem: accusative participle modifying *me* (note the BRACKETING of the prepositional phrases *pro summo poeta atque eruditissimo homine.* **hoc concursu...hac...hu-
manitate...hoc...praetore:** the ANAPHORA of the demonstrative pronoun (*hoc...hac...
hoc*) introduces a TRICOLON of ablative absolutes (here expressing attendant circumstance), modifying *dicentem.* Cicero avoids strict PARALLELISM by expanding the third
ablative absolute with the present active participle *exercente,* modifying *praetore* and
taking *iudicium* as its object.

34. **littera, ~ae,** *f., (usu. pl.)* what is learned from books or formal education, erudition or culture; literature.

    paulo, *(adv.)* by a little, somewhat.

    loquor, loqui, locutus, to speak, say.

35. **persona, ~ae,** *f.,* a role, part, or position (*assumed or adopted*).

    propter, *(prep. w. acc.)* because of, on account of.

    otium, ~i, *n.,* leisure (*esp. as devoted to cultural pursuits*).

36. ***** iudicium, ~i,** *n.,* a legal proceeding, a trial.

    periculum, ~i, *n.,* danger, hazard; (*pl.*) legal liability.

    tracto, ~are, ~avi, ~atus, to handle, have experience with.

    * prope, *(adv.)* almost, nearly, all but.

37. **inusitatus, ~a, ~um,** unusual, unfamiliar.

    * genus, generis, *n.,* type, style.

38. **tribuo, tribuere, tribui, tributus,** to grant, bestow.

    concedo, concedere, concessi, concessus, to concede, grant.

    * sentio, sentire, sensi, sensus, to realize, perceive, feel.

    perficio, perficere, perfeci, perfectus, to effect, bring about.

    * profecto, *(adv.)* undoubtedly, without question.

39. **segrego, ~are, ~avi, ~atus,** to separate, exclude.

    civis, civis, *m. or f.,* a citizen (*usu. of Rome*).

40. **ascisco, asciscere, ascivi, ascitus,** to enroll.

Optional Reading: On the *Exordium* (Appendix III, p. 106)

35 humanitatis ac litterarum paulo loqui liberius, et in eius modi persona quae propter otium ac studium minime in iudiciis periculisque tractata est uti prope novo quodam et inusitato genere dicendi. **4** Quod si mihi a vobis tribui concedique sentiam, perficiam profecto ut hunc A. Licinium non modo non segregandum, cum sit civis, a 40 numero civium verum etiam, si non esset, putetis asciscendum fuisse.

---

34. **paulo loqui liberius:** "to speak a little more freely." *paulo* (< *paulus*) is an ablative of degree of difference with the comparative adverb *liberius*. **loqui:** objective infinitive of *patiamini* (see 33 above), B 328. **et:** connects *loqui* and (36).

34–36. **in eius modi persona quae...:** "assuming a persona ("role") of the sort which..." i.e., by using a different style of speaking (*novum genus dicendi*) suited more to poets and scholars (*otium ac studium*) than lawyers and law courts (*iudiciis periculisque*). **minime...tractata est:** "is infrequently introduced..." **in iudiciis periculisque:** HENDIADYS for *in iudiciorum periculis*, "...into the legal hazards of the courts."

36–37. **uti...novo...et inusitato genere dicendi:** *genere* is the ablative object of *uti* ("to use"). Cicero repeats the claim he made at the beginning of the sentence, that in his defense he will employ a style of speaking not usually heard in a court of law.

37–41. **Quod si...sentiam:** "and if I (shall) perceive that this..." *si* begins the PROTASIS of a future more vivid (uses the indicative) condition, which is introduced by **Quod:** a CONNECTING (or linking) RELATIVE PRONOUN. Read *Id* (= it, B 251.6). *Quod* in turn serves as the accusative subject of **tribui concedique:** present passive infinitives of the indirect statement governed by *sentiam*.

perficiam...ut: the APODOSIS of the condition: "I shall bring it about that..." The main verb of the sentence, *perficiam* takes an *ut* clause of result (B 297.1), whose verb, *putetis*, in turn governs an extended accusative + infinitive indirect statement: *hunc... non modo non segregandum* (sc. *esse*)...*verum etiam...asciscendum fuisse* (for the passive periphrastic expressing necessity/obligation, cf. B 337.8). **cum sit civis...si non esset:** two circumstantial clauses; the first qualifies *non segregandum* (*esse*), the second *asciscendum fuisse*.

NARRATIO
(42–89)

Cicero begins the NARRATIO *at the point in Archias' life when Roman boys traditionally assumed the "toga of manhood"* (toga virilis), *usually age 16 or 17. From his birthplace at Antioch, Cicero gives a brief account of Archias' travels through Asia and Greece during his early career as a poet, before arriving in Rome in 102* B.C. *For a poet of his conspicuous celebrity it was not long before he secured the patronage of both consuls and other influential men from some of the leading families in Rome.*

42. **excedo, excedere, excessi, excessus,** to depart from, grow out of.
43. **** ars, artis,** *f.,* art, skill; (*pl.*) cultural pursuits, liberal studies.
    * aetas, aetatis, *f.,* the span of one's life; a lifetime.
    ** humanitas, humanitatis, *f.,* civilization, formal society.
    informo, ~are, ~avi, ~atus, to mold, shape.
44. **soleo, solere, solui, solitus,** (*w. inf.*) to be accustomed.
    scribo, scribere, scripsi, scriptus, to write.
    confero, conferre, contuli, collatus, (*refl. w.* **se**) to apply oneself.
45. **nascor, nati, natus,** to be born.
    celeber, ~bris, ~bre, busy, frequented, populous.
46. **copiosus, ~a, ~um,** rich, well-supplied.
    * eruditus, ~a, ~um, learned, accomplished.
    liberalis, ~e, (*w.* **studium**) of the liberal arts.
47. **adfluo, adfluere, adfluxi, adfluctus,** to abound, be rich.
    antecello, antecellere, (*w. dat.*) to excel, surpass.
    ** ingenium, ~i, *n.,* natural talent, ability.
48. **coepi, coepisse, coeptus,** (*w. inf.*) to begin.
    cunctus, ~a, ~um, the whole of, all.
    sic, (*adv.*) so, to such an extent.
49. **adventus, ~us,** *m.,* an arrival, visit, appearance.
    celebro, ~are, ~avi, ~atus, to throng, attend in large numbers, honor with ceremonies.
    fama, ~ae, *f.,* reputation, public opinion.
    *** ingenium, ~i, *n.,* natural talent, ability.
    exspectatio, exspectationis, *f.,* expectation.
50. **admiratio, admirationis,** *f.,* admiration, veneration.
51. **supero, ~are, ~avi, ~atus,** to excel, surpass, outdo.

Nam ut primum ex pueris excessit Archias atque ab
eis artibus quibus aetas puerilis ad humanitatem informari
solet, se ad scribendi studium contulit. Primum Antiochiae
45   —nam ibi natus est loco nobili—celebri quondam urbe et
copiosa atque eruditissimis hominibus liberalissimisque
studiis adfluenti, celeriter antecellere omnibus ingeni gloria
coepit. Post in ceteris Asiae partibus cunctaque Graecia sic
eius adventus celebrabantur ut famam ingeni exspectatio
50   hominis, exspectationem ipsius adventus admiratioque
superaret.

42–44. **ut primum ex pueris excessit:** "as soon as he left boyhood," i.e., grew up,
reached adolescence. **ab eis artibus quibus:** "from those studies by which..." Note
how the demonstrative pronoun *eis* ANTICIPATES the relative clause *quibus...solet* (the
antecedent is *artibus*), B 247.1. **aetas puerilis:** "period of boyhood." **se...contulit:** "he
applied himself to the study of writing." **Primum Antiochae:** locative, "first at Antioch," (for this city, see APPENDIX I). The sequence begun by *primum* is picked up by
post in the following sentence (see on 48 below).

45–47. **loco nobili:** i.e., Antioch; an ablative of source with *natus est* (B 215). **celebri...urbe...copiosa...adfluenti:** ablatives in APPOSITION to the locative *Antiochiae*, B
169.4. **celebri quondam urbe:** "once a bustling city." **hominibus...studiis:** ablatives
of means modifying *adfluenti* (note: "means" may be a person as well as a thing, B
218.10). **omnibus:** dative with the compound verb *antecellere* (B 187.3). **gloria:** ablative of respect, B 226.

48–51. **Post:** sequential to *primum* (line 44 above): "And next." **sic...celebraban-
tur ut...superaret:** note how the adverb *sic* ANTICIPATES the result clause: "his visits
were *so* attended *that*..." **ingeni:** genitive, construe with *famam*. **exspectatio...ad-
ventus admiratioque:** three nominative subjects with the singular verb *superaret*.
ipsius: genitive, construe with *adventus* and *admiratio*. (A genitive, or other oblique
case, generally follows the noun it modifies, as *hominis* [w. *exspectatio*], but in order
to avoid perfect symmetry, and perhaps to emphasize *ipsius*, Cicero here, as else-
where, uses the rhetorical device VARIATIO, reversing the word order in the second
and third members).

52. **tum,** (*adv.*) then, at that time (*in the past*).

    plenus, ~a, ~um, (*w. gen.*) full (*of*).

    *** **ars, artis,** *f.,* art, skill; (*pl.*) cultural pursuits, liberal studies.

    ** **disciplina, ~ae,** *f.,* formal instruction, training.

53. **vehementius,** (*comp. adv.* < **vehementer**) more enthusiastically.

54. **colo, colere, colui, cultus,** to cultivate, develop, foster.

    oppidum, ~i, *n.,* a town (*smaller than an* **urbs**).

    hic, (*adv*) here, in this place, at this point.

55. * **propter,** (*prep. w. acc.*) because of, on account of.

    tranquilitas, tranquilitatis, *f.,* a peaceful condition.

    neglego, neglegere, neglexi, neglectus, to neglect, fail to observe or respect.

56. **itaque,** (*adv.*) accordingly.

57. **civitas, civitatis,** *f.,* citizenship.

    ceterus, ~a, ~um, other, the rest or remaining.

    praemium, ~i, *n.,* reward, prize, legal benefit.

    dono, ~are, ~avi, ~atus, to award, (*w. acc. of recipient and abl. of gift*).

58. **iudico, ~are, ~avi, ~atus,** to judge, appraise.

    cognitio, cognitionis, *f.,* recognition.

59. **hospitium, ~i,** *n.,* the formal relationship between host (**patronus**) and guest (**cliens**).

    dignus, ~a, ~um, (*w. abl.*) worthy or deserving (*of*).

    existimo, ~are, ~avi, ~atus, to judge, consider, hold an opinion.

    celebritas, celebritatis, *f.,* renown, notoriety.

    * **fama, ~ae,** *f.,* fame, reputation.

60. **iam,** (*adv.*) now, at length; (*indicates the completion of a prior action or state of affairs*) by this time, by now, already.

    absens, absentis, not present, absent; (*esp.*) despite being absent, (*i.e., without benefit of meeting the other party*).

    notus, ~a, ~um, well-known, noted.

5   Erat Italia tum plena Graecarum artium ac dis-
ciplinarum, studiaque haec (et in Latio) vehementius tum
colebantur quam nunc (isdem in oppidis) et hic Romae
55   propter tranquillitatem rei publicae non neglegebantur.
Itaque hunc et Tarentini et Locrenses et Regini et Neapolitani civitate ceterisque praemiis donarunt, et omnes
(qui aliquid de ingeniis poterant iudicare cognitione atque
hospitio dignum existimarunt. Hac tanta celebritate
60   famae cum esset iam absentibus notus, Romam venit

52. **Italia:** specifically the region of southern Italy known as Magna Graecia because many of its towns were originally settled by Greek colonists. **tum:** i.e., before
the Social War. Archias arrived in Italy in 102 B.C., during the consulship of C. Marius and Q. Lutatius Catulus (see note on 60–61 below).

53–54. **et in Latio:** "also in Latium" (i.e., the area of central Italy containing Rome
and its environs); the *et* is adverbial, the two clauses joined by the enclitic connector
-que (w. *studia*). **isdem in oppidis:** "in these same towns," i.e., those of Latium. **hic
Romae:** "here at Rome," the locative, with the adverb *hic*, marks the culmination
of the geographical progression of the NARRATIO and prepares the audience for Archias' arrival in Rome.

55. **propter tranquillitatem rei publicae:** the peaceful interval between the political and civil upheaval caused by the revolutionary reforms of the Gracchi (133–
121 B.C.) and the Social War (90–89 B.C.). **non neglegebantur:** an example of the rhetorical figure LITOTES, the affirmation of something by the negation of its opposite.

56–59: **hunc:** i.e., Archias, direct object of *donarunt* (= *donaverunt*, a SYNCOPATED
form of the perfect tense) and *existimarunt* (= *existimaverunt*) with *dignum* (line 59)
serving as a predicate accusative: "thought him worthy..." (*B* 177.2). **Tarentini...Nea-
politani:** the inhabitants of the principle towns of Magna Graecia.

57–59. **civitate ceterisque praemiis:** ablatives of thing given (*B* 187.1.a) with
donarunt, "they presented him with citizenship and other awards." **cognitione
atque hospitio:** ablatives with *dignum* (*B* 226.2): "...worthy of their acquaintance
and hospitality" (note the BRACKETING of *hunc...dignum*).

59–60. **Hac tanta celebritate...cum esset...notus:** "when, because of the great
expansion of his reputation, he was already known even to men he had never met."
The ablative of cause (*celebritate*) precedes *cum*, the governing conjunction of the
clause, illustrating how Archias' reputation preceded him. **Romam:** with verbs of
motion, the names of cities, towns, peninsulas, and small islands with a single important city or town do not require a preposition, *B* 182.1a.

61. **nanciscor, nancisci, nactus,** to get attached to a person in a particular relationship or connection (*i.e., as an ally or supporter*).

 consul, consulis, *m.,* consul, the highest ranking magistrate in the Roman republican government.

62. * **scribo, scribere, scripsi, scriptus,** to write.

63. **gero, gerere, gessi, gestus,** to carry on, perform (**res gestae:** deeds, exploits, achievements).

 auris, auris, *f.,* the ear; **aures adhibere:** to listen to, pay attention.

 adhibeo, adhibere, adhibui, adhibitus, to offer, furnish, provide.

64. **statim,** (*adv.*) immediately, at once.

 praetextatus, ~a, ~um, wearing the **toga praetexta** (*worn by boys up to the official age of manhood, about 16 or 17*).

65. **recipio, recipere, recepi, receptus,** to receive, admit.

66. **lumen, luminis,** *n.,* brilliance, excellence.

 * **littera, ~ae,** *f.,* (*usu. pl.*) what is learned from books or formal education, erudition or culture; literature.

 natura, ~ae, *f.,* inborn abilities; natural endowments.

 virtus, virtutis, *f.,* moral excellence, character.

67. **adulescentia, ~ae,** *f.,* youth, young manhood; adolescence.

 faveo, favere, favi, fautus, (*w. dat.*) to show favor, give support.

68. **familiaris, ~e,** (*w. dat.*) congenial, welcome, intimate.

 senectus, senectutis, *f.,* the period of old age.

Mario consule et Catulo. Nactus est primum consules eos
quorum alter res ad scribendum maximas, alter cum res
gestas tum etiam studium atque auris adhibere posset.
Statim Luculli, cum praetextatus etiam tum Archias esset,
65 eum domum suam receperunt. Dedit etiam hoc non solum
lumen ingeni ac litterarum, verum etiam naturae atque virtutis ut domus, quae huius adulescentiae prima favit, eadem
esset familiarissima senectuti.

---

61. Mario consule et Catulo: "in the consulship of Marius and Catulus," i.e., 102
B.C. The usual construction for dating would be *Mario et Catulo consulibus,* and would
normally come first in the sentence. By altering the construction Cicero seems to im-
ply that Marius was the more powerful man, elected first at the polls (see APPENDIX
I); postponing it until the end of the sentence emphasizes Archias' arrival in Rome.

61–63. Nactus est: i.e., Archias came to Rome at a singularly propitious time.
consules eos quorum alter...alter: the demonstrative pronoun follows its noun
for emphasis while also ANTICIPATING the relative clause (see note on 42–44 above),
"those consuls, of whom the one (Marius)...the other (Catulus)." **adhibere posset:**
subjunctive in a relative clause of characteristic, B 283. *adhibere posset* applies to both
pronouns *alter...alter.*

62–64. res...maximas: "outstanding achievements (as material) for literary composition," (see note on 251 below). **cum...etiam tum...atque:** "not only (x)...but also
(y) and (z)." While Marius' *res maximae* are superior to the *res gestae* (sc. *ad scribendum*) of his colleague Catulus, Cicero is careful to note the enthusiasm (*studium*) and
attention (*auris* [= *aures*, the alternate form of the accusative plural of 3rd declension
nouns, B 37, 40]) that Catulus paid to Archias' poetry. The pairing of *studium* and
auris as objects of *adhibere* is an example of the rhetorical figure ZEUGMA, in which
a single verb governs two or more objects in different ways, "the other was able to
lend not only his achievements, but also his support and his ears."

64. Luculli: nominative plural; for the notables of this family see APPENDIX I.
cum...esset: *cum* concessive ("although") in an adversative clause (B 309.3), "although Archias was even then still wearing the *toga praetexta*," i.e., the toga adoles-
cents wore until the age of 16 or 17, when they assumed the *toga virilis.*

65. domum suam: with *domus* no preposition is required, B 182.1.b (cf. note on
60–61 above).

65–68. Dedit...senectuti: the text of the sentence is corrupt. The best sense seems
to be: *hoc* is the subject of *dedit* and ANTICIPATES the *ut* clause, a substantive clause
in APPOSITION to it: "Even this (*hoc*) showed brilliance (*lumen*) not only of his talent
and education, but also of his nature and character, namely that (*ut*) the same house
which first showed favor to him in his youth, was also a most intimate friend to him
in his old age." **adulescentiae:** dative with *favit.* **senectuti:** dative with *familiarissima.*

69. iucundus, ~a, ~um, (*w. dat.*) on friendly terms (*with*); congenial, agreeable (*to*).

70. **filius, ~i,** *m.,* a son.
71. **vivo, vivere, vixi, victus,** to live, be alive.
72. * **colo, colere, colui, cultus,** to cultivate (*e.g., someone's friendship*).
73. **totus, ~a, ~um,** (*usu. w. defining gen.*) the whole of, all; whole, complete.
    devincio, devincere, devinxi, devinctus, to hold, bind (*under obligation*).
    * **consuetudo, consuetudinis,** *f.,* a general convention of society, friendship.
74. **teneo, tenere, tenui, tentus,** to hold, maintain, keep.
    adficio, adficere, adfeci, adfectus, to effect, bring about; (*pass.*) to be treated (*by others*).
    honos, honoris, *m.,* respect, esteem, honor, glory.
75. **percipio, percipere, percepi, perceptus,** to perceive, take in or grasp with the mind.
76. **studeo, studere, studui,** (*w. inf.*) to devote oneself, be eager.
    * **forte,** (*adv.*) perhaps, by chance, as it might happen.
    simulo, ~are, ~avi, ~atus, (*w. inf.*) to pretend.
    interim, (*adv.*) meanwhile.

6 Erat (temporibus illis) iucundus Q. Metello, illi
70 Numidico, et eius Pio filio, audiebatur a M. Aemilio, vivebat cum Q. Catulo et patre et filio, a L. Crasso colebatur. Lucullos vero et Drusum et Octavios et Catonem et
totam Hortensiorum domum devinctam consuetudine
cum teneret, adficiebatur summo honore, quod eum non
75 solum colebant, qui aliquid percipere atque audire
studebant, verum etiam si qui forte simulabant. Interim

69–72. Erat...colebatur: the sentence contains four independent clauses (*erat...
iucundus :: audiebatur :: vivebat :: colebatur*) of which Archias is the subject, PARATACTI-
CALLY arranged in ASYNDETON (i.e., without any connective particles such as *et*, *atque*,
etc.). **Q. Metello...filio:** datives with the adjective *iucundus*. **Q. Catulo...filio:** "Q.
Catulus, both the father and the son," i.e., they shared the same name. It was common for Roman sons to have the same name as their fathers. **Pio filio:** *pius*, from
pietas, "dutifulness to one's gods, family, and state." The son of Metellus Numidicus
helped secure his father's return from exile, hence the cognomen, *pius*. (For more
historical details on all those listed in this paragraph, see APPENDIX I.) **audiebatur:**
i.e., during recitations of his poetry. **M. Aemilio [Scauro]** (*Marcus Aemilius Scaurus*):
patrician, *novus homo*, consul in 115 B.C., a well-known public figure. Cicero is attempting here to add to Archias' honor and prestige by putting Scaurus in one of
the poet's audiences. **Q. Catulo** (*Quintus Catulus*): enjoyed the fine arts, philosophy,
art, literature, and himself was author of some poetry and history. He was also an
adequate orator. **L. Crasso** (*Lucius Crassus*): consul in 95 B.C., made his name as a
superb orator. He serves as Cicero's model of a public speaker in the *de Oratore*.

72–74. Lucullos...cum teneret: Cicero postpones *cum* ("since"), the conjunction
that governs the clause and should therefore come first, to emphasize the impres-
sive list of Archias' *patroni*, some of the leading men in Rome at the time. **Catonem:** Cato, father of *Cato Uticensis*, contemporary of Cicero. **Hortensiorum:** the
very well-known Hortensius (who defended Verres) was a famous orator and rival
of Cicero. He also was a childhood friend of Lucullus. **devinctam consuetudine:**
"bound by close social ties." The participle *devinctam* (< *devincio*), a predicate accusative adjective (*B* 177.2), agrees with *domum* but must be understood with all the
names that precede it.

74–76. adficiebatur: the main verb of the sentence, "he was treated." **quod:**
"because." **non solum...verum etiam:** balances the *qui* and *si qui* (= *aliqui*, see note
on 1 above) clauses, the subjects of *colebant*. **si qui forte simulabant:** i.e., who
only pretended (with an implied complementary infinitive phrase, *aliquid percipere
atque audire*).

77. **satis,** *(adv.)* sufficiently.

    intervallum, ~i, *n.,* an intervening period of time, an interval.

78. **proficiscor, proficisci, profectus,** to start a journey, set out, depart.

    provincia, ~ae, *f.,* a province; the provincial assignment of a pro-magistrate.

79. **decedo, decedere, decessi, decessus,** to go away, depart, leave.

80. **aequus, ~a, ~um,** *(of actions, laws, etc.)* fair, just, reasonable.

    * **ius, iuris,** *n.,* that which is sanctioned, law; *(of cities, communities)* privileges of citizenship; *(w. defining gen.)* a legal code, system, or its branches.

    foedus, foederis, *n.,* a formal agreement between states, peoples, or cities; *(w.* **aequus)** a treaty in which the two parties are, at least in theory, on equal terms.

    ascribo, ascribere, ascripsi, ascriptus, to enroll as a citizen.

81. **volo, velle, volui,** to want, wish, desire *(w. inf.).*

    * **dignus, ~a, ~um,** *(w. abl.)* worthy, deserving *(of).*

82. **auctoritas, auctoritatis,** *f.,* the quality of leadership, authority; personal influence; prestige.

    gratia, ~ae, *f.,* popularity, esteem or the influence derived thereof.

83. **impetro, ~are, ~avi, ~atus,** to obtain by request or application.

    lex, legis, *f.,* the law; legal reasoning or argument.

84. **foederatus, ~a, ~um,** federated, bound by treaty to Rome.

85. **domicilium, ~i,** *n.,* a permanent residence, domicile.

86. **sexaginta,** *(indecl. adj.)* sixty.

    dies, diei, *m. or f.,* day.

    * **apud,** *(prep. w. acc. usu. denoting position or relationship)* at *(the house of);* in *(the army of);* before, in front of *(a magistrate, etc.).*

    ** **praetor, praetoris,** *m.,* the Roman magistrate, second only to the consul, who usually presided over a public court.

    profiteor, profiteri, professus, to submit one's name, register, enroll.

satis longo intervallo, cum esset cum M. Lucullo in Siciliam profectus et cum ex ea provincia cum eodem
Lucullo decederet, venit Heracleam. Quae cum esset
80   civitas aequissimo iure ac foedere, ascribi se in
eam civitatem voluit idque, cum ipse per se dignus
putaretur, tum auctoritate et gratia Luculli ab Hera-
cliensibus impetravit. 7 Data est civitas Silvani lege et Carbonis: Si qui foederatis civitatibus ascripti fuissent, si tum
85   cum lex ferebatur in Italia domicilium habuissent et
si sexaginta diebus apud praetorem essent professi.

77–79. **satis longo intervallo:** ablative of time, "after sufficient time had passed."
cum...cum...cum...cum: the structural balance of this sentence revolves around the
anaphora of *cum*, whose function alternates between the conjunction ("since"), and
the preposition ("with"). The verbs of the two *cum* clauses (*esset...profectus* :: *decederet*) create the antithesis that is underscored by *in Siciliam...ex ea provincia*. **cum M.
Lucullo...cum eodem Lucullo:** the repetition of the prepositional phrase emphasizes
Archias' loyalty to Lucullus, whom he accompanied to and from his province. **venit
Heracleam:** the main clause is postponed until final position to highlight Archias'
arrival in Heraclea, the location of his disputed citizenship. (see Appendix I).

79–81. **Quae...foedere:** "And since it (i.e., Heraclea) was a city with full civic privileges through its treaty (with Rome)." After Pyrrhus' defeat of the Roman forces at
Heraclea in 280 b.c., Rome extended full and unconditional citizenship (*aequissimo iure
et foedere*) to the city in 278 b.c. **iure ac foedere:** ablatives of quality (*B* 224.1). **quae:** (=
et ea) the connecting relative, referring to *civitas*, "Since it was..." **foedere, ascribi:**
echoes the language of the law below (cf. 87–89).

81–83. **idque:** "it" (what he wanted, i.e., *ascribi in eam civitatem*, = citizenship), direct
object of *impetravit*. **cum...tum:** here links a general statement and a particular application of it, "as he was thought to be worthy (of citizenship) on his own merits, so with
the support and influence of Lucullus he obtained it from the Heracleans."

83–84. **Data est civitas:** "Citizenship was granted" (note the emphatic position
of the verb). **Silvani lege et Carbonis:** M. Plautius Silvanus and C. Papirius Carbo,
tribunes of 89 b.c., authors of the law (see Appendix I). Roman magistrates gave their
name to laws they had passed. Cicero uses the cognomen of the sponsors whereas the
official title of the law gives the nomen (*Lex Plautia Papiria de Civitate Sociis Danda*) in
the feminine form to modify *lex*.

84–86. **Si...professi:** the *Lex Plautia Papiria de Civitate Sociis Danda* of 89 b.c. granted
full Roman citizenship to all citizens of allied states who resided in Italy at the time the
law was passed, provided they reported to the praetor within sixty days. Cicero para-
phrases the law as a condition with a compound protasis and apodosis supplied by *data
est civitas*. **ascripti fuissent...habuissent...essent professi:** pluperfect subjunctives in
past sequence because of the tense of the governing verb (*data est*). **Si qui:** = *aliqui*, "if any"
(the indefinite pronoun must also be supplied as the subject of the following two *si* clauses). **tum cum...ferebatur:** "at that time, when..." the imperfect indicative emphasizes
the specific time when the law was passed. **sexaginta diebus:** ablative of time, "within
sixty days." **apud...professi:** the applicant had to register publicly before the praetor.

87. *** domicilium, ~i,** *n.,* a permanent residence, domicile.

    * iam, (*adv.*) at length, by now, already.

    annus, ~i, *m.,* year.

88. *** profiteor, profiteri, professus,** to state openly, declare publicly; (*w.* **apud praetorem**) to submit one's name, register.

    familiaris, ~e, intimate, closely associated (*by friendship, etc.*).

Optional Reading: On the *Narratio* (Appendix III, p. 108)

REFUTATIO

(90—143)

In his refutatio, *or counter-argument, Cicero responds to four issues raised by the prosecution: (1) the lack of any written proof of Archias' citizenship at Heraclea; (2) the question of whether he maintained a domicile at Rome in compliance with the* Lex Plautia Papiria; *(3) whether he appeared before the* praetor *within the period of sixty days prescribed by the law; and (4) the absence of his name from the census records taken at Rome.*

90. ****civitas, civitatis,** *f.,* citizenship.

    * lex, legis, *f.,* the law; any legal argument.

91. **amplius,** (*comp. adv.* < **amplus**) more, further; in addition.

    * causa, ~ae, *f.,* the case.

    infirmo, ~are, ~avi, ~atus, to weaken, invalidate; void, annul.

92. *** ascribo, ascribere, ascripsi, ascriptus,** to enroll as a citizen.

93. **nego, ~are, ~avi, ~atus,** to deny.

    adsum, adesse, afui, afuturus, to be present, at hand.

    * vir, viri, *m.,* a man; hero; husband.

    * auctoritas, auctoritatis, *f.,* the quality of leadership, authority; personal influence; prestige.

    religio, religionis, *f.,* reverence for what is divine; conscientiousness; the quality of evoking awe or respect.

    fides, fidei, *f.,* faith, confidence, a trust or agreement

94. **opinor, ~ari, ~atus,** to hold as an opinion, to suppose; to believe.

    scio, scire, scivi (~ii), scitus, to know (*as fact*); to have certain knowledge of.

95. **intersum, interesse, interfui, interfuturus,** to be among, attend; be present (*as an onlooker*).

Cum hic domicilium Romae multos iam annos haberet,
professus est apud praetorem Q. Metellum, familiar-
issimum suum.

---

90   8 Si nihil aliud nisi de civitate ac lege dicimus,
nihil dico amplius: causa dicta est. Quid enim horum
infirmari, Gratti, potest? Heracleaene esse tum ascriptum negabis? Adest vir summa auctoritate et religione
et fide, M. Lucullus, qui se non opinari sed scire, non
95   audisse sed vidisse, non interfuisse sed egisse dicit.

87–89. **Cum...haberet:** "Since he continued to maintain a domicile at Rome..."
By using language similar to that of the law, Cicero implies Archias' compliance
with it. **hic:** i.e., Archias. **multos...annos:** accusative of duration of time, B 181. **fa-**
miliarissimum suum: the phrase, in APPOSITION to *Metellum*, emphasizes the close
relationship Archias enjoyed with the PRAETOR of 89 B.C.

90 ff. Cicero moves from the NARRATIO to the REFUTATIO, where he will counter
the specific charges raised by the prosecution.

90–91. **nihil aliud nisi:** "nothing other than." **de civitate ac lege:** Archias' citizenship at Heraclea and compliance with the *Lex Plautia Papiria* (see note on 83–86
above). **dicimus...dico:** while Cicero does use first person singular and plural forms
interchangeably, because he may have been one of several *patroni* speaking on behalf of Archias, he may be using *dicimus* collectively; on the other hand, he may
be including the prosecution. **causa dicta est:** "the case has been pled," i.e., "the
defense rests."

91–92. **Quid:** subject of *potest*. **horum:** partitive genitive, "what of these things,"
i.e., Archias' enrollment at Heraclea (*de civitate*) and his compliance with the *Lex
Plautia Papiria* at Rome (*ac lege*). **Gratti:** vocative (< *Grattius*), the prosecutor, about
whom nothing more is known.

92–93. Cicero addresses the first charge of the prosecution: the question of Archias' citizenship at Heraclea. **Heracleaene:** locative + the interrogative enclitic -*ne*.
esse...ascriptum: perfect passive infinitive in indirect statement (sc. *eum*, i.e., Archias, as subject), dependent on *negabis*.

93–95. Cicero presents witnesses (*adest, adsunt*) who will testify that Archias was
in fact a citizen of Heraclea. **vir...M. Lucullus:** note how the "bookend" arrangement of the nominatives BRACKETS the three ablatives of description, creating CHI-
ASMUS. Notice also the pleasing balance of the TRICOLON in the indirect statement,
describing the validity of M. Lucullus as a witness: *non opinari sed scire, non audisse*
sed vidisse, non interfuisse sed egisse.... **audisse** = *audivisse*. **egisse:** Lucullus had a
direct role in obtaining citizenship for Archias.

96. **legatus, ~i,** *m.,* an ambassador, envoy, delegate.

97. ** **causa, ~ae,** *f.,* cause, reason, pretext; (*leg.*) a case, trial; (*abl. w. gen.*) for the sake (*of*).

   mandatum, ~i, *n.,* a commission, charge; official business or orders (*usu. conveyed by* **legati**).

   testimonium, ~i, *n.,* evidence given by a witness in court.

98. ** **ascribo, ascribere, ascripsi, ascriptus,** to enroll as a citizen.

99. **tabula, ~ae,** *f.,* a written document; (*pl.*) public records.

   desidero, ~are, ~avi, ~atus, to desire, want.

100. **incendio, incendere, incensi, incensus,** to burn.

   tabularium, ~i, *n.,* the record-office; public registry.

   intereo, interire, interii, interiturus, (*of things*) to be destroyed; (*of persons*) to die, perish.

   * **scio, scire, scivi (~ii), scitus,** to know (*as fact*); to have certain knowledge of.

101. **quaero, quaerere, quaesivi (~ii), quaesitus,** to search for, hunt, seek; to try to obtain; to ask for.

102. **taceo, tacere, tacui, tacitus,** to keep silent, be quiet.

   ** **littera, ~ae,** *f.,* (*usu. pl.*) what is learned from books or formal education, erudition or culture; literature.

103. **flagito, ~are, ~avi, ~atus,** to ask for, demand.

   amplus, ~a, ~um, large, spacious, extensive; (*of persons, status, etc.*) magnificent, distinguished, great.

   ** **vir, viri,** *m.,* a man; hero; husband.

   religio, religionis, *f.,* reverence for what is divine; conscientiousness; the quality of evoking awe or respect.

104. **integer, ~gra, ~grum,** (*of places*) in an undiminished state, not affected by war.

   municipium, ~i, *n.,* a self-governing community or township awarded the rights of Roman citizenship (*usu. without the right to vote,* **civitas sine suffragio**).

   ius iurandum, a sworn oath (< **ius, iuris,** *n.,* "law" + **iurare**).

   * **fides, fidei,** *f.,* faith, confidence; a trust or agreement.

105. **depravo, ~are, ~avi, ~atus,** to corrupt.

   repudio, ~are, ~avi, ~atus, to refuse, reject; to regard as false.

   * **tabula, ~ae,** *f.,* a written document; (*pl.*) public records.

106. * **soleo, solere, solui, solitus,** (*w. inf.*) to be accustomed (*to do something*).

   corrumpo, corrumpere, corrupi, corruptus, to tamper with, corrupt.

Optional Reading: On Evidence and Witnesses (Appendix III, p. 110)

Adsunt Heraclienses legati, nobilissimi homines, huius
iudici causa cum mandatis et cum publico testimonio
venerunt, qui hunc ascriptum Heracleae esse dicunt. Hic tu
tabulas desideras Heracliensium publicas, quas Italico bello
100   incenso tabulario interisse scimus omnes? Est ridiculum
ad ea quae habemus nihil dicere, quaerere quae habere
non possumus, et de hominum memoria tacere, litterarum
memoriam flagitare et, cum habeas amplissimi viri re-
ligionem, integerrimi municipi ius iurandum fidemque,
105   ea quae depravari nullo modo possunt repudiare, tabulas
quas idem dicis solere corrumpi desiderare.

96–97. **Adsunt Heraclienses legati:** the embassy from Heraclea. The CHIASTIC
structure of this sentence (*adsunt...legati...qui...dicunt*) mirrors that of the previous
(*adest vir...qui...dicit*). **huius iudici causa:** "for the sake of this trial" (*causa* = ablative of
cause, B 198.1; 219). **cum mandatis et...publico testimonio:** "with official orders and
public testimony," the exact nature of which Cicero does not disclose.

98–106. Cicero's response to the first charge of the prosecution: the absence of
any documentation to confirm Archias' citizenship at Heraclea.

98–100. **Hic:** the adverb, "at this point." **tu:** Grattius, the prosecutor. **tabulas...
publicas:** the public records of Heraclea, where Archias' citizenship would have
been recorded. **Italico bello:** ablative of time during which, B 231.1. The reference
is to the Social War (90–89 B.C.), when the allied cities of Rome revolted over the
issue of citizenship. **incenso tabulario:** ablative absolute, "with the burning of the
records office."

100–106. Cicero ridicules the prosecution for demanding records that everyone
(including the prosecution) knows were destroyed when the *tabularium* at Heraclea burned during the Social War. **Est ridiculum:** the predicate of the main clause
whose subjects are a TRICOLON of antithetical pairs of infinitives arranged in ASYN-
DETON (*nihil dicere...quaerere :: tacere... flagitare :: repudiare...desiderare*).

101–102. **ad ea:** construe with *nihil dicere*, "to say nothing in contradiction to
those things which we have" (*est ridiculum ad ea [quae habemus] nihil dicere; ea* = evidence). **quae habemus:** antecedent = *ea*. **quae habere non possumus:** object clause
of *quaerere*. **de...memoria:** construe with *tacere*, "to remain silent with regard to the
memory of men."

103–106. **cum habeas...:** "although you have," subject = Grattius. **amplissimi viri:**
i.e., M. Lucullus. **integerrimi municipi:** i.e., Heraclea, whose citizens were granted
Roman citizenship after the Social War. **ea:** object of *repudiare* and antecedent of
quae...possunt. **nullo modo:** "in no way." **tabulas:** object of *desiderare* and antecedent
of *quas...corrumpi*. **idem:** i.e., Grattius, subject pronoun of *dicis* ("the self-same you
says"); it conveys more emphatically (rather than *ipse* as "you yourself") the irony of
Grattius' demand for the records in the first place.

107. ** **domicilium, ~i,** *n.,* permanent residence, domicile.

    tot, *(indecl. adj.)* so many.

    * **annus, ~i,** *m.,* year.

108. **ante,** *(prep. w. acc.)* before, previous to.

    sedes, sedis, *f.,* where one lives, a dwelling place, home.

    fortuna, ~ae, *f.,* *(pl.)* wealth, property.

109. **conloco, ~are, ~avi, ~atus,** to settle, establish, set up.

    ** **profiteor, profiteri, professus,** to submit one's name, register, enroll.

    immo, *(adv. particle, often w.* **vero,** *implying complete denial of the preceding statement)* on the contrary.

110. **vero,** *(adv. particle, often w.* **immo,** *with adversative force),* however, on the other hand.

    ** **tabula, ~ae,** *f.,* a written document; *(pl.)* public records.

    professio, professionis, *f.,* a formal declaration before a magistrate.

111. **conlegium, ~i,** *n.,* a board or body of magistrates.

    *** **praetor, praetoris,** *m.,* the Roman magistrate, immediate to the office of consul, who often presided over a public court.

    obtineo, obtinere, obtinui, obtentus, to have, possess.

112. ** **auctoritas, auctoritatis,** *f.,* the quality of leadership, authority; personal influence, prestige.

    neglegentius, *(comp. adv.* < **neglegens**) somewhat carelessly, without due caution.

    adservo, ~are, ~avi, ~atus, to keep safe, guard, protect.

113. **incolumis, ~e,** safe, unharmed *(from legal prosecution),* intact.

114. **levitas, levitatis,** *f.,* unreliability, frivolity, carelessness.

    damnatio, damnationis, *f.,* condemnation in a court of law.

    calamitas, calamitatis, *f.,* misfortune, disaster, ruin, calamity.

115. ** **fides, fidei,** *f.,* faith, confidence; a trust or agreement.

    resigno, ~are, ~avi, ~atus, *(w.* **fidem**) to break the binding force *(of an agreement, etc).*

    sanctus, ~a, ~um, scrupulous, upright, virtuous.

    modestus, ~a, ~um, restrained, temperate, mild.

116. **diligentia, ~ae,** *f.,* attentiveness, diligence.

117. ** **iudex, iudicis,** *m.,* one appointed to decide a case, a juror.

118. **litura, ~ae,** *f.,* a rubbing out, erasure; a correction.

    commoveo, commovere, commovi, commotus, to stir the emotions; to disturb, trouble, vex, make anxious.

9 An domicilium Romae non habuit is qui tot annis
ante civitatem datam sedem omnium rerum ac fortunarum
suarum Romae conlocavit? An non est professus? Immo
110 vero eis tabulis professus quae solae ex illa professione
conlegioque praetorum obtinent publicarum tabularum
auctoritatem. Nam cum Appi tabulae neglegentius adservatae dicerentur, Gabini, quam diu incolumis fuit,
levitas, post damnationem calamitas omnem tabularum
115 fidem resignasset, Metellus, homo sanctissimus modes-
tissimusque omnium, tanta diligentia fuit ut ad L. Len-
tulum praetorem et ad iudices venerit et unius nominis
litura se commotum esse dixerit. His igitur in tabulis

107–109. The second issue raised by the prosecution: whether Archias had a
residence at Rome at the time the *Lex Plautia Papiria* was passed (for the law see on
83–86 above). **An...non habuit?:** "or did he not have...?" *B* 162.4a. **Romae:** locative
(as also at line 109). **is:** i.e., Archias. **tot annis ante civitatem datam:** the interval
between Archias' arrival in Rome (102 B.C.) and the granting of his citizenship at
Heraclea (89 B.C.).

109–112. **An non est professus?:** The third issue: "Or did Archias not make
declaration to the PRAETOR (i.e., within sixty days of the passing of the *Lex Plautia
Papiria*)?" **Immo vero...professus:** sc. *est.* **eis tabulis:** ablative of instrument with
professus (note how the demonstrative *eis* ANTICIPATES the following relative clause):
"On the contrary, he registered in *those* documents..." **quae solae...auctoritatem:** "...
which are the only ones from that registration and that board of PRAETORS (of 89 B.C.)
that still have the force of public records." The implication is that despite the care-
less manner in which Appius and Gabinius, PRAETORS of 89 B.C., conducted their
registration (see below), the diligent oversight of their colleague Metellus assures
the validity of the appearance of Archias' name on the list.

112–115. **Nam:** introduces an explanation of the previous sentence, i.e., the
questionable enforcement of the *Lex Plautia Papiria* by certain PRAETORS of 89 B.C.
cum: "although," governs both *dicerentur* and *resignasset* (= *resignavisset*). **Appi:**
genitive, construe with *tabulae*. **adservatae:** sc. *esse.* **Gabini:** genitive, construe
with both *levitas* and *calamitas*, subjects of *resignasset*. **quam diu incolumis fuit:**
"as long as he (Gabinius) was safe (from prosecution)." **fidem resignavisset:** "had
removed credibility."

115–118. **Metellus...fuit:** the main clause. **tanta diligentia:** ablative of description. **ut...venerit et...dixerit:** a result clause triggered by *tanta*, "Metellus was a man
of *such* diligence *that*," (for the perfect subjunctive cf. *B* 268.6). **litura:** ablative of
cause, modifying *commotum esse*, an infinitive in indirect statement governed by
dixerit. **His:** construe with *tabulis*.

119. * **litura, ~ae,** *f.,* a rubbing out, erasure; a correction.
120. * **ita,** (*adv.*) so, thus, in this way; as follows.

   dubito, ~are, ~avi, ~atus, (*w. acc.*) to doubt, question; (*w.* **de**) to be in doubt about.

   praesertim, (*adv. emphasizing single words or subordinate clauses*) especially; (*w.* **cum**) especially since; (*w.* **si**) especially if.
121. **quoque,** (*adv. emphasizes the word it follows*) also, even, too.

   *** **ascribo, ascribere, ascripsi, ascriptus,** to enroll as a citizen.

   * **etenim,** (*conj.*) and indeed; the fact is.
122. **mediocris, ~e,** ordinary, average, common, undistinguished.

   humilis, ~e, humble, lowly; insignificant.
123. **praeditus, ~a, ~um,** (*w. abl.*) endowed (*with*).

   gratuito, (*adv.* < **gratuitus**) without payment, for nothing.

   impertio, impertire, impertivi (~ii), impertitus, to present, offer.
124. **credo, credere, credidi, creditus,** (*w. acc. and inf.*) to believe, suppose (*often used parenthetically with sarcastic overtones*).
125. **scaenicus, ~a, ~um,** of or connected with the stage; of actors, stage performers.

   artifex, artificis, *m.,* an artisan; (*w.* **scaenicus**) an actor.

   largior, largiri, largitus, to bestow, confer, grant.

   ** **soleo, solere, solui, solitus,** (*w. inf.*) to be accustomed.
126. **summus, ~a, ~um,** (*superl.* < **superior**) the highest, greatest, supreme.

   nolo, nolle, nolui, (*w. inf.*) to be unwilling, not to want.

nullam lituram in nomine A. Licini videtis. **10** Quae cum
120   ita sint, quid est quod de eius civitate dubitetis, praesertim cum aliis quoque in civitatibus fuerit ascriptus? Etenim cum mediocribus multis et aut nulla aut humili aliqua
arte praeditis gratuito civitatem in Graecia homines impertiebant, Reginos credo aut Locrensis aut Neapolitanos
125   aut Tarentinos, quod scaenicis artificibus largiri solebant, id
huic summa ingeni praedito gloria noluisse! Quid? Cum

---

119. **nullam lituram:** i.e., no evidence of erasure or forgery.

119–120. **Quae cum ita sint:** (= *et cum ea ita sint*) "and since these things are so..."
While *cum* governs the clause, and therefore should come first, conventional rules
of syntax require that the CONNECTING RELATIVE PRONOUN (*quae*) begin the sentence,
B 251.6. **quid est quod:** "what is that which..." **dubitetis:** subjunctive in a relative
clause of characteristic (B 283.2) with the previous *quod* (neuter singular accusative)
as its direct object.

120–121. **praesertim cum:** "especially since." **aliis:** separated from its noun *civitatibus* in order to BRACKET *quoque*. **fuerit ascriptus:** perfect subjunctive emphasizes
the sequence of events: Archias was already a citizen of other cities before the *Lex
Plautia Papiria* was even passed.

121–124. **Etenim:** used when stating the obvious, it sets an ironic tone, picked up
by *credo* (see 124–126 below). **cum:** temporal (with its indicative verb, *impertiebant*)
"at a time when." **mediocribus...praeditis:** dative, indirect object of *impertiebant*.
The word order BRACKETS the ablative phrase *aut nulla aut humili aliqua arte*, which
modifies (means or instrument) *praeditis*, and explains the critical *mediocribus*. **et:**
connects *mediocribus* and *praeditis*. **in Graecia:** i.e., Magna Graecia. **impertiebant:**
imperfect for repeated action in the past, B 260.2.

124–126. **credo:** verb of the main clause, it continues the sarcastic tone of *etenim*
(cf. note on 121–124). **Reginos...Locrensis...Neapolitanos...Tarentinos:** accusative
subjects of *noluisse*, an indirect statement dependent on *credo* (*Locrensis* = *Locrenses*,
see note on 62–63 above). These are various peoples of Magna Graecia mentioned
earlier in section 5. **quod:** direct object of *largiri*, antecedent of **id:** (= *civitatem*) direct
object of an understood *largiri*, which must be supplied from the preceding *quod*
clause as the complementary infinitive of *noluisse*. **scaenicis artificibus:** i.e., actors,
dative indirect object of *largiri*.

huic...praedito: i.e., Archias, dative indirect object of *largiri noluisse*. Note how
huic...praedito BRACKETS *summa ingeni*, the ANTITHESIS of *mediocribus...praeditis* of the
preceding *cum* clause (observe how Cicero places *gloria*, an ablative of means with
praedito, and modified by *summa*, outside the BRACKET to avoid strict PARALLELISM
with the *cum* clause); the point of contrast is between the undistinguished multi-
tude (*mediocribus multis...praeditis*) and the exceptional individual (*huic...praedito*).

126. **Quid?:** "Well, what about..." a transition that sustains the ironic tone of the
previous sentence while anticipating the following question. **cum:** temporal (cf. the
cum clause at 121–124 above).

127. * **ceterus, ~a, ~um,** other, the rest or remaining.

    ** **lex, legis,** *f.,* the law; legal reasoning or argument.

128. * **municipium, ~i,** *n.,* a community with the rights of Roman citizenship without the right to vote (**civitas sine suffragio**).

    *** **tabula, ~ae,** *f., (sing.)* a document; *(pl.)* public records.

129. **inrepo, inrepere, inrepsi,** to slip in; to insinuate oneself *(into a position, etc.).*

    * **utor, uti, usus,** *(w. abl.)* to use, employ, exploit.

    * **quidem,** *(particle)* indeed, certainly, to be sure *(emphasizes the word it immediately follows);* **ne...quidem,** not even *(emphasizes the word or phrase it brackets).*

130. ** **scribo, scribere, scripsi, scriptus,** to write.

    semper, *(adv.)* always.

    * **volo, velle, volui,** to want, wish, desire *(w. inf.).*

131. **reicio, reicere, reieci, reiectus,** to refuse to admit, reject.

    census, ~us, *m.,* registration of Roman citizens and their property *(usu. every five years);* written records of the census.

    requiro, requirere, requisivi (~ii), requisitus, to ask for, inquire about; to try to obtain; to demand.

    scilicet, *(exclamatory particle affirming an obvious fact and often w. sarcastic overtones)* to be sure! obviously! of course!

132. **obscurus, ~a, ~um,** not clear, uncertain, doubtful; obscure.

    proximus, ~a, ~um, *(of place)* nearest, next; *(of periods of time)* immediately preceding, last.

    censor, censoris, *m.,* one of two magistrates whose duties included the taking of the **census** *(i.e., registering citizens according to their property).*

    clarissimus, ~a, ~um, *(superl. adj. <* **clarus***)* most distinguished.

133. **imperator, imperatoris,** *m.,* a commanding officer, general.

    ** **apud,** *(prep. w. acc.)* at *(the house of);* in *(the army of);* before, in the presence of *(a magistrate, etc.).*

    exercitus, ~us, *m.,* a military force, an army.

    superior, superioris, *(comp. adj. <* **superus***)* earlier, previous.

134. **quaestor, quaestoris,** *m.,* the lowest-ranking elected magistrate, often assigned as a deputy to a higher magistrate.

    primus, ~a, ~um, first; *(w. gen.)* the first part *(of something).*

135. * **populus, populi,** *m.,* people *(usu. the Roman people).*

    censeo, censere, censui, census, to conduct a census; *(pass.)* to be registered in a census.

ceteri non modo post civitatem datam sed etiam post legem Papiam aliquo modo in eorum municipiorum tabulas inrepserunt, hic qui ne utitur quidem illis in quibus
130   est scriptus, quod semper se Heracliensem esse voluit, reicietur? **11** Census nostros requiris. Scilicet! Est
enim obscurum proximis censoribus hunc cum clarissimo imperatore L. Lucullo apud exercitum fuisse, superioribus cum eodem quaestore fuisse in Asia, primis
135   Iulio et Crasso nullam populi partem esse censam.

127–130. The antithetical structure of this sentence (*ceteri... inrepserunt* :: *hic...
reicietur?*) mirrors the preceding (*multis...praeditis* :: *huic... praedito*). **ceteri:** i.e., those
who acquired Roman citizenship by questionable means. **non modo...sed etiam:**
see note on 26–28 above. **post civitatem datam:** even after receiving Roman citizenship they still sought the citizenship of those cities of Magna Graecia, which Archias already enjoyed. **post legem Papiam:** the *Lex Papia de Peregrinis*, passed in 65 B.C.
by the TRIBUNE C. Papius, was the basis for the prosecution of Archias; it challenged
false claims to citizenship and called for the expulsion from Rome of all foreigners.
aliquo modo: "by any means necessary." **eorum municipiorum:** Rhegium, Locri,
Neapolis, and Tarentum. **hic:** i.e., Archias, subject of *reicietur*. **ne...quidem:** see note
on 18–19 above. **utitur:** an "historical present," *B* 359.3, 268.3. **illis:** ablative object of
utitur (antecedent = *tabulas*). **quod:** "because."

131. **reicietur?:** in the final position to emphasize the irony, as if to say, "This is
the thanks Archias gets for going through proper channels to obtain his citizenship?" **Census nostros:** the fourth issue: the absence of Archias' name from the last
three census reports taken at Rome between 89 B.C., when he was enrolled at Heraclea, and 62 B.C., the date of the trial (see note on 131–135 below). Citizen lists were
collected and made official for taxation purposes by censors (who were appointed
every five years). **requiris:** 2nd person singular (subject is Grattius, the prosecutor).

131–135. **Scilicet!:** "To be sure!" sets up the sarcastic tone of **est obscurum:** predicate of the subjective infinitives *fuisse...fuisse...esse censam*. **proximis censoribus...
superioribus...primis:** a TRICOLON of ablatives: "under the last censors" (70 B.C.),
"under the previous ones" (86 B.C.), "under the first ones" (89 B.C.), i.e., the census
taken after the passing of the *Lex Plautia Papiria*. Note how each of these ablatives
introduces an accusative + infinitive clause (*hunc...fuisse* :: [*hunc*]...*fuisse* :: *nullam...
partem esse censam*) that serve as the subjects of *est obscurum*. Cicero maintains PARAL-
LELISM between the first two members of the TRICOLON with the repetition of *hunc...
fuisse*, and the reference to Lucullus (*cum...imperatore* :: *cum eodem quaestore*), but al-
ters the construction in the third with a change of subject (*partem*) and the voice of
the infinitive (*esse censam*).

Iulio et Crasso: L. Iulius Caesar and P. Licinius Crassus, censors of 89 B.C. (see
APPENDIX I). **imperatore:** as PROCONSUL in Asia, Cilicia, Bithynia, and Pontus; having
led an army in the Third Mithridatic War (74–63 B.C.), he was relieved of his command in 66 B.C. **quaestore:** as proquaestor under Sulla in the First Mithridatic War
(88–84 B.C.).

136. **quoniam,** *(conj.)* since, because.

  ** **ius, iuris,** *n.,* law; *(w. defining gen.)* a legal code, system.

  *** **civitas, civitatis,** *f.,* citizenship.

  confirmo, ~are, ~avi, ~atus, to establish, confirm.

137. **indico, ~are, ~avi, ~atus,** to make known, show, point out.

  * **censeo, censere, censui, census,** to conduct a census; *(pass.)* to be enrolled or registered.

  * **ita,** *(adv.)* so, thus, in this way; as follows.

  ** **iam,** *(adv.)* now, at length; by now; already.

  * **gero, gerere, gessi, gestus,** to carry on, do, perform.

138. * **civis, civis,** *m. or f.,* a citizen, *(usu. of Rome).*

  criminor, ~ari, ~atus, to accuse, make an allegation.

  ne...quidem, not even *(emphasizes the word it brackets).*

139. * **verso, ~are, ~avi, ~atus,** to turn; *(pass.)* to be engaged, involved *(in an action or activity).*

  testamentum, ~i, *n.,* a will.

140. **saepe,** *(adv.)* often, continuously.

  *** **lex, legis,** *f.,* the law; legal reasoning or argument.

  adeo, adire, adii, aditus, to enter, come into *(a certain position).*

  hereditas, hereditatis, *f.,* inheritance, hereditary possession.

141. **beneficium, ~i,** *n.,* formal thanks or commendation; a reward.

  aerarium, ~i, *n.,* the treasury.

  defero, deferre, detuli, delatus, to confer, recommend.

142. * **consul, consulis,** *m.,* consul, the highest magistrate in the Roman republican government.

  * **quaero, quaerere, quaesivi (~ii), quaesitus,** to search for, hunt for; to seek out; to try to obtain; to ask for.

  argumentum, ~i, *n.,* evidence; the basis for a charge.

143. **revinco, revincere, revici, revictus,** to convict of a falsehood.

Optional Reading: On the Four Types of Logical Proof (Appendix III, p. 112)

Sed, quoniam census non ius civitatis confirmat ac tantum
modo indicat eum, qui sit census, ita se iam tum gessisse pro
cive, eis temporibus is quem tu criminaris ne ipsius quidem
iudicio in civium Romanorum iure esse versatum et testa-

140   mentum saepe fecit nostris legibus, et adiit hereditates civium
Romanorum, et in beneficiis ad aerarium delatus est a L. Lucullo pro consule. Quaere argumenta, si quae potes; numquam
enim hic neque suo neque amicorum iudicio revincetur.

136–138. **Sed, quoniam...pro cive:** "But since the census does not confirm citizenship, and in fact merely indicates that whoever happened to be recorded was
at that time conducting himself in the manner of a citizen..." **census:** nominative
singular. **ius civitatis:** i.e., citizenship. **tantum modo:** "merely." **eum...se...gessisse:**
indirect statement with *indicat*. **qui sit census:** subjunctive in a relative clause of
characteristic. **pro cive:** in APPOSITION to *ita*.

138–142. **eis temporibus:** ablative of time during which (*B* 231.1), "during those
times," i.e., when the census was being taken. **is...pro consule:** the TRIPARTITE main
clause, where Cicero describes Archias' involvement in three activities reserved
for Roman citizens, is outlined thus: *is...testamentum ...fecit...et adiit hereditates...et...in
beneficiis delatus est.* **quem:** the subject of *esse versatum*, the infinitive of the indirect
statement dependent on *criminaris*. **ne...iudicio:** "not even in his own opinion." **in
civium...iure esse versatum:** i.e., to be entitled to the rights and privileges of a
Roman citizen. **testamentum...legibus:** i.e., every time Archias revised his will,
he did so in accordance with Roman law. **adiit...Romanorum:** only a Roman citizen could inherit from a Roman citizen. **in beneficiis...delatus est:** Lucullus, on
returning to Rome after losing his command against Mithridates to Pompey in 66
B.C., included Archias among those of his staff whom he recommended to the senate for monetary reward.

142–143. **quae:** neuter accusative plural (= *aliqua*, see note on 1 above), the antecedent is *argumenta*. **potes:** sc. *invenire*. **hic:** i.e., Archias. **suo:** construe with *iudicio*.
numquam...neque...neque: with this emphatic denial of the prosecution's case, Cicero concludes his *refutatio*.

CONFIRMATIO
(144–375)

The CONFIRMATIO *marks a dramatic shift in the course of the speech, as Cicero departs from the case proper to deliver a disquisition on the value of the liberal arts in an ordered society.*

145. **delecto, ~are, ~avi, ~atus,** to delight, charm; (*pass. w. abl.*) to be delighted (*by*), take pleasure (*in*).

 suppedito, ~are, ~avi, ~atus, to supply, make available.

146. * **forensis, ~e,** of, or connected to, the law courts.

 strepitus, ~us, *m.,* noise, clamor, uproar.

 reficio, reficere, refeci, refectus, to restore, refresh, revive.

 * **auris, auris,** *f.,* the ear.

 convicium, ~i, *n.,* noise, clamor, shouts (*usu. angry*).

 defetiscor, defetisci, defessus, to be worn out, suffer exhaustion.

147. **conquiesco, conquiescere, conquievi,** to rest, relax.

 * **existimo, ~are, ~avi, ~atus,** to judge, consider, hold an opinion.

 suppeto, suppetere, suppetivi (~ii), (*of people*) to be available; (*of something*) to present itself when needed or required.

148. **cotidie,** (*adv.*) every day, daily, day by day.

 varietas, varietatis, *f.,* a variety; the quality of being many different things, (*i.e., forms, aspects, natures, etc.*).

149. **doctrina, ~ae,** *f.,* formal teaching, instruction.

 excolo, excolere, excolui, excultus, to improve, cultivate.

 * **fero, ferre, tuli, latus,** to carry, bear, convey; to endure.

150. **contentio, contentionis,** *f.,* conflict, contention; a disagreement.

 relaxo, ~are, ~avi, ~atus, to relieve the tension, relax, unbend.

151. **fateor, fateri, fassus,** to confess, acknowledge; to admit.

 * **dedo, dedere, dedidi, deditum,** to devote, commit oneself (*to something*).

 ** **ceterus, ~a, ~um,** other, the rest or remaining.

 pudeo, pudere, pudui, (*usu. impers.*) to fill with shame, shame.

12 Quaeres a nobis, Gratti, cur tanto opere hoc
145 homine delectemur. Quia suppeditat nobis ubi et animus
ex hoc forensi strepitu reficiatur et aures convicio defessae
conquiescant. An tu existimas aut suppetere nobis posse
quod cotidie dicamus in tanta varietate rerum, nisi animos
nostros doctrina excolamus, aut ferre animos tantam posse
150 contentionem, nisi eos doctrina eadem relaxemus? Ego
vero fateor me his studiis esse deditum. Ceteros pudeat,

144–145. Cicero begins the CONFIRMATIO with an OCCUPATIO, a rhetorical device
that anticipates an opponent's objection. **quaeres:** future: "you will ask..." **tanto
opere:** an adverbial expression, "so greatly," lit., "with such effort." **Quia suppeditat...ubi:** "Because he supplies us (with the means) whereby..." (*ubi* [= *ut ibi*] introduces a BIPARTITE [*et...et*] relative clause of purpose [B. 282.2] whose subjects [*animus...aures*], when construed with their respective verbs [*reficiatur...conquiescant*], are
examples of SYNECDOCHE). **ex...strepitu:** i.e., the din of the courts of the forum.

147–150. **An:** see note on 107–109 above. **aut...aut:** "either...or," balances the two
indirect statements, governed by *existimas*, whose parallel structure is maintained
by the repetition of *posse* in each clause and the two corresponding *nisi* clauses that
follow, both of which contain the ablative *doctrina* and share the same direct object
(*animos :: eos*).

suppetere nobis posse: "could be available to us," "at our disposal," the subject
is the following *quod* clause. **cotidie...rerum:** i.e., in the daily routine of the courts.
doctrina: ablative of means or instrument, "academic pursuits," "study," i.e., of literature (so also in the following *nisi* clause). **ferre...posse:** the subject is *animos*, the
antecedent of *eos*, direct object of *relaxemus* in the following *nisi* clause.

150–151. **Ego...deditum:** an emphatic assertion that serves as the response to the
preceding rhetorical question (cf. *ne nos quidem huic uni studio...dediti fuimus* [18–19
above]). **Ceteros pudeat:** "Let it shame the rest," an impersonal "jussive" subjunctive (B 275.1), whose subject may be loosely understood as the following *si* clause.

152. *** **littera, ~ae,** *f.,* (*usu. pl.*) what is learned from books or formal education, erudition or culture; literature.

     abdo, abdere, abdidi, abditus, to put away; to bury; (*reflex.*) to devote oneself completely (*to*).

153. * **communis, ~e,** common, shared jointly by two parties.

     adfero, adferre, attuli, adlatus, to bring (as a contribution).

     fructus, ~us, *m.,* advantage, gain, profit; enjoyment, gratification, pleasure.

     aspectus, ~us, *m.,* the range of vision, sight, view.

154. **profero, proferre, protuli, prolatus,** to produce, bring before the public.

     ** **annus, ~i,** *m.,* year.

155. * **vivo, vivere, vixi, victus,** to live, be alive.

     *** **iudex, iudicis,** *m.,* one appointed to decide a case, a juror.

     commodum, ~i, *n.,* advantage, interest.

156. * **otium, ~i,** *n.,* leisure (*esp. as devoted to cultural pursuits*).

     abstraho, abstrahere, abstraxi, abstractus, to distract, divert.

     voluptas, voluptatis, *f.,* organized pleasures; formal entertainment.

     avoco, ~are, ~avi, ~atus, to call away one's attention, distract, divert.

157. **somnus, ~i,** *m.,* sleep.

     retardo, ~are, ~avi, ~atus, to hold back, inhibit, discourage.

     quare (*interrog. and rel. adv.*) for what reason, wherefore.

     tandem, (*adv.*) at length, at last.

Optional Reading: On the Benefits of Reading Poetry (Appendix III, p. 114)

si qui ita se litteris abdiderunt ut nihil possint ex eis neque
ad communem adferre fructum neque in aspectum lucemque proferre; me autem quid pudeat qui tot annos ita
155 vivo, iudices, ut a nullius umquam me tempore aut commodo aut otium meum abstraxerit aut voluptas avocarit
aut denique somnus retardarit? **13** Quare quis tandem me

152–154. **si qui:** "if anyone." **qui...abdiderunt:** the antecedent is *ceteros* (*qui* =
aliqui, see note on 1 above). **ut...proferre:** ANTICIPATED by *ita*. **nihil:** direct object of
both *adferre* and *proferre*. **ex eis:** the antecedent is *litteris*. **ad communem...fructum:**
"for the common benefit," i.e., in the service of the state. **in aspectum lucemque:**
HENDIADYS for *in aspectum lucis*.

154–157. **me...quid pudeat qui...ita...ut:** although the interrogative pronoun *quid*
("why") should begin the clause, Cicero postpones it in order to mirror the structure
of the preceding sentence, thereby emphasizing the ANTITHESIS between *ceteros* and
me. **qui...vivo:** a conditional relative clause (*B* 312.2) that can be loosely understood
as the subject of *pudeat*: "I who have lived my life" = "if I have lived my life" (cf. note
on *Ceteros pudeat* above). **ut:** a result clause, ANTICIPATED by *ita*.

a nullius...commodo: "from the time (of need) or interest of no one," i.e., from
being ready to help anyone. **me:** direct object of *abstraxerit*, *avocarit* (= *avocaverit*), and
retardarit (= *retardaverit*). **aut...aut...aut...aut:** the first connects *tempore* and *commodo*,
the last three set in symmetry the three verbs of the *ut* clause and their subjects.
otium: not simply "leisure," but the commitment of one's leisure time to cultural
pursuits, study, etc. **voluptas:** i.e., the pursuit of social activities, idle entertainment.
somnus: i.e., sloth.

158. **reprehendo, reprehendere, reprehensi, reprehensus,** to find fault with, rebuke; to mark with disapproval.

iure, (*adv.* < **ius**) according to the law; with good reason, rightly.

suscenseo, suscensere, suscensui, to be angry (*with*).

***ceterus, ~a, ~um, other, the rest or remaining.

159. **obeo, obire, obivi (~ii), obitus,** to take on, deal with, carry out.

festus, ~a, ~um, festal; on or suitable for festivals (*i.e., public holidays*).

* dies, diei, *m. or f.,* day.

ludus, ~i, *m.,* (*pl.*) public games, festivals, holidays.

160. *** celebro, ~are, ~avi, ~atus,** to throng, attend in large numbers, honor with ceremonies.

requies, requietis, *f.,* rest, repose, relaxation.

161. **corpus, corporis,** *n.,* the body.

* concedo, concedere, concessi, concessus, to concede, grant.

162. *** tribuo, tribuere, tribui, tributus,** to grant, bestow.

tempestivus, ~a, ~um, timely, occurring at the right time; (*w.* **convivium**), a dinner party starting at an early hour (*i.e., an elaborate banquet*).

convivium, ~i, *n.,* a dinner party, banquet, feast.

alveolus, ~i, *m.,* a gaming board.

163. **pila, ~ae,** *f.,* a ball (*for play or exercise, etc.*).

-met, (*encl. particle*) attached for emphasis to pronouns.

recolo, recolere, recolui, recultus, to resume a practice, pursuit, etc.

164. **sumo, sumere, sumpsi, sumptus,** to undertake (*an activity, etc.*); to take on, assume (*a duty, responsibility, etc.*).

magis, (*adv.*) more (*w.* **quam** *or abl. of comp.*).

165. *** quoque,** (*adv. emphasizes the word it follows*), also, even, too.

cresco, crescere, crevi, cretus, to grow; (*w.* **ab** *or* **de**), to arise from.

facultas, facultatis, *f.,* ability, skill.

166. **quantuscumque, ~acumque, ~umcumque,** (*rel. adj.*) of whatever size; however great (*or small*).

* periculum, ~i, *n.,* danger, hazard; (*leg. usu. pl.*) legal liabilities; the risks or hazards of litigation.

reprehendat, aut quis mihi iure suscenseat, si, quantum ceteris ad suas res obeundas, quantum ad festos dies ludorum
160 celebrandos, quantum ad alias voluptates et ad ipsam requiem animi et corporis conceditur temporum, quantum alii
tribuunt tempestivis conviviis, quantum denique alveolo,
quantum pilae, tantum mihi egomet ad haec studia recolenda
sumpsero? Atque id eo mihi concedendum est magis quod
165 ex his studiis haec quoque crescit oratio et facultas quae,
quantacumque est in me, numquam amicorum periculis

157–164. **reprehendat...suscenseat:** potential subjunctives in the APODOSIS of a
present general ("should-would") condition, B 280.2. **si...sumpsero:** the PROTASIS of
the condition BRACKETS an extended *quantum...tantum* correlative construction continuing the ANTITHESIS of *ceteros* :: *me*. The *quantum...tantum* correlative construction contains two TRICOLA whose six members are introduced by the ANAPHORA of
quantum.

⇒ **First TRICOLON** (158–161): "as much time as is devoted by others for..." In each
clause **quantum** is the subject. **ceteris:** dative of agent with *conceditur*, B 189. **ad...**
obeundas: "for the purpose of attending to their own affairs." **ad...celebrandos:**
"for the purpose of attending festivals." **ad...voluptates et...corporis:** "to other idle
distractions and the relaxation of mind and body" (note the shift in construction
from *ad* + gerundive, expressing purpose, to *ad* + accusative, a simple prepositional
phrase). **requiem:** (= *requietem*). **conceditur:** must be supplied in the first two *quan-*
tum clauses. **temporum:** partitive genitive, construe also with each preceding *quan-*
tum (note: its placement at the end of the first TRICOLON and the beginning of the
second indicates that it also modifies each *quantum* of the second TRICOLON).

⇒ **Second TRICOLON** (161–163): "as much time as some give to..." Cicero shifts
to an active construction where each **quantum** functions as the direct object of its
clause. **alii tribuunt:** the subject and verb of all three *quantum* clauses. **conviviis...**
alveolo...pilae: dative indirect objects of *tribuunt*.

163–164. **tantum...sumpsero:** the resolution of the correlative construction, "that
much (time) I myself apply to the cultivation of these pursuits." **mihi egomet:** Cicero uses both the dative (indirect object) and nominative of the personal pronoun
(with the -*met* enclitic for emphasis) to correspond to *ceteris* and *alii* above. **id:** the
antecedent is the preceding *tantum* clause. **eo...magis:** "by so much the more" (*eo*
= ablative of degree of difference with the comparative adverb *magis*), B 223. **quod:**
causal, ANTICIPATED by *eo...magis*.

165–166. **haec:** the singular pronoun introduces a compound subject (*oratio et*
facultas) and ANTICIPATES the following *quae* clause. **oratio et facultas:** HENDIADYS for
orationis facultas, "capacity for public speaking." **periculis:** ablative with *defuit; pe-*
riculis refers here to legal entanglements (or in that sense, "hazards" in which his
friends became involved—see note on 34–36 above).

167. **desum, deesse, defui,** (*w. dat. of person, situation, etc.*) to fail (*in respect of*), be neglectful in one's duty (*to*) or support (*of*); to be lacking, not forthcoming.

    levis, ~e, unimportant, of little consequence; insignificant; trivial; slight.

    *** quidem, (*particle*) indeed, certainly, to be sure (*usu. emphasizes the word it immediately follows*); **ne...quidem,** not even (*usu. emphasizes the word or phrase it brackets*).

    certe, (*adv.* < **certus**) without doubt, surely.

168. *** summus, ~a, ~um,** (*superl. adj.* < **superior**), the highest, greatest, supreme.

    fons, fontis, *m.,* the source (*usu. of a river*); origin.

    haurio, haurire, hausi, haustus, to draw (*usu. water*); to take in; to derive.

    ** sentio, sentire, sensi, sensus, to realize, perceive; to feel (*with the senses*).

169. *** praeceptum, ~i,** *n.,* instruction, precept.

    * adulescentia, ~ae, *f.,* youth, young manhood; adolescence.

170. **suadeo, suadere, suasi, suasus,** (*w. dat. of person*) to persuade, give advice (*to*); to advise; to urge.

    magno opere or **magnopere,** (*adv.* < **magnus** + **opus**) especially, particularly.

    expeto, expetere, expetivi (~ii), expetitus, to seek after, desire; to try to obtain.

171. **laus, laudis,** *f.,* praise or praiseworthiness; renown; distinction.

    honestas, honestatis, *f.,* honesty; moral rectitude; integrity.

    persequor, persequi, persecutus, to seek to obtain; to strive to accomplish.

172. **cruciatus, ~us,** *m.,* pain, anguish, agony; the act of physical torture.

    mors, mortis, *f.,* death.

    exsilium, ~i, *n.,* the condition of banishment, exile.

    parvus, ~a, ~um, small in size, amount, quantity; of little worth; insignificant, of no consequence.

173. *** salus, salutis,** *f.,* safety, security.

    * tot, (*indecl. adj.*) so many.

174. **dimicatio, dimicationis,** *f.,* struggle.

    profligatus, ~a, ~um, ruined; desperate.

175. **cotidianus, ~a, ~um,** daily, every day.

    impetus, ~us, *m.,* attack, assault; violence or violent behavior.

    obicio, obicere, obieci, obiectus, to throw, hurl, cast; (*refl.*) to offer, expose oneself.

    plenus, ~a, ~um, (*w. gen.*) full, stocked.

    liber, libri, *m.,* book; a written account.

defuit. Quae si cui levior videtur, illa quidem certe quae
summa sunt ex quo fonte hauriam sentio. **14** Nam nisi mul-
torum praeceptis multisque litteris mihi ab adulescentia
170 suasissem nihil esse in vita magno opere expetendum nisi
laudem atque honestatem, in ea autem persequenda omnis
cruciatus corporis, omnia pericula mortis atque exsili parvi esse ducenda, numquam me pro salute vestra in tot ac
tantas dimicationes atque in hos profligatorum hominum
175 cotidianos impetus obiecissem. Sed pleni omnes sunt libri,

---

167–168. Quae...sentio: "And if this (capacity) seems to anyone somewhat trivial,
I certainly am aware from what source I derive those things (of it) that are of the
highest importance." **Quae:** the CONNECTING RELATIVE (= *et ea*), subject of *videtur*, singular because its compound antecedent (*oratio et facultas*) expresses a single idea
through HENDIADYS (cf. *laudem atque honestatem, in ea*, note 169–173 below). **cui:** = *alicui* (see note on 1 above). **levior:** when not used to make a comparison, a comparative adjective can describe a quality of considerable ("rather," "somewhat") or excessive ("too") degree, *B* 240.1. **illa:** neuter accusative plural, object of *hauriam* (cf. *quod
sentio quam sit exiguum* [1–2 above]). **quae:** the antecedent is *illa*. **summa:** contrast
with *levior*. **ex quo...hauriam:** an indirect question governed by **sentio:** the main
verb of the APODOSIS of the condition.

168–175. An extended past contrary-to-fact condition (*B* 304.1), whose PROTASIS
(*nisi...mihi...suasissem*) and APODOSIS (*numquam me... obiecissem*) BRACKET two indirect
statements (*nihil esse...expetendum nisi laudem atque honestatem :: omnis cruciatus...om-
nia pericula...parvi esse ducenda*) arranged in ASYNDETON.

169–173. **praeceptis multisque litteris:** ablatives of means. **mihi:** dative object of
suasissem. **magno opere:** "greatly," an adverbial phrase (often written as one word).
nisi...honestatem: (sc. *expetendam esse*) not another PROTASIS, but a modifying clause
introducing an exception to *nihil*. **in ea...persequenda:** introduces the second indirect statement with *suasissem*, "in the pursuit of which" (*ea* is singular because
the compound antecedent, *laudem atque honestatem*, while not strictly an instance of
HENDIADYS, still conveys a single idea [cf. *oratio et facultas...quae*, note 165–167 above]).
omnis cruciatus...omnia pericula: accusative plural subjects of the second indirect
statement (*omnis* = *omnes*, see note on 62–63 above). Note the ANTITHESIS of *omnis...
omnia* and *nihil* (subject of the first indirect statement). **parvi esse ducenda:** "ought
to be considered of little importance" (*parvi* = genitive of indefinite value, *B* 203.1).

173–175. **numquam...obiecissem:** the APODOSIS of the condition. **me:** direct object of *obiecissem*. **vestra:** i.e., that of the *iudices*, but Cicero includes his entire audience. **in...dimicationes atque in hos...impetus:** the repetition of *in* balances the two
prepositional phrases, but the addition of the demonstrative *hos* marks a shift from
a general statement (*tot ac tantas*) to something more specific, perhaps an allusion to
Cicero's suppression of the Catilinarian conspiracy, and its consequences, during
his consulship in 63 B.C.

176. **sapiens, sapientis,** wise, educated; (*as subst.*) a wise man.

exemplum, ~i, *n.,* model, example; (*leg.*) a precedent.

vetustas, vetustatis, *f.,* tradition; the people, customs, or institutions of the distant past; antiquity.

177. **iaceo, iacere, iacui, iaciturus,** to lie, lie dead; be situated.

tenebrae, ~arum, *f., (usu. pl.)* darkness, shadows; obscurity.

* **lumen, luminis,** *n.,* light, light of day; any source of illumination; brilliance, excellence.

accedo, accedere, accessi, accessurus, to draw near, approach; be added.

178. **imago, imaginis,** *f.,* the death-masks of their ancestors that Romans displayed in the *atria* of their houses and carried in funeral processions.

intueor, intueri, intuitus, to watch, gaze at; to examine, consider, reflect upon (*as an example*).

179. **imitor, ~ari, ~atus,** to copy the conduct of, imitate.

fortis, ~e, brave, fearless.

*** **vir, viri,** *m.,* a man; hero; husband.

180. **exprimo, exprimere, expressi, expressus,** to make, produce; to express, portray (*in painting, sculpture, etc.*).

scriptor, scriptoris, *m.,* a writer, author.

relinquo, relinquere, reliqui, relictus, to leave, leave behind.

181. **administro, ~are, ~avi, ~atus,** to manage, perform the duties of, administer.

propono, proponere, proposui, propositus, (*refl. w. dat.*) to hold up to oneself (*as a model*).

182. **cogitatio, cogitationis,** *f.,* the act of thinking, thought; reflection; acknowledgment; recognition.

183. **excellens, excellentis,** outstanding, excellent.

* **conformo, ~are, ~avi, ~atus,** to shape, mold; (*w.* **animus, mens,** *etc.*) to educate oneself.

plenae sapientium voces, (plena exemplorum vetustas;
quae iacerent in tenebris omnia, nisi litterarum lumen ac-
cederet. Quam multas nobis imagines non solum ad intuendum verum etiam ad imitandum fortissimorum virorum
180 expressas scriptores et Graeci et Latini reliquerunt! Quas
ego mihi semper in administranda re publica proponens
animum et mentem meam ipsa cogitatione hominum excel-
lentium conformabam.

175–177. **pleni** (p. 41)**...plenae...plena:** the three clauses, arranged in ASYNDETON, mark a dramatic shift in tempo from the lengthy PERIODICITY of the previous sentence. **sapientium:** genitive plural, with *voces,* "the voices of wise men." **exemplorum:** partitive genitive, construe with all three forms of *plenus.* **quae:** the CONNECTING RELATIVE (= *et ea*), neuter nominative plural (antecedent = *exemplorum*). **iacerent...accederet:** imperfect subjunctives in a present contrary-to-fact condition, B 304.1. **omnia:** modifies *quae,* its emphatic postponement until the end of the clause is an example of HYPERBATON.

178–180. **Quam:** the adverb, construe with *multas:* "How many..." **nobis:** the dative has two possibilities: (1) agent with the gerunds (*intuendum...imitandum*); (2) indirect object of *reliquerunt.* **imagines...expressas:** an artistic metaphor from sculpture (cf. 368–369); the separation of the participle from its subject BRACKETS the two gerunds, set in symmetry by *non solum...verum etiam,* expressing purpose (B 338.3), and modifying the participle: "created not only to be viewed, but also to be imitated." **fortissimorum virorum:** genitive plural with *imagines.* **et Graeci et Latini:** nominative plural, modifying *scriptores,* "writers, both Greek and Latin."

180–183. **Quas:** the CONNECTING RELATIVE (= *et eas*), direct object of *proponens* (the antecedent is *imagines*). **mihi:** dative of reference with *proponens,* B 188.1: "And holding these always before me," i.e., as examples. **in administranda re publica:** an allusion to his consulship in the preceding year. **ipsa...excellentium:** "by the very contemplation of outstanding men," construe with *conformabam.*

184. ** **quaero, quaerere, quaesivi (~ii), quaesitus,** to inquire, ask.

   quispiam, quaepiam, quippiam (quidpiam), an unspecified person or thing; someone, something; anyone, anything.

   ** **summus, ~a, ~um,** (*superl. adj.* < **superior**) the highest, greatest, supreme.

185. * **virtus, virtutis,** *f.,* virtue, moral excellence; character; courage, bravery.

   prodo, prodere, prodidi, proditus, to hand down, transmit.

   * **doctrina, ~ae,** *f.,* formal teaching, instruction; a branch or area of learning.

186. **effero, efferre, extuli, elatus,** to lift up; to carry off, remove.

   * **laus, laudis,** *f.,* praise or praiseworthiness; renown; distinction.

   erudio, erudire, erudivi (~ii), eruditus, to instruct, educate.

   difficilis, ~e, not easy, difficult; hard, painful; dangerous.

187. * **confirmo, ~are, ~avi, ~atus,** to establish, confirm.

   certus, ~a, ~um, fixed, definite, certain; (*of individuals*) resolute, trusty, faithful.

   respondeo, respondere, respondi, responsus, to answer, respond.

188. * **excellens, excellentis,** outstanding, excellent.

   ** **virtus, virtutis,** *f.,* moral excellence, character.

189. **sine,** (*prep. w. abl.*) without.

   * **natura, ~ae,** *f.,* inborn abilities; natural endowments.

   habitus, ~us, *m.,* quality, character.

   ** **prope,** (*adv.*) almost, nearly, all but.

190. **moderatus, ~a, ~um,** temperate, restrained, moderate.

   gravis, ~e, heavy, ponderous; (*of people*) venerable, serious, severe, distinguished.

   * **exsto, exstare, exstiti,** to emerge, stand out, exist (*in a given manner or capacity*).

   * **fateor, fateri, fassus,** to confess, acknowledge; to admit, declare.

191. **adiungo, adiungere, adiunxi, adiunctus,** to add, mention in addition.

   saepius, (*comp. adv.* < **saepe**) more often.

192. **valeo, valere, valui, valiturus,** to be strong; to have power, influence.

15 Quaeret quispiam: "Quid? Illi ipsi summi viri,
185   quorum virtutes litteris proditae sunt, istane doctrina
quam tu effers laudibus eruditi fuerunt?" Difficile est hoc
de omnibus confirmare, sed tamen est certum quid respondeam. Ego multos homines excellenti animo ac virtute fuisse et sine doctrina, naturae ipsius habitu prope
190   divino per se ipsos et moderatos et gravis exstitisse fateor;
etiam illud adiungo: saepius ad laudem atque virtutem
naturam sine doctrina quam sine natura valuisse doctrinam.

184–186. **Quaeret quispiam:** Cicero again uses the rhetorical figure OCCUPATIO
(cf. *quaeres,* 144–145 above) to anticipate and then rebut an argument against the value of literary pursuits. The objection, framed as a question in direct statement, asks
whether Rome's illustrious *summi viri* would have achieved their historic greatness
without benefit of a liberal arts education.

    "Quid?": see note on 126 above. **Illi ipsi summi viri:** the subject of the main
clause is emphatically introduced by both a demonstrative and intensive pronoun,
the former serving also to ANTICIPATE the relative *quorum* clause. **litteris:** ablative of
means with *proditae sunt,* "recorded in literature." **istane doctrina:** the ablative of
means, modifying *eruditi fuerunt,* is introduced by the intensive pronoun *ista,* AN-
TICIPATING the following relative *quam* clause, while the placement of the enclitic interrogative particle *-ne* (*B* 162.2.c) focuses the question on *doctrina:* "was it by means
of this particular education...?" **laudibus:** construe with *eruditi fuerunt:* "educated to
greatness," or perhaps "raised to glory."

    186–188. **hoc:** neuter accusative singular, object of *confirmare,* the subjective in-
finitive of *difficile est.* **quid respondeam:** an indirect question, subject of *est certum.*

    188–190. **Ego...fateor:** the HYPERBATON of subject and verb BRACKETS two indirect
statements in ASYNDETON. **homines:** the subject of both *fuisse* and *exstitisse.* **excellenti animo ac virtute:** ablatives of quality or description, used predicatively to modify
homines (*B* 224.1). **sine doctrina, naturae...habitu:** the distinction is between greatness achieved through learning (*doctrina*), or natural endowment (*naturae*). **divino:**
construe with *habitu.* **et moderatos et gravis:** accusative plural complements of *homines* (*gravis* = *graves,* see note on 62–63 above).

    191–192. **illud:** object of *adiungo* and antecedent of the following indirect state-
ment (*B* 246.2). **saepius...quam:** "more often...than..." the comparative construction
balances the two clauses of the BIPARTITE indirect statement. **valuisse:** the verb of
both *naturam* and *doctrinam,* construe with *ad laudem atque virtutem,* "has had the
power to achieve glory and excellence."

193. **contendo, contendere, contendi, contentus,** to assert, allege, maintain.

     ** **natura, ~ae,** *f.,* inborn abilities; natural endowments.

     eximius, ~a, ~um, special, remarkable, outstanding, exceptional.

194. **inlustris, ~e,** illustrious, famous, distinguished.

     * **accedo, accedere, accessi, accessurus,** to draw near, approach.

     conformatio, conformationis, *f.,* training through formal instruction; education.

195. ** **doctrina, ~ae,** *f.,* formal teaching, instruction; a branch or area of learning.

     nescioquid, indecl., *n.,* something or other (< **nescio, nescire, nescivi (~ii), nescitus** [to not know, be ignorant] + **quid** [something] (*often used to describe something ineffable or inscrutable*).

     praeclarus, ~a, ~um, illustrious, glorious, distinguished.

196. *** **soleo, solere, solui, solitus,** (*w. inf.*) to be accustomed.

     exsisto, exsistere, exstiti, to come into being, emerge, arise.

198. * **moderatus, ~a, ~um,** temperate, restrained, moderate.

199. **continens, continentis,** self-restrained, temperate.

     * **fortis, ~e,** brave, fearless.

200. **doctus, ~a, ~um,** educated, learned.

     senex, senis, *m.,* an old man (*a term of distinction usu. applied to historical figures with allusion to their venerability*).

201. ** **profecto,** (*adv.*) surely, certainly; without doubt.

     * **percipio, percipere, percepi, perceptus,** to take possession of, acquire.

     ** **colo, colere, colui, cultus,** to cultivate, develop, foster.

     *** **virtus, virtutis,** *f.,* moral excellence, character.

202. **adiuvo, ~are, ~avi, ~atus,** to help, aid; (*w. dat.*) to help, give aid (*to*); (*w.* **ad** *or* **in** + *acc.*) to facilitate progress toward, contribute to.

203. * **confero, conferre, contuli, collatus;** (*refl. w.* **se**) to betake oneself, to go.

     * **fructus, ~us,** *m.,* advantage, gain, profit; enjoyment, gratification, pleasure.

     ostendo, ostendere, ostendi, ostentus, to show, reveal; (*pass.*) be evident.

204. **delectatio, delectationis,** *f.,* the gaining of pleasure or delight; a source of enjoyment.

     peto, petere, petivi (~ii), petitus, to seek; to aim for, attack.

tempora

Atque idem ego hoc contendo: cum ad naturam eximiam et inlustrem accesserit ratio quaedam conformatioque
195   doctrinae, tum illud nescioquid praeclarum ac singulare solere exsistere. **16** Ex hoc esse hunc numero quem patres nostri viderunt, divinum hominem, Africanum, ex hoc C. Laelium, L. Furium, moderatissimos homines et continentissimos, ex hoc fortissimum virum et illis
200   temporibus doctissimum, M. Catonem illum senem. Qui profecto si nihil ad percipiendam colendamque virtutem litteris adiuvarentur, numquam se ad earum studium *imperfect h.bj* contulissent. Quod si non hic tantus fructus ostenderetur, et si ex his studiis delectatio sola peteretur, tamen,

---

193–196. **idem:** construe with *ego* (see note on 103–106 above). **hoc:** object of *contendo* and antecedent of the following indirect statement (cf. *illud*, 191 above). **cum... tum:** "when...then." **accesserit:** "has been added (to)." **ratio...doctrinae:** "a certain system of training and education imparted by instruction." **illud nescioquid:** subject of *solere*, intentionally vague despite the demonstrative, "that certain something or other." **praeclarum ac singulare:** construe with *nescioquid*.

196–200. A list of historical *exempla* connected by the ANAPHORA of *ex hoc* (for the biographies of the individuals mentioned see APPENDIX I).

196–197. **Ex hoc...numero:** "from this number," where we would say "in this number," or "among these." **esse hunc:** a continuation of the indirect statement dependent on *contendo* from the previous sentence. **divinum hominem, Africanum:** in APPOSITION to *hunc*.

198–199. **ex hoc:** sc. *numero esse.* **moderatissimos...continentissimos:** plurals in APPOSITION to the compound antecedent *C. Laelium, L. Furium.*

199–200. **fortissimum...doctissimum:** in APPOSITION to *Catonem*, so also *illum senem.* **illis temporibus:** ablative of time during which (*B* 231.1), construe with *doctissimum.*

200–203. **Qui:** nominative plural, CONNECTING RELATIVE (= *et ii*), referring to all the individuals just mentioned. **si...adiuvarentur...contulissent:** a contrary-to-fact condition referring to the past. The imperfect subjunctive of the PROTASIS refers to a continued act, the pluperfect subjunctive of the APODOSIS describes completed action, *B* 304.2. **nihil:** adverbial, "not at all." **ad...virtutem:** "in their progress toward achieving and cultivating excellence." **litteris:** ablative of means with *adiuvarentur.* **se...contulissent:** see note on 42–44 above. **earum:** the antecedent is *litteris.*

203–205. **Quod si...ostenderetur...peteretur:** "But if..." a contrary-to-fact condition with a BIPARTITE PROTASIS.

205. **opinor, ~ari, ~atus,** to hold as an opinion, believe.

    remissio, remissionis, *f.,* the act of relaxing; (*w.* **animi**) the relaxation of the mind.

    humanus, ~a, ~um, human, of man or mankind, civilized.

    liberalis, ~e, gentlemanly, decent; characteristic of a liberal arts education.

206. * **iudico, ~are, ~avi, ~atus,** to judge, appraise.

207. ** **aetas, aetatis,** *f.,* the span of one's life or lifetime.

    ** **adulescentia, ~ae,** *f.,* youth, young manhood; adolescence.

208. **acuo, acuere, acui, acutus,** to stir up, arouse, incite; (*of the senses*) to sharpen, make keen.

    * **senectus, senectutis,** *f.,* the period of old age.

    oblecto, ~are, ~avi, ~atus, to delight, amuse, entertain.

    secundus, ~a, ~um, favorable, advantageous.

209. **orno, ~are, ~avi, ~atus,** to adorn, decorate (*with honors, etc.*).

    perfugium, ~i, *n.,* a place of refuge, shelter; a sanctuary.

    solacium, ~i, *n.,* relief in sorrow, solace; a consolation.

    praebeo, praebere, praebui, praebitus, to offer, supply.

    * **delecto, ~are, ~avi, ~atus,** to charm, delight, please.

210. **impedio, impedire, impedivi (~ii), impeditus,** to obstruct.

    foris, (*adv.*) abroad; outside; away from home.

    pernocto, ~are, ~avi, ~atus, to spend the night.

    peregrinor, ~ari, ~atus, to go or travel abroad.

211. **rusticor, ~ari, ~atus,** to live or stay in the country.

212. **attingo, attingere, attigi, attactus,** to touch, make contact (*with*).

    sensus, ~us, *m.,* the faculties of perception; any of the five senses.

213. **gusto, ~are, ~avi, ~atus,** to taste.

    * **miror, ~ari, ~atus,** to wonder. *at, to admire*

    ** **debeo, debere, debui, debitus,** (*w. inf.*) to be under obligation to do something.

214. **agrestis, ~e,** boorish, coarse, unrefined, unsophisticated.

215. **durus, ~a, ~um,** (*of people*) dull, slow, obtuse.

    * **mors, mortis,** *f.,* death.

    nuper, (*adv.*) recently, lately; (*as adjective*) recent.

    * **commoveo, commovere, commovi, commotus,** to disturb.

216. * **senex, senis,** *m.,* an old man.

    morior, mori, mortuus, to die, be killed.

    ** **propter,** (*prep. w. acc.*) because of, on account of.

    ** **excellens, excellentis,** outstanding, excellent.

217. **venustas, venustatis,** *f.,* the quality of being charming.

Optional Reading: On the Benefits of Reading and Cultivating a Reading Lifestyle (Appendix III, p. 116)

205 ut opinor, hanc animi remissionem humanissimam ac liberalissimam iudicaretis. Nam ceterae neque temporum sunt
neque aetatum omnium neque locorum; at haec studia adulescentiam acuunt, senectutem oblectant, secundas res
ornant, adversis perfugium ac solacium praebent, delectant
210 domi, non impediunt foris, pernoctant nobiscum, peregrinantur, rusticantur.

17 Quod si ipsi haec neque attingere neque sensu nostro gustare possemus, tamen ea mirari deberemus, etiam
cum in aliis videremus. Quis nostrum tam animo agresti ac
215 duro fuit ut Rosci morte nuper non commoveretur? qui
cum esset senex mortuus, tamen propter excellentem ar-
tem ac venustatem videbatur omnino mori non debuisse.

205–206. **ut opinor:** a parenthetical aside: "as I suppose." **hanc...remissionem:** the use of the demonstrative pronoun (*hanc*) ANTICIPATES the contrast with *ceterae* in the next sentence. **humanissimam ac liberalissimam:** predicate adjectives of *remissionem*.

206–211. The structure of this sentence, whose two members are arranged in ASYNDETON, turns on the antithesis of *ceterae* :: *at haec*.

206–207. **ceterae:** (sc. *remissiones*) "other sources of relaxation of the mind," i.e., those not derived *ex studiis*. **temporum...aetatum...locorum:** (sc. *omnium*) genitives of quality (B 203) as predicate adjectives of *ceterae*.

207–211. In contrast to the simple structure of the first member, the second member of the ANTITHESIS is made up of a series of nine short, independent clauses, of which **studia** is the subject, arranged PARATACTICALLY and organized in two TRICOLA. **adulescentiam...foris:** the first TRICOLON contains the first six clauses, arranged in three contrasting pairs (*adulescentiam* :: *senectutem; secundas* :: *adversis; domi* :: *foris*). **adversis:** (sc. *rebus*) ablative (here expressing attendant circumstance) with *praebent* (B 223). **domi:** locative, "at home." **pernoctant...rusticantur:** the second TRICOLON, with three intransitive verbs, differs significantly from the first in structure and tempo.

212–214. **Quod si:** "But if..." **ipsi:** nominative plural (sc. *nos*), "we ourselves." **haec** (with implied *studia*): neuter accusative plural referring again to *studia liberalia*, object of *attingere* and *gustare* (complementary infinitives of *possemus*), antecedent of **ea:** object of *mirari* (complementary infinitive of *deberemus*). **etiam cum:** "even when."

214–217. **Quis nostrum:** "Who of us" (cf. *vestrum*, 22–23 above). **tam:** construe with *agresti ac duro*, ablatives of description. **ut:** result clause, ANTICIPATED by *tam*. **nuper:** the adverb used adjectivally with *morte*, "by the recent death." **qui:** CONNECTING RELATIVE (= *et is*), the antecedent is *Rosci* (one of Rome's most celebrated actors, see APPENDIX I). **morte:** ablative of cause (B 219) with *commoveretur*. **cum...tamen:** "although...nevertheless." **senex:** "as an old man," in APPOSITION to an understood *Roscius*. Take *mortuus* with *esset*, as pluperfect tense of the deponent. **videbatur...debuisse:** "it seemed that he ought not to have died at all."

218. * **corpus, corporis,** *n.,* the body.
motus, ~us, *m.,* motion, movement.
amor, amoris, *m.,* love, affection; the object of love or desire.
concilio, ~are, ~avi, ~atus, to procure, get; to win over, obtain.
219. **incredibilis, ~e,** incredible, beyond belief.
celeritas, celeritatis, *f.,* swiftness, speed.
220. * **neglego, neglegere, neglexi, neglectus,** to neglect, fail to observe or respect.
quotiens, (*interrog. and rel. adv.*) how many times? how often?
221. ** **utor, uti, usus,** (*w. abl.*) to use, employ, exploit.
benignitas, benignitatis, *f.,* kindness, indulgence.
* **quoniam,** (*conj.*) since, because.
222. ** **genus, generis,** *n.,* type, style.
diligenter, (*adv.*) diligently, with care.
attendo, attendere, attendi, attentus, (*w. acc.*) to listen to, pay attention to.
223. *** **scribo, scribere, scripsi, scriptus,** to write.
224. **versus, ~us,** *m.,* a line of verse, poetry.
225. **revoco, ~are, ~avi, ~atus,** to call back, recall (*esp. for an encore*).
226. **commuto, ~are, ~avi, ~atus,** to change, exchange one for another.
verbum, ~i, *n.,* word, utterance.
sententia, ~ae, *f.,* thought, feeling, idea; a sentence, phrase.
227. **accurate,** (*adv.*) with attention to detail; meticulously, carefully.
cogitate, (*adv.*) with thought; carefully.
228. **probo, ~are, ~avi, ~atus,** to approve, commend.
vetus, veteris, long-standing, well-established; veteran.
* **scriptor, scriptoris,** *m.,* a writer, author.
** **laus, laudis,** *f.,* praise or praiseworthiness; renown; distinction.
pervenio, pervenire, perveni, perventus, to arrive (*at a place, situation, station, etc.*); to attain (*a position*).

Recite

Ergo ille corporis motu tantum amorem sibi conciliarat a nobis
omnibus; nos animorum incredibilis motus celeritatemque
220 ingeniorum neglegemus? **18** Quotiens ego hunc Archiam
vidi, iudices—utar enim vestra benignitate, quoniam me
in hoc novo genere dicendi tam diligenter attenditis—quotiens ego hunc vidi, cum litteram scripsisset nullam, magnum numerum optimorum versuum de eis ipsis rebus
225 quae tum agerentur dicere ex tempore, quotiens revocatum eandem rem dicere commutatis verbis atque senten-
tiis! Quae vero accurate cogitateque scripsisset, ea sic vidi
probari ut ad veterum scriptorum laudem perveniret. Hunc

218–220. Another BIPARTITE sentence whose two members, joined in ASYNDETON,
are set in contrast by the ANTITHESIS of *ille* :: *nos*.

Ergo: "therefore." It introduces a statement that logically follows from what has
preceded (*B* 344.1.b). **ille:** i.e., Roscius. **corporis motu:** i.e., by his acting. **conciliarat:**
(= *conciliaverat*) "had won for himself (*sibi*) such great love (*tantum amorem*) from
us all (*a nobis omnibus*). **nos:** corresponds antithetically to *ille* but picks up and emphasizes *a nobis omnibus* in the preceding sentence. **animorum...motus:** parallel to
corporis motu; the point of the ANTITHESIS is the physical activity of the actor's body
vs. the intellectual activity of the poet's mind. **incredibilis:** accusative plural (= *in-
credibiles*, see note on 62–63 above), modifying *motus*.

220–227. A complex sentence addressing Archias' talent as a poet: an extended
indirect statement with two accusative + infinitive predicate clauses interrupted
first by a parenthetical aside (*utar...attenditis*), then by a *cum* clause, and then by a
quae clause. The skeleton of the sentence is: *Quotiens ego hunc Archiam vidi... (cum
litteram scripsisset) numerum... de...rebus (quae...agerentur) dicere* :: *quotiens* [sc. *ego hunc
vidi*] *eandem rem dicere...*

Quotiens: exclamatory, "how often!" **hunc Archiam:** accusative subject of the
indirect statement. **utar:** future, as explained by the following *quoniam* clause. **vestra
benignitate:** ablative, object of *utar*. **cum:** concessive, "although." **numerum:** object
of *dicere*, the verb of the indirect statement dependent on *vidi*. **quae tum agerentur:**
i.e., current events (the antecedent is *rebus*, indicated by the demonstrative *eis*). **dicere ex tempore:** i.e., he improvised. **revocatum:** (sc. *hunc*) "called back for an encore."
eandem rem dicere: "recite the same material." **commutatis verbis...sententiis:** an
ablative absolute expressing means: "with altered words and altered phrases."

227–228. **Quae...scripsisset:** the relative clause precedes *ea*, its antecedent in the
main clause, for emphasis. **sic:** construe with *probari*. **ut...perveniret:** result clause,
ANTICIPATED by *sic*. **ad veterum scriptorum laudem:** *laudem* here has the sense "the
level of renown." **Hunc:** i.e., Archias.

229. **diligo, diligere, dilexi, dilectus,** to hold dear, love, cherish.

    admiror, ~ari, ~atus, to admire, hold in high esteem or regard.

230. ***** summus, ~a, ~um,** the highest, greatest, supreme.

231. **** eruditus, ~a, ~um,** learned, accomplished.

    * accipio, accipere, accepi, acceptus, to take, receive.

232. ***** doctrina, ~ae,** *f.,* formal teaching, instruction.

    ** praeceptum, ~i, *n.,* instruction, precept.

    consto, ~are, ~iti, (*w.* **ex** + *abl.*) to consist (*of*).

    *** natura, ~ae, *f.,* inborn abilities; natural endowments.

233. *** valeo, valere, valui, valiturus,** to be strong; have influence.

    * mens, mentis, *f.,* the mind.

    vis, vis, *f.,* (*w.* **animus, mens**) intellectual ability.

    excito, ~are, ~avi, ~atus, to rouse, stir (*the senses*); to inspire.

    * quasi, (*adv.*) as it were, in a manner of speaking.

234. **spiritus, ~us,** *m.,* divine inspiration.

    inflo, ~are, ~avi, ~atus, to blow into, fill with breath; to inspire.

    * quare (*interrog. and rel. adv.*) for what reason, wherefore.

    * sanctus, ~a, ~um, scrupulous, upright, virtuous.

235. **appello, ~are, ~avi, ~atus,** to name, call.

    donum, ~i, *n.,* a gift, award.

236. **munus, muneris,** *n.,* duty; gift, tribute, offering; prize, reward

    commendo, ~are, ~avi, ~atus, to entrust, recommend.

237. ***** apud,** (*prep. w. acc.*), among, before.

    * humanus, ~a, ~um, human, of man or mankind, civilized.

239. **barbaria, ~ae,** *f.,* lack of civilization, brutality, barbarism.

    violo, ~are, ~avi, ~atus, to violate.

    saxum, ~i, *n.,* stone, rock, boulder.

    solitudo, solitudinis, *f.,* the state of being alone, solitude; (*of places*) **a deserted** place, uninhabited country.

240. *** respondeo, respondere, respondi, responsus,** to answer.

    bestia, ~ae, *f.,* a beast, animal, creature (*distinct from man*).

    * saepe, (*adv.*) often, continuously.

    immanis, ~e, huge, vast; monstrous, dreadful.

    cantus, ~us, *m.,* singing, a song.

    flecto, flectere, flexi, flectus, to bend, turn, influence.

241. **consisto, consistere, constiti,** to come to a stop, stand still.

    instituo, instituere, institui, institutus, to form, instruct, teach.

242. **moveo, movere, movi, motus,** to move, arouse, excite.

243. **vindico, ~are, ~avi, ~atus,** to lay claim to, assert one's title to.

    ** repeto, repetere, repetivi (~ii), repetitus, to demand.

ego non diligam, non admirer, non omni ratione
230 defendendum putem? Atque sic a summis hominibus
eruditissimisque accepimus, ceterarum rerum studia ex
doctrina et praeceptis et arte constare; poetam natura ipsa
valere et mentis viribus excitari et quasi divino quodam
spiritu inflari. Quare suo iure noster ille Ennius "sanctos"
235 appellat poetas, quod quasi deorum aliquo dono atque
munere commendati nobis esse videantur.

19 Sit igitur, iudices, sanctum apud vos, humanissimos homines, hoc poetae nomen quod nulla
umquam barbaria violavit. Saxa atque solitudines voci
240 respondent, bestiae saepe immanes cantu flectuntur atque
consistunt; nos instituti rebus optimis non poetarum voce
moveamur? Homerum Colophonii civem esse dicunt
suum, Chii suum vindicant, Salaminii repetunt, Smyrnaei

229–230. **non diligam...admirer...putem:** deliberative subjunctives (B 277),
"should I not...?" **defendendum:** sc. *esse hunc*, an indirect statement dependent
on *putem.*

230–234. **sic...accepimus:** the governing construction of the following four accusative + infinitive constructions, ANTICIPATED by *sic*, "thus we have learned from
the greatest and most learned men that..." **studia:** neuter accusative plural, subject
of *constare.* **ex doctrina et praeceptis et arte:** construe with *constare*, "consist of..." (B
218.4). **poetam:** subject of *valere, excitari,* and *inflari.* **natura ipsa:** ablative of means
with *valere* (in contrast to *ex doctrina...etc.*), "derives his power from nature itself."
viribus: ablative plural (< **vis**); with *mentis*: "by means of the powers of his imagina-
tion." **quasi...spiritu:** see note on 21–22 above (so also for **quasi...munere** below).

234–236. **suo iure:** i.e., because Ennius himself was a poet (for Ennius' life and
career see APPENDIX I). **quod...videantur:** a causal clause in indirect statement takes
the subjunctive (B 314.1).

237–239. **Sit:** the independent "jussive" subjunctive (B 275). **sanctum:** predicate
adjective of *nomen*, the subject of *sit.* **humanissimos homines:** in APPOSITION to *vos.*
hoc: the pronoun ANTICIPATES the following relative *quod* clause. **barbaria:** note the
ANTITHESIS with *humanissimos.*

239–241. **Saxa...respondent:** i.e., echo the sound of his voice. **voci:** (sc. *poetae*) dative with *respondent.* **cantu:** ablative of means with *flectuntur.* **instituti:** nominative
plural masculine, construe with *nos.*

242–243. For the *Colophonii, Chii, Salaminii,* and *Smyrnaei* see APPENDIX I.
Homerum...civem esse...suum: an indirect statement, dependent on *dicunt.* **Chii
suum vindicant:** sc. *Homerum civem esse.*

244. ** **confirmo, ~are, ~avi, ~atus,** to establish, confirm.

* **itaque,** (*adv.*) accordingly.

delubrum, ~i, *n.,* a shrine, temple.

245. * **oppidum, ~i,** *n.,* a town.

dedico, ~are, ~avi, ~atus, to dedicate.

permultus, ~a, ~um, a great many, very many.

praeterea, (*adv.*) moreover; besides; after that.

pugno, ~are, ~avi, ~atus, to fight, contend.

246. * **contendo, contendere, contendi, contentus,** to assert, argue (*a point, an issue, etc.*); to take issue (*over something*).

alienus, ~a, ~um, a stranger, non-citizen; of another race, etc.

247. ** **mors, mortis,** *f.,* death.

* **expeto, expetere, expetivi (~ii), expetitus,** to seek after, desire; to try to obtain.

vivus, ~a, ~um, alive, living.

voluntas, voluntatis, *f.,* free will, choice; personal inclination.

248. * **praesertim,** (*adv.*) especially; (*w.* **cum**) especially since.

* **repudio, ~are, ~avi, ~atus,** to refuse, reject, disregard as false.

olim, (*adv.*) for a long time past, since long ago, formerly.

249. ** **confero, conferre, contuli, collatus,** to devote, bring, apply.

250. *** **laus, laudis,** *f.,* praise, glory, renown, distinction.

** **celebro, ~are, ~avi, ~atus,** to praise, extol, celebrate (*in speech, song, poetry, etc.*).

251. **adulescens, adulescentis,** young, youthful.

* **attingo, attingere, attigi, attactus,** to touch upon, treat, address, deal with (*a subject, issue, etc.*).

* **durus, ~a, ~um,** insensitive, unresponsive.

252. * **iucundus, ~a, ~um,** (*w. dat.*) congenial, agreeable (*to*).

245 vero suum esse confirmant itaque etiam delubrum eius in
oppido dedicaverunt, permulti alii praeterea pugnant inter
se atque contendunt. Ergo illi alienum, quia poeta fuit, post
mortem etiam expetunt; nos hunc vivum qui et voluntate et
legibus noster est repudiamus, praesertim cum omne olim
studium atque omne ingenium contulerit Archias ad populi
250 Romani gloriam laudemque celebrandam? Nam et Cimbricas res adulescens attigit et ipsi illi C. Mario qui durior ad haec studia videbatur iucundus fuit. **20** Neque

244–246. suum esse: sc. *Homerum civem*, an indirect statement dependent on *con-firmant*. **itaque:** see note on *ergo*, 217–220 above. **delubrum eius:** a shrine to Homer. **dedicaverunt:** subject = *Smyrnaei*. **pugnant...contendunt:** i.e., for the right to claim Homer's citizenship.

246–250. The point of this BIPARTITE sentence, containing two independent claus-es, is the ANTITHESIS between those ancient Greeks (*illi*) who in rivalry with each other sought (*expetunt*) Homer's citizenship—albeit posthumously (*post mortem*), and even though he was a foreigner (*alienum*)—and present-day Romans (*nos*), who would refuse (*repudiamus*) citizenship to Archias who unlike Homer is neither dead nor a foreigner (*vivus...noster est*).

illi: i.e., the *Colophonii, Chii, Salaminii,* and the *Smyrnaei.* **hunc:** i.e., Archias. **praesertim cum:** see note on 120–121 above. **contulerit:** perfect subjunctive. **populi Romani:** genitive; construe with both *gloriam* and *laudem* (note how the phrase is BRACKETED by *ad...celebrandam*).

250–252. Cimbricas res: object of *attigit*; the reference is to the military campaign conducted by Marius and Q. Lutatius Catulus against the Cimbri in 101 B.C. (cf. note on 62–63 above). **adulescens attigit:** (sc. *versibus*) "though still a youth he took up in his poetry..." **ipsi illi C. Mario...iucundus fuit:** an important point for Cicero to bring out is Marius' approval of Archias' poem about his Cimbrian campaign; by using two demonstrative pronouns to introduce his name, Cicero reminds his audi-ence of the weight Marius' opinion carried. **durior:** "rather insensitive" (for this use of the comparative see note on *levior*, 167–168). **haec studia:** i.e., poetry.

253. **quisquam, quicquam,** (*indef. pron.*) anyone, anything (*at all*).

    aversus, ~a, ~um, (*w.* **a** + *abl.*) estranged (*from*), averse (*to*).

    mando, ~are, ~avi, ~atus, to hand over, entrust.

254. * **versus, ~us,** *m.,* a line of verse, poetry.

    labor, laboris, *m.,* labor, task; effort, struggle; trial, hardship.

    praeconium, ~i, *n.,* a public announcement or proclamation.

255. * **patior, pati, passus,** to allow (*w. inf.*).

256. **aiunt,** (< **aio,** to say) a defective verb, i.e., found only in someforms, most commonly the third person singular (**ait**) or plural (**aiunt**), and usually with an indefinite subject.

    *** **quaero, quaerere, quaesivi (~ii), quaesitus,** to inquire.

    acroama, acroamatis, *n.,* an act; any form of entertainment.

257. **libenter,** (*adv.*) freely, gladly.

258. **optime,** (*superl. adv.* < **bene**) competently, most satisfactorily.

    praedico, ~are, ~avi, ~atus, to announce, declare publicly.

    ** **itaque,** (*adv.*) accordingly.

    item, (*adv.*) in addition, as well; in the same manner, likewise.

    eximie, (*adv.*) especially, exceptionally, outstandingly.

259. * **diligo, diligere, dilexi, dilectus,** to hold dear, love, cherish.

    ** **gero, gerere, gessi, gestus,** to carry on, do, perform.

260. *** **celebro, ~are, ~avi, ~atus,** to praise, extol, celebrate (*in speech, song, poetry, etc.*).

261. * **varietas, varietatis,** *f.,* a variety; the quality of being many different things, (*i.e., forms, aspects, natures, etc.*).

    terra, ~ae, *f.,* land, the earth; a country.

    mare, maris, *n.,* the sea.

    ** **verso, ~are, ~avi, ~atus,** to turn; (*pass.*) to be engaged in.

262. * **totus, ~a, ~um,** (*usu. w. defining gen.*) the whole (*of something*), all; whole, complete.

    * **exprimo, exprimere, expressi, expressus,** to make, produce; to express, portray (*in painting, sculpture, etc.*).

    * **liber, libri,** *m.,* book; a written account.

263. ** **fortis, ~e,** brave, fearless.

    * **clarissimus, ~a, ~um,** (*superl.* < **clarus**) most distinguished (*usu. men of senatorial rank*).

enim quisquam est tam aversus a Musis qui non mandari
versibus aeternum suorum laborum praeconium facile
255   patiatur. Themistoclem illum, summum Athenis virum,
dixisse aiunt, cum ex eo quaereretur quod acroama aut
cuius vocem libentissime audiret: eius a quo sua virtus
optime praedicaretur. Itaque ille Marius item eximie L.
Plotium dilexit, cuius ingenio putabat ea quae gesserat
260   posse celebrari. **21** Mithridaticum vero bellum magnum
atque difficile et in multa varietate terra marique versatum
totum ab hoc expressum est; qui libri non modo L. Lucul-
lum, fortissimum et clarissimum virum, verum etiam

253–257. **tam:** construe with *aversus.* **qui...patiatur:** relative clause of result (*B*
284.2), anticipated by *tam.* **summum...virum:** in apposition to *Themistoclem.* **Athenis:** locative. **dixisse:** perfect infinitive in indirect statement, dependent on **aiunt,**
the main verb of the sentence with an indefinite subject, "they say." **cum...quae-
reretur:** an impersonal passive construction, "when it was asked of him." **quod...
aut cuius...audiret:** two indirect questions dependent on *quaereretur,* "which act or
whose voice he would most gladly hear." Cicero introduces the first with an interrogative relative adjective (*quod*), the second with an interrogative relative pronoun
(*cuius*), B 90. **eius:** sc. *vocem libentissime se audire,* the understood indirect statement
of *dixisse,* verb of the indirect statement governed by *aiunt.* **a quo...praedicaretur:** a
relative clause of characteristic (*B* 283), anticipated by *eius.*

258–260. **item:** i.e., as Themistocles did. **ingenio:** ablative of means with *celebrari.* **ea...posse celebrari:** indirect statement dependent on *putabat.* **quae gesserat:**
sc. *Marius.*

260–262. **Mithridaticum...bellum:** the third war waged by Rome against Mithridates, King of Pontus (see Appendix I), from 74–63 b.c. Although begun under the
command of Lucullus, the victory went to Pompey who relieved Lucullus of his *imperium* in 66 b.c. (see note on 137–142 above). **magnum atque difficile et...versatum:**
a tricolon of adjectives modifying *bellum;* typical of his style, Cicero expands the
third member with a participial phrase. **totum:** predicative; translate adverbially:
"entirely." **ab hoc expressum est:** i.e., in a poem by Archias. **qui:** connecting relative (= *et hi*).

264. **inlustro, ~are, ~avi, ~atus,** to give glory to, embellish, make famous.

    ** **populus, populi,** *m.,* people, (*usu. the Roman people*).

265. **aperio, aperire, aperui, apertus,** to open up (*a territory*); to make available, place at one's disposal.

    impero, ~are, ~avi, ~atus, to order, command; to lead an army.

    regius, ~a, ~um, kingly, characteristic of a king; royal, on a regal scale.

    ops, opis, *f.,* power, resource; (*usu. pl.*) wealth.

266. **regio, regionis,** *f.,* a geographical position; a territory, region.

    vallo, ~are, ~avi, ~atus, to surround, hem in; to fortify (*w. a rampart, palisade, etc.*).

    * **exercitus, ~us,** *m.,* a military force, an army.

267. **dux, ducis,** *m.,* a military leader, commander.

    manus, ~us, *f.,* a military force, an army.

    innumerabilis, ~e, countless, endless.

268. **copiae, ~arum,** *f.,* (*pl.*) troops, soldiers, an army.

    fundo, fundere, fudi, fusus, (*w.* **copias**) to rout, defeat utterly.

269. **consilium, ~i,** *n.,* counsel; advice; an advisory body.

    * **impetus, ~us,** *m.,* attack, assault; violence or violent behavior.

    * **regius, ~a, ~um,** kingly, characteristic of a king; royal.

270. ** **totus, ~a, ~um,** (*usu. w. defining gen.*) the whole (*of*), all.

    os, oris, *n.,* mouth, lips; face; (*pl.*) expression.

    fauces, faucium, *f.,* (*usu. pl.*) throat, jaws; (*of a house*) the entry-way; (*of a mountain, etc.*) a pass, an approach.

    eripio, eripere, eripui, ereptus, to snatch away.

    * **servo, ~are, ~avi, ~atus,** to defend; to save, keep safe.

populi Romani nomen inlustrant. Populus enim Romanus
265 aperuit Lucullo imperante Pontum et regiis quondam opibus
et ipsa natura et regione vallatum, populi Romani exercitus
eodem duce non maxima manu innumerabilis Armeniorum
copias fudit, populi Romani laus est urbem amicissimam
Cyzicenorum eiusdem consilio ex omni impetu regio atque
270 totius belli ore ac faucibus ereptam esse atque servatam.

264–270. A complex sentence structured around a TRICOLON of independent
clauses in ASYNDETON, each containing a reference to Lucullus and introduced by
the ANAPHORA of a form of the phrase *populus Romanus*.

⇒ 1. **Populus enim Romanus...vallatum** (264–266): **Lucullo imperante:** ablative
absolute. **Pontum...vallatum:** note how the HYPERBATON BRACKETS the TRICOLON of
ablatives (formally composed with *et...et...et*) which, because they require the resolution of a passive participle, produce the figure of ANTICIPATION. **natura et regione:**
HENDIADYS for *natura regionis*.

⇒ 2. **populi Romani...fudit** (266–268). **eodem duce:** ablative absolute, "with
the same man as leader," i.e., Lucullus. **non maxima manu:** LITOTES, "with not the
greatest force" = "a very limited force." **innumerabilis:** accusative plural (= *innu-
merabiles*, see note on 62–63 above), construe with *copias*. The ANTITHESIS between
Lucullus' *non maxima manu* and the *innumerabilis copias* of Mithridates is no fiction
or mere rhetorical flourish on Cicero's part: with an army numbering barely 10,000
Lucullus routed a force of over 200,000 men; he was awarded a triumph by the
senate in 63 B.C.

⇒ 3. **populi Romani...servatam** (268–271). **urbem...ereptam esse atque servatam:** an accusative + infinitive construction either in APPOSITION to, or explanatory
of *laus est*, which governs it: "It is to the credit of the Roman people that the city
was snatched...and saved." **Cyzicenorum:** genitive plural, modifying *urbem* (for the
inhabitants, see APPENDIX I). **eiusdem:** i.e., Lucullus. **regio:** i.e., of Mithridates. **ore
ac faucibus:** sc. *ex*.

271. ** **fero, ferre, tuli, latus,** to carry, bear, convey; to endure; (*pass.*) to relate, proclaim publicly.

　* **praedico, ~are, ~avi, ~atus,** to announce, proclaim publicly.

272. **dimico, ~are, ~avi, ~atus,** to struggle, contend, fight.

　interficio, interficere, interfeci, interfectus, to kill.

　* **dux, ducis,** *m.,* a military leader, commander.

　deprimo, deprimere, depressi, depressus, to press or force down; (*of ships*) to sink.

273. **hostis, hostis,** *m.* or *f.,* enemy, foe.

　classis, classis, *f.,* a naval force, fleet.

　* **incredibilis, ~e,** incredible, beyond belief.

　pugna, ~ae, *f.,* a fight, battle.

274. **tropaeum, ~i,** *n.,* a trophy commemorating a victory.

　monumentum, ~i, *n.,* memento, monument, commemorative.

275. **triumphus, ~i,** *m.,* the triumphal procession, parade honoring a victorious general; the victory itself.

　* **effero, efferre, extuli, elatus,** to lift up, raise; to carry off.

　*** **populus, populi,** *m.,* people, (*usu. the Roman people*).

276. ** **fama, ~ae,** *f.,* fame, reputation.

277. **carus, ~a, ~um,** dear, valued, beloved (*w. dat.*).

　* **superior, superioris,** (*comp.* < **superus**) preceding in time; (*w. proper names*) the elder.

278. *** **itaque,** (*adv.*) accordingly.

　sepulcrum, ~i, *n.,* tomb.

　constituo, constituere, constitui, constitutus, (*of people*) to establish (*in a position, etc.*); (*of objects, statues, etc.*) to erect.

279. **marmor, marmoris,** *n.,* marble; something made of marble, a statue.

　* **certe,** (*adv.* < **certus**) without doubt, surely.

280. **laudo, ~are, ~avi, ~atus,** to praise.

　* **orno, ~are, ~avi, ~atus,** to adorn, decorate.

Nostra semper feretur et praedicabitur L. Lucullo dimicante, cum interfectis ducibus depressa hostium classis est, incredibilis apud Tenedum pugna illa navalis, nostra sunt tropaea, nostra monumenta, nostri triumphi. Quae
275 quorum ingeniis efferuntur, ab eis populi Romani fama celebratur.

22 Carus fuit Africano superiori noster Ennius, itaque etiam in sepulcro Scipionum putatur is esse constitutus ex marmore. At eis laudibus certe non solum
280 ipse qui laudatur sed etiam populi Romani nomen ornatur.

271–274. **Nostra...navalis:** the first clause in a series of four arranged in ASYNDETON, each introduced by an ANAPHORA of the first-person plural possessive pronoun. **nostra:** nominative feminine singular, translate as a predicate adjective of **pugna:** subject of **feretur** and **praedicabitur:** "will be spoken of and proclaimed as ours," i.e., as victors. **L. Lucullo dimicante:** ablative absolute. **cum...depressa...est:** a temporal clause. **interfectis ducibus:** ablative absolute (i.e., the admirals of the enemy fleet).

incredibilis...illa navalis: construe with *pugna*. **apud Tenedum:** the island of Tenedos (see APPENDIX I), the site of the naval battle (note the attributive position of the prepositional phrase, BRACKETED between the adjective and its noun). **nostra monumenta, nostri triumphi:** sc. *sunt*.

274–275. **Quae:** CONNECTING RELATIVE (= *et ea*), neuter nominative plural (i.e., *tropaea, monumenta*, etc.), subject of *efferuntur*. **quorum...ab eis:** the relative clause precedes its antecedent (*eis*) in the main clause; while *quorum* governs the clause, *quae* precedes because it serves to link this sentence to the previous: "And by whose talents these things are made known, by these same men the fame of the Roman people is celebrated."

277–279. **Carus...Ennius:** note how the structure BRACKETS **Africano superiori:** dative with the predicate adjective *carus*, B 192.1 (for Publius Cornelius Scipio Africanus the elder, see APPENDIX I). **esse:** complementary infinitive with *putatur*. **constitutus:** nominative because the subject of *esse* is the same as *putatur*, its governing verb, B 328.2 and 332.

279–280. **eis laudibus:** ablative of means with *ornatur*; the reference is to Ennius' epic poem the *Annales*, through which he glorified not only his patrons, individual Romans whom Cicero enumerates in this sentence and the following two (for whom see APPENDIX I), but also the Roman people as a whole. **non solum...sed etiam:** balances *ipse* and *nomen*, subjects of *ornatur*, singular because of its proximity to *nomen*. **qui laudatur:** i.e., Scipio Africanus Major.

281. **caelum, ~i,** *n.,* sky; heaven.

    proavus, ~i, *m.,* a great-grandfather.

    tollo, tollere, sustuli, sublatum, to remove, take away; to raise, lift up; to elevate to a position of superiority.

    * **honos, honoris,** *m.,* respect, esteem, honor, glory.

282. * **adiungo, adiungere, adiunxi, adiunctus,** to add, attribute; to mention in addition.

283. * **sine,** (*prep. w. abl.*) without.

    ** **communis, ~e,** common, shared jointly by two parties.

284. **decoro, ~are, ~avi, ~atus,** to decorate (*with honors, etc.*), embellish, praise, extoll.

285. * **recipio, recipere, recepi, receptus,** to receive, admit.

286. ** **expeto, expetere, expetivi (~ii), expetitus,** to seek after, desire; to try to obtain.

287. * **constituo, constituere, constitui, constitutus,** (*of people*) to establish (*in a position, etc.*); (*of objects, statues, etc.*) to erect.

    eicio, eicere, eieci, eiectus, to throw out, drive away, banish.

288. **minor, minus** (*comp. adj.* < **parvus**) smaller, less.

    * **fructus, ~us,** *m.,* advantage, gain, profit, enjoyment.

289. **versus, ~us,** *m.,* a line of verse, poetry.

    ** **percipio, percipere, percepi, perceptus,** to take, acquire.

    vehementer, (*adv.*) seriously, gravely.

    erro, ~are, ~avi, ~atus, to err, be wrong, make a mistake.

In caelum huius proavus Cato tollitur; magnus honos populi Romani rebus adiungitur. Omnes denique illi Maximi, Marcelli, Fulvii non sine communi omnium nostrum laude decorantur. Ergo illum qui haec fecerat, 285 Rudinum hominem, maiores nostri in civitatem receperunt; nos hunc Heracliensem, multis civitatibus expetitum, in hac autem legibus constitutum, de nostra civitate eiciamus?

23 Nam si quis minorem gloriae fructum putat ex Graecis versibus percipi quam ex Latinis, vehementer errat,

---

281–282. **In caelum...tollitur:** (sc. *laudibus*) i.e., by Ennius' *Annales*. **proavus Cato:** Cato the elder, great-grandfather of Cato Uticensis, Cicero's contemporary, who was present, apparently (*huius*), in court. **populi Romani:** genitive with **rebus:** dative with *adiungitur*, "great glory is added to the achievements of the Roman people," i.e., by the poetry of Ennius.

282–284. **denique:** "finally," signals the last installment of Ennius' patrons. **Omnes...illi Maximi, Marcelli, Fulvii:** all men of prominent Roman families who distinguished themselves as commanders in the field and received recognition in the poetry of Ennius (see Appendix I). **sine...laude:** note how the hyperbaton of the preposition and its object brackets **omnium nostrum:** an objective genitive modifying *laude*.

284–287. **Ergo...eiciamus?:** The two independent clauses of this sentence, arranged in asyndeton, share many parallel structures in order to feature the antithesis of "they" (*maiores nostri*) and "we" (*nos*).

284–285. **Ergo:** indicates that what follows is a conclusion inferred from the points raised in the previous three sentences, "therefore," "for this reason" (construe with only the first of the two clauses). **illum:** i.e., Ennius, object of *receperunt*. **qui haec fecerat:** i.e., who wrote the poetry. **Rudinum hominem:** the phrase, in apposition to *illum*, is best translated with concessive force, "although (he was) a man from Rudiae" (for Ennius' life see Appendix I). **in civitatem receperunt:** i.e., granted him citizenship (despite being from Rudiae).

286–287. **hunc:** i.e., Archias. **Heracliensem:** in apposition to *hunc* (corresponding to *Rudinum hominem* in the previous clause). **expetitum...constitutum:** both passive participles modify *hunc*. **multis civitatibus:** dative of agent with the passive participle *expetitum*, B 189.2. **in hac:** sc. *civitate*. **de nostra civitate eiciamus?:** contrast with *in hac* [*civitate*], and *in civitatem receperunt* from the previous clause.

288–289. **Nam:** the particle, which usually presents an explanation of the preceding sentence, here introduces the rhetorical device occupatio, as Cicero anticipates the argument that Ennius, because he wrote in Latin, was more worthy of Roman citizenship than Archias, who wrote in Greek. **si...Latinis:** the protasis of a present general condition (B 302.1). **quis:** = *aliquis* (see on 1 above). **minorem:** comparative adjective (< *parvus*), modifying **fructum:** subject of **percipi:** passive infinitive of the indirect statement dependent on *putat*. **quam:** "than," a relative adverb introducing the comparandum. **ex Latinis:** sc. *versibus gloriae fructum percipi*. **vehementer errat:** the apodosis of the condition, "he is gravely mistaken."

290. **propterea,** (*adv.*) therefore; (*w.* **quod**) because of the fact that.

   lego, legere, legi, lectus, to read.

   fere, (*adv.*) nearly, almost, virtually.

   gens, gentis, *f.,* family, race, clan.

291. **finis, finis,** *m.,* end, limit; (*of countries, territories, etc.*) the boundary, border.

   * **exiguus, ~a, ~um,** small, scanty, slight, insignificant.

   sane, (*adv.*) certainly, truly, absolutely.

   * **contineo, continere, continui, contentus,** to hold together (*by bonds of relationship*); to contain, hold, keep.

   ** **quare** (*interrog. and rel. adv.*) for what reason, wherefore.

292. *** **gero, gerere, gessi, gestus,** to carry on, perform.

   orbis, orbis, *m.,* circle, circuit, course; **orbis terrae** (*or* **terrarum**), the world.

   * **regio, regionis,** *f.,* a geographical position; a territory, region.

   definio, definire, definivi (~ii), definitus, to limit, bound; to define.

293. *** **debeo, debere, debui, debitus,** (*w. inf.*) to be under obligation to do something.

   quo, (*interrog. and rel. adv.*) to what place, where; (*abl. sing. of rel. pron. used as conj.*) whereby, in order that.

   telum, ~i, *n.,* a weapon (*dagger, knife, spear, etc.*).

   * **pervenio, pervenire, perveni, perventus,** to arrive (*at a place, situation, station, etc.*); to attain (*a position*).

294. *** **fama, ~ae,** *f.,* reputation, public opinion.

   penetro, ~are, ~avi, ~atus, to work a way, make one's way (*to or into a place, etc.*); to reach, enter, penetrate.

295. * **amplus, ~a, ~um,** (*w. dat. of person*) magnificent, great.

296. ** **certe,** (*adv.* < **certus**) without doubt, surely.

   *** **causa, ~ae,** *f.,* (*abl. w. gen.*) for the sake (*of*).

   * **dimico, ~are, ~avi, ~atus,** to struggle, contend, fight.

297. ** **periculum, ~i,** *n.,* danger.

   incitamentum, ~i, *n.,* that which urges, a stimulus, incentive.

   * **labor, laboris,** *m.,* labor, task; effort, struggle; trial, hardship.

298. ** **scriptor, scriptoris,** *m.,* a writer, author.

290   propterea quod Graeca leguntur in omnibus fere genti-
      bus, Latina suis finibus exiguis sane continentur. Quare,
      si res eae quas gessimus orbis terrae regionibus definiun-
      tur, cupere debemus, quo hominum nostrorum tela perven-
      erint, eodem gloriam famamque penetrare, quod cum ipsis
295   populis de quorum rebus scribitur haec ampla sunt, tum
      eis certe qui de vita gloriae causa dimicant hoc maximum
      et periculorum incitamentum est et laborum. 24 Quam
      multos scriptores rerum suarum magnus ille Alexander
      secum habuisse dicitur. Atque is tamen, cum in Sigeo

290–291. **propterea quod:** "because of the fact that..." **Graeca...Latina:** (sc. *scripta*). **in...gentibus:** Greek was the predominant language of the eastern half of the Mediterranean. **sane:** with *continentur*.

291–292. **si...definiuntur:** the PROTASIS of a present general condition (*B* 302.1). **quae gessimus:** the antecedent is *res* (note how the demonstrative *eae*, inserted after its noun for emphasis, ANTICIPATES the clause). **orbis terrae:** genitive with *regionibus*.

292–294. **cupere:** complementary infinitive with *debemus*, the main verb of the APODOSIS. **quo...pervenerint:** "where..." the adverbial relative clause precedes its antecedent *eodem* for emphasis (the usual order would be *eodem...quo*: "to the same place...where." **hominum nostrorum:** i.e., soldiers. **gloriam...penetrare:** accusative + infinitive object clause of *cupere*, *B* 331 IV.

294–297. **quod:** "because." **cum...tum:** a correlative construction introducing two co-existing circumstances of which *tum* indicates the more noteworthy, "not only...but especially." **ipsis populis:** dative with *ampla*. **de...scribitur:** an impersonal construction, "about whose achievements it is written" (the antecedent of *quorum* is *populis*). **haec:** neuter nominative plural (antecedent = *tela* or a vague "these things"). **qui...dimicant:** the antecedent is *eis*. **gloriae causa:** "for the sake of glory" (see note on 95–98 above). **hoc:** neuter nominative (note: the singular pronoun, which has no precise antecedent, refers to the idea expressed by the main clause of the sentence [*cupere...penetrare*]), i.e., wanting our glory and reputation to reach where our weapons have reached. **maximum:** modifies *incitamentum*. **et...et:** "both...and," connects *periculorum* and *laborum*, objective genitives of *incitamentum*, *B* 200.

297–300. **Quam:** the adverb, construe with *multos*, "How many..." **scriptores:** direct object of **habuisse:** complementary infinitive of *dicitur* (for the construction see note on 277–279 above). **magnus ille Alexander:** i.e., Alexander the Great (see APPENDIX I). **secum:** (a common inversion of *cum se*) "with him," i.e., accompanying him on his military campaigns. **is:** i.e., Alexander. **tamen:** the adverb lends an ironic tone (strengthened by *atque*) to the sentence.

300. **tumulus, ~i,** *m.,* a burial-mound, grave, tomb.

    asto, astare, astiti, *(w.* **ad** + *acc.)* to stand at or on *(a place, etc.).*

    fortunatus, ~a, ~um, fortunate, lucky, successful.

    inquam, inquis, inquit, *(defective verb)* to say.

    * **adulescens, adulescentis,** young, youthful.

301. * **Homerus, ~i,** *m.,* Homer, the poet who wrote the *Iliad.*

    praeco, praeconis, *m.,* a public announcer, an auctioneer.

    invenio, invenire, inveni, inventus, to come upon, find, discover.

302. **vere,** *(adv.)* truly, in truth.

    * **exsisto, exsistere, exstiti,** to come into being, emerge, arise.

303. ** **corpus, corporis,** *n.,* the body.

    contego, contegere, contexi, contectus, to cover; to entomb, bury.

    obruo, obruere, obrui, obrutus, to bury, hide, conceal *(i.e., in obscurity).*

304. * **fortuna, ~ae,** *f., (pl.)* wealth, property.

305. **adaequo, ~are, ~avi, ~atus,** to equate, make *(someone, something)* equal *(to someone, something else).*

    nonne, *(interrog. particle introducing a question that expects a positive answer)* Is it not the case that...?

306. **contio, contionis,** *f.,* a public assembly, rally.

    miles, militis, *m., (sing.)* a soldier; *(pl.)* the army.

    * **dono, ~are, ~avi, ~atus,** to award, *(w. abl. of thing given).*

300   ad Achillis tumulum astitisset: "O fortunate," inquit, "adulescens, qui tuae virtutis Homerum praeconem in-
veneris!" Et vere: nam nisi Ilias illa exstitisset, idem
tumulus qui corpus eius contexerat nomen etiam obruisset. Quid? Noster hic Magnus qui cum virtute fortunam
305   adaequavit, nonne Theophanem Mytilenaeum, scriptorem
rerum suarum, in contione militum civitate donavit, et

299–302. **cum in Sigeo** (p. 65)**...astitisset:** "when he had stood at Sigeum," a
promontory and town in the Troad, near the site of Troy (see APPENDIX I). **Achillis:**
genitive (note how Cicero BRACKETS the form between the preposition *ad* and its
object *tumulum*). For Achilles, the central figure of Homer's *Iliad* who died at Troy,
see APPENDIX I. **fortunate:** the vocative (< **fortunatus**) is regularly the same as the
nominative (cf. *adulescens*) except for nouns and adjectives in ~*us* of the second declension *B* 19.1. **qui...inveneris:** "you who acquired Homer (as) the herald of your
valor." A relative clause of characteristic, here expressing cause, takes the subjunctive (*B* 283.3). **tuae virtutis:** objective genitive of *praeconem*. **Homerum praeconem:**
invenire takes two accusatives, a direct object (*Homerum*) and predicate accusative
(*praeconem*), *B* 177.1.

302–303. **nam:** signals an explanation of the previous sentence. **nisi...exstitisset:**
the PROTASIS of a past contrary-to-fact condition, *B* 304.1. **Ilias:** nominative singular;
the *Iliad*, Homer's epic poem about the Trojan War. **qui...contexerat:** the antecedent
is **tumulus**, which also functions as the subject of **obruisset:** the verb of the APODO-
SIS. **eius:** i.e., Achilles.

304. **Quid?:** see note on 126 above. **Noster hic Magnus:** i.e., Cn. Pompeius Magnus (see APPENDIX I). Note how *hic Magnus* echoes *magnus ille* of the previous sentence. Cicero is using the adjective, which was Pompey's cognomen, to help smooth
the transition from the preceding anecdote about Alexander to the present one
about Pompey; so also, *noster hic* looks forward to the phrase *nostri illi* (307 below),
which introduces the second independent clause of this BIPARTITE sentence.

304–305. **qui...adaequavit:** "who balanced his good luck with his valor..." **nonne:** Cicero postpones the interrogative particle, which introduces a question that
expects a positive answer (*B* 162.2.a), until after the relative clause in order to emphasize the importance of Pompey's public image. **Theophanem Mytilenaeum:**
Theophanes of Mytilene, who wrote a history of Pompey's military achievements in
Greek (see APPENDIX I). **scriptorem:** in APPOSITION to *Theophanem*.

306. **rerum suarum:** objective genitive dependent on *scriptorem*. **in contione
militum:** "before an assembly of the army." At Rome, a *contio* was always an open
rally to which the people were summoned by a magistrate to hear public debate;
since citizenship was a privilege that could only be granted by the people, Pompey,
because he was on campaign in the Mithridatic War, could only grant citizenship
to Theophanes before a military assembly. **civitate donavit:** for the construction see
note on 57–59 above.

307. ***** fortis, ~e,** brave, fearless.

rusticus, ~a, ~um, of or belonging to the country; rustic, uncultured, unrefined.

dulcedo, dulcedinis, f., pleasantness (*to the mind, etc.*); an object causing agreeable sensations or emotions.

308. **** commoveo, commovere, commovi, commotus,** to disturb, arouse; (*pass.*) to be moved (*to action, etc.*); to be alarmed.

** quasi, (*adv.*) as if, as it were; in a manner of speaking.

particeps, participis, m., a participant, member (*of a group, office, etc.*).

309. **clamor, clamoris, m.,** shout, outcry; protest; applause.

approbo, ~are, ~avi, ~atus, to approve, express approval.

310. *** credo, credere, credidi, creditus,** (*often used parenthetically with sarcastic overtones*) to believe, suppose.

311. *** imperator, imperatoris, m.,** a commanding officer, general.

* perficio, perficere, perfeci, perfectus, to effect, bring about; to finish, bring to completion, complete.

313. *** peto, petere, petivi (~ii), petitus,** to seek; to aim for, attack.

** repudio, ~are, ~avi, ~atus, to refuse, reject, disregard as false.

314. **libellum, ~i, n.,** book; (*spec.*) a small book, pamphlet.

315. **subicio, subicere, subieci, subiectus,** (*w. acc. object, dat. of person*) to furnish, supply (*something to someone*).

epigramma, epigrammatis, n., a short poem, epigram.

316. **alternus, ~a, ~um,** occuring in alternation with something else; (*of poetry, w. versus, etc.*) a reference to the alternating metrics of elegaic verse.

* versus, ~us, m., a line of verse, poetry.

longiusculus, ~a, ~um, a little longer (*in length, duration, extent, etc.*).

* statim, (*adv.*) immediately, at once.

317. **vendo, vendere, vendidi, venditus,** to sell, offer for sale.

iubeo, iubere, iussi, iussus, to order, command.

* praemium, ~i, n., reward, prize, legal benefit.

** tribuo, tribuere, tribui, tributus, to grant, bestow.

condicio, condicionis, f., a condition, term, stipulation (*followed by* **ut, ne**).

nostri illi fortes viri, sed rustici ac milites, dulcedine quadam gloriae commoti quasi participes eiusdem laudis magno
illud clamore approbaverunt?

310   **25** Itaque, credo, si civis Romanus Archias legibus
non esset, ut ab aliquo imperatore civitate donaretur perficere non potuit. Sulla cum Hispanos et Gallos donaret,
credo, hunc petentem repudiasset. Quem nos in contione vidimus, cum ei libellum malus poeta de populo
315 subiecisset, quod epigramma in eum fecisset tantum modo
alternis versibus longiusculis, statim ex eis rebus, quas tum
vendebat, iubere ei praemium tribui—sed ea condicione

307–309. **nostri illi fortes viri:** i.e., Pompey's soldiers. **sed:** sets *rustici ac milites*
in ANTITHESIS to *fortes viri,* translate concessively: "although," "even though." **quadam...quasi:** see note on 21–22 above. **gloriae commoti...participes...laudis:** (note
the CHIASMUS) i.e., they would also benefit from the renown that Pompey would
enjoy as a result of Theophanes' history. **illud:** i.e., the granting of Theophanes'
citizenship.

310–312. **credo:** inserted as a parenthetical aside, with no effect on the syntax of
the sentence, the verb casts an ironic tone over the sentence (so also at 313 below).
si...non esset: the PROTASIS of a past contrary-to-fact condition (*B* 304.1). **ut...donare-
tur:** result clause dependent on *perficere.* **ab aliquo imperatore:** "from some general
or other." **civitate:** see note on 57–59 above. **perficere non potuit:** the APODOSIS of the
condition (for the indicative mood, cf. *B* 304.2–3).

312–313. **Sulla:** L. Cornelius Sulla Felix (see APPENDIX I). **cum...donaret:** (sc. *civitate*) a concessive clause. **credo:** see note on 310–312 above. **hunc:** i.e., Archias. **petentem:** the conditional use of the participle (= *si petivisset*), *B* 337.2.b.

313–318. **Quem:** (sc. *Sullam*) the CONNECTING RELATIVE (= *et eum*), it is the accusative subject of the infinitive *iubere,* an indirect statement dependent on *vidimus.*
cum...subiecisset: a temporal clause, *B* 288.1.B. **ei:** i.e., Sulla; dative indirect object
with *subiecisset.* **libellum:** note the contempt of the diminutive. **de populo:** construe
with *malus poeta,* "some bad poet from the crowd." **quod...fecisset:** a causal clause,
"because he had written an epigram about him." An epigram was usually a short
poem composed in elegiac couplets (alternating lines of hexameter and pentameter
verse [cf. *alternis versibus longiusculis*]). **ex eis rebus:** construe with **tribui:** present
passive (objective) infinitive of *iubere.* **quas tum vendebat:** the antecedent is *rebus.*
As dictator in 82 B.C., Sulla sold at public auction the possessions of the political
enemies whom he had proscribed (see APPENDIX I). **ei:** dative (i.e., the *malus poeta*),
indirect object of *tribui.* **praemium:** accusative, subject of *tribui.* **sed...scriberet** (p. 70):
"but on one condition: that he not write anything else." **ea condicione:** an ablative
of manner specifying the condition(s) under which *praemium tribui* (*B* 220.3), here
taking the form of a negative indirect command *ne...scriberet.*

318. **postea,** (*adv.*) later on, thereafter.

    sedulitas, sedulitatis, *f.*, assiduity, attention to detail; earnestness, diligence.

319. ** **dignus, ~a, ~um,** (*w. abl.*) worthy, deserving (*of*).

320. * **copia, ~ae,** *f.*, (*sing.*) abundance, plenty.

    ** **expeto, expetere, expetivi (~ii), expetitus,** to seek after, desire; to try to obtain.

321. * **familiaris, ~e,** intimate, closely associated or attached (*by bonds of kinship or friendship, etc.*).

322. ** **dono, ~are, ~avi, ~atus,** to award, (*w. acc. of recipient, abl. of gift*).

    * **impetro, ~are, ~avi, ~atus,** to obtain by request or application.

323. ** **praesertim,** (*adv.*) especially.

    cupio, cupere, cupivi, cupitus, (*w. inf.*) to desire, want.

324. * **nascor, nati, natus,** to be born.

    pinguis, ~e, slow-witted, dull, obtuse; (*of literary works, style, etc.*) clumsy, unrefined, coarse.

    sono, ~are, ~avi, ~atus, to give out a sound, utterance (*usu. of a particular nature or quality*).

325. **peregrinus, ~a, ~um,** foreign, alien.

    ** **auris, auris,** *f.*, the ear.

    dedo, dedere, dedidi, deditum, to devote oneself to.

326. **dissimulo, ~are, ~avi, ~atus,** to hide, conceal.

    obscuro, ~are, ~avi, ~atus, to cover up, conceal; to obscure, make unclear.

    prae, (*prep. w. abl.*) before, in front of.

327. **fero, ferre, tuli, latus,** to convey, bestow; to bear, endure.

    traho, trahere, traxi, tractus, to drag, draw, pull.

ne quid postea scriberet. Qui sedulitatem mali poetae duxerit aliquo tamen praemio dignam, huius ingenium et
320 virtutem in scribendo et copiam non expetisset? 26 Quid? a Q. Metello Pio, familiarissimo suo, qui civitate multos donavit, neque per se neque per Lucullos impetravisset? qui praesertim usque eo de suis rebus scribi cuperet ut etiam Cordubae natis poetis pingue quiddam sonantibus atque
325 peregrinum tamen auris suas dederet. Neque enim est hoc dissimulandum quod obscurari non potest, sed prae nobis ferendum: trahimur omnes studio laudis, et optimus

---

318–320. **quid:** = *aliquid* (see note on 1 above). **Qui...dignam:** a conditional relative clause (= *si is...*) serving as the PROTASIS of a past contrary-to-fact condition, *B* 312.2 (note how the HYPERBATON of *sedulitatem...dignam* BRACKETS the entire clause). **duxerit:** here the verb means "to consider" and governs two accusatives: (1) the direct object *sedulitatem* and, (2) *dignam*, a predicate adjective serving as the object complement (*B* 177.2). **aliquo...praemio:** ablative, construe with *dignam*, "worthy of some sort of reward." **huius...expetisset:** the APODOSIS, or main clause, of the condition. **huius:** i.e., Archias. **copiam:** "abundance," referring perhaps to the prolific literary output of Archias.

320–322. **a Q. Metello Pio:** a prepositional phrase denoting source or agency, construe with *impetravisset*. **familiarissimo suo:** in APPOSITION to *Metello Pio*. **qui... donavit:** for the construction see note on 57–59 above. **impetravisset:** (sc. *civitatem*) the subject is Archias.

322–325. **qui praesertim:** (= *cum praesertim is*) "especially since he." **usque eo...ut:** "to such an extent...that." **scribi:** an impersonal passive infinitive, complementary with *cuperet*. **Cordubae:** the locative; construe with *natis*: "born at Cordova." **poetis:** dative plural, indirect object of *dederet*. **pingue...peregrinum:** the two adjectives are used here as internal accusatives of the participle *sonantibus* (*B* 176.4), "sounding a certain thick and foreign (sound)." **auris:** = *aures* (see note on 62–63 above).

325–328. **hoc:** neuter nominative; the pronoun serves as the antecedent of the following *quod* clause. **ferendum:** (sc. *hoc est*) contrasts with *dissimulandum*. **trahimur... ducitur** (p. 73): a direct statement in APPOSITION to *hoc*, consisting of two independent clauses BRACKETED by the "bookend" arrangement of the two passive verbs in first and last position. **optimus quisque maxime** (p. 73): the indefinite pronoun *quisque* with two superlatives implies a proportion, "the more patriotic the man, the greater the influence that glory will have over him," *B* 252.5.c. **laudis:** objective genitive with *studio*, an ablative of means with the passive *trahimur*.

328. **maxime,** (*superl. adv.* < **magis**) most, very much, especially.

329. * **libellum, ~i,** *n.,* book; (*spec.*) a small book, pamphlet.

  contemno, contemnere, contempsi, contemptus, to treat with contempt, regard of little value.

330. **inscribo, inscribere, inscripsi, inscriptus,** to write, inscribe (*a name, title, etc., on something*).

  praedicatio, praedicationis, *f.,* an announcement, public address.

  nobilitas, nobilitatis, *f.,* renown, celebrity.

331. **despicio, despicere, despexi, despectus,** to despise, look down on, view with contempt.

  ** **praedico, ~are, ~avi, ~atus,** to announce, proclaim publicly.

   nomino, ~are, ~avi, ~atus, to name, call by name.

332. ** **volo, velle, volui,** to want, wish, desire (*w. inf.*).

  ** **imperator, imperatoris,** *m.,* a commanding officer, general.

333. **carmen, carminis,** *n.,* a song or poem.

  templum, ~i, *n.,* a temple; the inaugurated site of a temple; any inaugurated location.

334. * **monumentum, ~i,** *n.,* memento, monument, commemorative.

  aditus, ~us, *m.,* a means of approach, access; an entry-way.

  exorno, ~are, ~avi, ~atus, (*of things*) to adorn, decorate, beautify; (*of people*) to enhance, embellish, decorate (*i.e., w. honors, offices, etc.*).

335. **comes, comitis,** *m.,* a friend, companion, comrade.

  bello, ~are, ~avi, ~atus, to wage war, take part in battle.

  * **dubito, ~are, ~avi, ~atus,** (*w. acc.*) to doubt, question; (*w.* **de**) to be in doubt about.

336. **manubiae, ~arum,** *f.,* (*pl.*) booty, spoils.

  consecro, ~are, ~avi, ~atus, to vow, consecrate, devote (*i.e., as an offering to a god, etc.*).

  *** **quare** (*interrog. and rel. adv.*) for what reason, wherefore.

quisque maxime gloria ducitur. Ipsi illi philosophi etiam
in eis libellis quos de contemnenda gloria scribunt nomen
330   suum inscribunt; in eo ipso in quo praedicationem no-
bilitatemque despiciunt praedicari de se ac nominari
volunt. 27 Decimus quidem Brutus, summus vir et imperator, Acci, amicissimi sui, carminibus templorum ac
monumentorum aditus exornavit suorum. Iam vero ille qui
335   cum Aetolis Ennio comite bellavit Fulvius non dubitavit
Martis manubias Musis consecrare. Quare, in qua urbe

328–332. **Ipsi illi philosophi:** probably either the Stoics or the Epicureans (see
APPENDIX I); while Cicero does not specify which group he means, the emphatic
replication of demonstrative pronouns suggests that his audience knew whom he
meant. **in eis libellis:** construe with *inscribunt*. **quos...scribunt...inscribunt:** note
how Cicero plays on the two verbs to mock the philosophers for their pretense of
virtue (so also with *praedicationem... praedicari* below). **in eo ipso in quo:** "in that
very place where..." **praedicari...nominari:** (an example of HYSTERON PROTERON) impersonal passive infinitives, complementary with *volunt* (cf. *scribi*, 322–325 above),
"they seek commendation and recommendation for themselves."

332–334. **Decimus...suorum:** Cicero uses Decimus Iunius Brutus Callaicus, consul in 138 B.C. (see APPENDIX I), as another example of individual aspiration for glory.
quidem: the particle links this sentence to the previous one, its placement between
praenomen and *nomen* creating a minor HYPERBATON that draws attention to the name.
summus vir et imperator: in APPOSITION to *Brutus*. **Acci:** possessive genitive with
carminibus: ablative of means, construe with *exornavit* (for Lucius Accius, a Roman
tragedian and contemporary of Brutus, see APPENDIX I). **amicissimi sui:** genitive, in
APPOSITION to *Acci*. **aditus:** accusative plural, object of *exornavit*. **suorum:** construe
with *templorum ac monumentorum*, suspended until last for emphasis.

334–336. **Iam vero:** "furthermore," an animated form of transition introduces the
last of the historical *exempla*. **ille...Fulvius:** the HYPERBATON produced by the insertion of the relative clause (*qui...bellavit*) between the demonstrative adjective and its
noun creates a dramatic suspense (for M. Fulvius Nobilior, consul 189 B.C., see note
on 282–284 and APPENDIX I). **cum:** the preposition (for the Aetolians see APPENDIX I).
Ennio comite: ablative absolute (for Ennius see on 284–285 and APPENDIX I). **Martis:**
genitive, construe with **Musis:** dative indirect object of **consecrare:** complementary
infinitive of *dubitavit*. (Note the ALLITERATION of *Martis manubias Musis*.)

336–338. **Quare:** signals the conclusion, or summation, of the historical *exempla*.

337. *** **imperator, imperatoris,** *m.,* a commanding officer, general.

    *****prope,** (*adv.*) almost, nearly, all but.

    armatus, ~a, ~um, armed; (*as subst.*) an armed man, a soldier.

338. * **delubrum, ~i,** *n.,* a shrine, temple.

    *****colo, colere, colui, cultus,** to cultivate, develop, foster.

    togatus, ~a, ~um, wearing a toga; living as a citizen (*i.e., Roman*).

339. ** **honos, honoris,** *m.,* respect, esteem, honor, glory.

    ** **salus, salutis,** *f.,* a means of deliverance (*usu. judicial*); security.

    ** **abhorreo, abhorrere, abhorrui,** to be adverse to (*w.* **a** + *abl.*).

340. **libentius,** (*comp. adv.* < **libenter**) more freely, rather willingly.

341. * **indico, ~are, ~avi, ~atus,** to make known, show, point out.

    * **amor, amoris,** *m.,* love, affection; the object of love or desire.

    nimis, (*adv.*) very much, too much, exceedingly.

    acer, acris, acre, sharp, harsh, keen.

342. **fortasse,** (*adv.*) perhaps.

    honestas, honestatis, *f.,* moral rectitude, decency; honor or honorableness.

    * **confiteor, confiteri, confessus,** to confess, admit.

343. **consulatus, ~us,** *m.,* consulship, the office of consul.

    simul, (*adv.*) at the same time, at once.

344. **imperium, ~i,** *n.,* dominion, the power of government; military command.

    universus, ~a, ~um, whole, altogether.

345. ** **attingo, attingere, attigi, attactus,** to touch upon, treat, address, deal with (*a subject, issue, etc.*).

    ** **versus, ~us,** *m.,* a line of verse, poetry.

    incoho (inchoo), ~are, ~avi, ~atus, to start, begin work on (*a task, topic, etc.*).

imperatores prope armati poetarum nomen et Musarum delubra coluerunt, in ea non debent togati iudices a Musarum honore et a poetarum salute abhorrere.
340 **28** Atque ut id libentius faciatis, iam me vobis, iudices, indicabo et de meo quodam amore gloriae nimis acri
fortasse, verum tamen honesto vobis confitebor. Nam quas
res nos in consulatu nostro vobiscum simul pro salute huius urbis atque imperi et pro vita civium proque universa
345 re publica gessimus, attigit hic versibus atque inchoavit.

336–339. in qua urbe (p. 73)**...in ea:** "in which city...in this (city)." *Urbe*, technically the antecedent of *qua*, has been attracted into the relative clause. The symmetrical structure of the sentence revolves around the parallel arrangement of contrasting
elements in the two clauses. **prope armati:** "all but still in armor," i.e., fresh from battle. **Musarum delubra:** i.e., the Temple of Hercules Musarum on the Circus Flamin-
ius next to the Porticus Metelli in Rome, built by M. Fulvius Nobilior in 187 B.C. with
the spoils of his campaign against the Aetolians and Cephallenians (see APPENDIX I).

togati iudices: using the series of historical *exempla* illustrating the respect paid
to poets by Rome's most distinguished military men, Cicero tries to impress upon
the *iudices* the action they should take toward Archias. Cicero avoids strict parallelism between the two clauses by reversing the word order of the contrasting phrases
(*imperatores...armati :: togati iudices; Musarum...poetarum :: poetarum...Musarum*).

340–342. ut...faciatis: a purpose clause through which Cicero directly addresses
the *iudices*. **id:** the pronoun stands for what Cicero said in the preceding sentence
(i.e., *non a Musarum honore et a poetarum salute abhorrere*). **me vobis...indicabo:** "I
shall reveal myself (i.e., my own feelings) to you." **quodam:** as a qualifying term the
adjective helps to tone down the notion of an *amor gloriae*. **nimis acri fortasse:** "perhaps too keen" (*acri* = ablative masculine, singular, construe with *amore*). **honesto:**
ablative masculine, singular, referring back to *amore* (in contrast to *acri*).

342–345. quas...gessimus: the relative clause functions as the direct object of
both *attigit* and *inchoavit*. **res...in consulatu nostro:** i.e., Cicero's suppression of the
Catilinarian conspiracy during his consulship in 63 B.C. **hic:** i.e., Archias. **attigit...
versibus atque inchoavit:** Cicero had hopes that Archias would compose an epic
poem about his consulship, but if Archias did begin the work, as *inchoavit* certainly
implies, he never saw it through.

346. * **iucundus, ~a, ~um,** (*w. dat.*) congenial, agreeable (*to*).

347. ** **perficio, perficere, perfeci, perfectus,** to effect, bring about.

     adorno, ~are, ~avi, ~atus, to decorate, adorn, praise.

348. **merces, mercedis,** *f.,* reward, prize; fee

     ** **labor, laboris,** *m.,* labor, task; effort, struggle; trial, hardship.

     *** **periculum, ~i,** *n.,* danger, hazard; (*pl.*) legal liability.

     * **desidero, ~are, ~avi, ~atus,** to desire, want.

     praeter, (*prep. w. acc.*) by; beyond; before.

349. **detraho, detrahere, detraxi, detractus,** to take away, remove, deprive; to cause the loss (*of something*).

350. ** **exiguus, ~a, ~um,** small, scanty, slight, insignificant.

     curriculum, ~i, *n.,* a course, track, race; (*fig. w.* **vitae**) the course or race of life.

     brevis, ~e, brief, short.

351. * **exerceo, exercere, exercui, exercitus,** to carry on, perform, execute.

     *** **certe,** (*adv.* < **certus**) without doubt, surely, certainly.

352. **praesentio, praesentire, praesensi, praesensus,** to apprehend beforehand; to predict, have a presentiment of.

     posterus, ~a, ~um, (*of time*) in the future, posterity.

     ** **regio, regionis,** *f.,* a geographical position; a territory, region.

353. * **spatium, ~i,** *n.,* a period, interval.

     circumscribo, ~scribere, ~scripsi, ~scriptus, to define, mark the bounds of, delimit.

     * **cogitatio, cogitationis,** *f.,* the act of thinking, thought; reflection; acknowledgement; recognition.

     termino, ~are, ~avi, ~atus, to set the limits of; to define; to mark the boundaries.

354. **frango, frangere, fregi, fractus,** to break, crush, destroy.

355. **cura, ~ae,** *f.,* care, anxiety, distress, trouble (*usu. daytime*).

     vigilia, ~ae, *f.,* (*usu. pl.*) the action or fact of keeping watch; watchful attention, vigilance (*usu. at night*).

     ango, angere, anxi, anctus, to cause mental pain or distress; to vex, irk, afflict; (*pass.*) to be distressed, feel anxious.

Quibus auditis, quod mihi magna res et iucunda visa est,
hunc ad perficiendum adornavi. Nullam enim virtus aliam
mercedem laborum periculorumque desiderat praeter hanc
laudis et gloriae. Qua quidem detracta, iudices, quid est
350 quod in hoc tam exiguo vitae curriculo et tam brevi tantis nos in laboribus exerceamus? 29 Certe, si nihil animus
praesentiret in posterum, et si, quibus regionibus vitae
spatium circumscriptum est, isdem omnis cogitationes terminaret suas, nec tantis se laboribus frangeret neque tot
355 curis vigiliisque angeretur nec totiens de ipsa vita

346–347. **Quibus auditis:** (sc. *a me*) the subject of this ablative absolute is the
CONNECTING RELATIVE *quibus* (= *et eis*), whose antecedent is *versibus*. **quod:** "because."
mihi: construe with *visa est*. **res:** i.e., Archias' poem about Cicero's consulship. **hunc
ad perficiendum adornavi:** a puzzling phrase, and the text is suspect. *Adornavi* (<
adornare: to prepare, outfit, supply, furnish, etc.), has been added by modern editors in the place of various troublesome manuscript readings. Although the meaning of *adornavi* in this context is still not completely clear, the general sense is that
because Cicero approved of what Archias had already written, he offered some kind
of support (financial? historical details?) so that Archias could finish the poem.

347–349. **Nullam...aliam mercedem:** ANTICIPATES *praeter hanc* (sc. *mercedem*).
laborum periculorumque: objective genitives with *mercedem*, "reward for its toils
and dangers," B 200. **laudis et gloriae:** subjective genitives with *hanc* (sc. *mercedem*)
"the reward of praise and glory," B 199 (note how the two pairs of genitives modify
mercedem in different ways).

349–351. **Qua...detracta:** the subject of the ablative absolute, *qua*, is a CONNECTING
RELATIVE (= *et ea*) whose antecedent is *mercedem*. **quid est quod:** "why is it that...?"
(lit.: "what is there as to which..."). **in hoc:** with *curriculo*. **vitae:** genitive, modifying *curriculo*. **et:** connects *tam exiguo* and *tam brevi*, both of which modify *curriculo*.
tantis: ablative plural, with *in laboribus*. **nos:** object of **exerceamus:** deliberative subjunctive, B 277.

351–356. **Certe...dimicaret** (p. 79): a present contrary-to-fact condition with two
PROTASES and an APODOSIS containing a TRICOLON of independent clauses symmetri-
cally arranged through the ANAPHORA *nec tantis...neque tot...nec totiens*. This sentence
introduces the last section before the PERORATIO and is an example of the rhetorical
figure EXPOLITIO, exploring the idea raised at 347–349, that virtue seeks no other
reward than that of praise and glory (*nullam aliam mercedem desiderat virtus praeter
hanc laudis et gloriae*).

animus: the subject of both PROTASES (*praesentiret, terminaret*), as well as *frangeret,
angeretur,* and *dimicaret,* the three verbs of the APODOSIS. **in posterum:** "into the future."
quibus regionibus...isdem: "by which boundaries...by these very same (boundaries)." For the attraction of *regionibus* into the relative clause, see note on *urbe* (336–339)
above. **vitae:** genitive modifying *spatium*. **omnis:** = *omnes* (see note on 62–63 above).

356. *** dimico, ~are, ~avi, ~atus,** to struggle, contend, fight.

   insideo, insidere, insedi, insessus, (*w.* **in** + *abl.*) to be present (*in a situation, with an individual*).

357. **** dies, diei,** *m. or f.,* day.

   stimulus, ~i, *m.,* something that rouses to fury, passion, or action; a spur, goad.

   concito, ~are, ~avi, ~atus, to excite, stir up; to rouse, incite.

358. **admoneo, admonere, admonui, admonitus,** to warn, caution, admonish (*w. acc. of person, abl. or gen. of thing*); to remind (*w. acc.+ inf.*).

   dimitto, dimittere, dimisi, dimissus, to give up, let go; to pass away (*into obscurity, etc.*).

359. **commemoratio, commemorationis,** *f.,* a recollection, memory.

360. **posteritas, posteritatis,** *f.,* the future; future generations.

   * adaequo, ~are, ~avi, ~atus, to equate, make (*someone, something*) equal (*to someone, something else*).

   * parvus, ~a, ~um, small in size, amount, quantity; of little worth; insignificant, of no consequence.

362. ***** labor, laboris,** *m.,* labor, task; effort, struggle; trial, hardship.

   *** verso, ~are, ~avi, ~atus, to turn; (*pass.*) to be engaged in.

363. **extremus, ~a, ~um,** occuring at the end, last, final.

   ** spatium, ~i, *n.,* a period, interval.

   tranquillus, ~a, ~um, calm, undisturbed, tranquil.

   otiosus, ~a, ~um, at leisure, idle.

364. *** spiritus, ~us,** *m.,* divine inspiration.

   * morior, mori, mortuus, to die, be killed.

dimicaret. Nunc insidet quaedam in optimo quoque virtus,
quae noctes ac dies animum gloriae stimulis concitat
atque admonet non cum vitae tempore esse dimittendam commemorationem nominis nostri, sed cum omni
360 posteritate adaequandam. **30** An vero tam parvi animi
videamur esse omnes qui in re publica atque in his vitae periculis laboribusque versamur ut, cum usque ad
extremum spatium nullum tranquillum atque otiosum
spiritum duxerimus, nobiscum simul moritura omnia

356–360. Nunc: adversative, "But as it is." **quoque:** ablative, from *quisque*, "each."
in optimo quoque: "in all the best men" (note the BRACKETING of *quaedam...virtus*).
quae...adaequandam: a relative clause defining *virtus* (ANTICIPATED by *quaedam*)
with the indicative (*concitat, admonet*), B 283.1. **noctes ac dies:** plural accusatives denoting duration of time (*B* 181) best rendered in English as singular: "night and day"
and corresponding to *curis vigilisque*. **gloriae stimulis:** "with the spurs of glory,"
means or instrument with *concitat*.

non cum...tempore...sed cum...posteritate: *non...sed* sets the two prepositional
phrases in parallel symmetry, each governed by its own verb: *cum vitae tempore* (w.
esse dimittendam); *cum omni posteritate* (w. *adaequandam*). **commemorationem:** accusative subject of the passive periphrastic infinitives *esse dimittendam...adaequandam*, the
indirect statement governed by *admonet*.

360–365. An: the first of two rhetorical questions (cf. 365–369 below) expressing
the central point of the EXPOLITIO. **tam parvi animi:** genitive of quality or characteristic (*B* 203.3), construe with *esse*, complementary infinitive of **videamur:** a deliberative subjunctive, "Are we to appear to be of such small spirit..?" **qui...versamur:**
modifies an understood *nos*, subject of the main clause; because the clause states a
fact about a definite antecedent, it takes the indicative (see note on 356–360 above).
in re publica atque in his...laboribusque: the two phrases form a sort of HENDIADYS
and are best translated as a single idea: "in these dangers and toils of public life."

ut...arbitremur? (p. 81): a result clause, governed by *videamur* and ANTICIPATED
by *tam*. Note how the clause is first postponed by the insertion of the adjectival *qui*
clause, and then interrupted by the insertion of an adverbial *cum* clause (concessive), an example of HYPOTAXIS. **usque ad...spatium:** (with implied *vitae*) "right up to
the end of our life." **nullum tranquillum atque otiosum:** modifies *spiritum*, direct
object of *duxerimus* (*spiritum ducere* = "to draw a breath"). **nobiscum simul:** "together
with us." **moritura omnia:** (sc. *esse*) an accusative + infinitive indirect statement
dependent on *arbitremur*.

365. **arbitror, ~ari, ~atus,** to think, suppose.

    statua, ~ae, *f.,* a statue.

    * imago, imaginis, *f.,* the death-masks of their ancestors that Romans displayed in the *atria* of their houses and carried in funeral processions.

366. **simulacrum, ~i,** *n.,* an image, statue, representation.

    *** corpus, corporis, *n.,* the body.

    studiose, *(adv.)* earnestly, assiduously; with serious application.

367. *** relinquo, relinquere, reliqui, relictus,** to leave, leave behind.

    * consilium, ~i, *n.,* counsel; advice; an advisory body.

368. **effigies, effigiei,** *f.,* an image, representation, likeness.

    malo, malle, malui, to prefer.

    ** exprimo, exprimere, expressi, expressus, to make, produce; to express, portray *(in painting, sculpture, etc.).*

369. **politus, ~a, ~um,** refined, elegant.

370. **spargo, spargere, sparsi, sparsus,** to scatter, sprinkle.

    dissemino, ~are, ~avi, ~atus, to scatter, disseminate; to broadcast.

    * arbitror, ~ari, ~atus, to think, suppose.

371. *** orbis, orbis,** *m.,* circle, circuit, course; **orbis terrae** (*or* **terrarum**), the world.

    sempiternus, ~a, ~um, lasting forever, perpetual, eternal.

372. *** sensus, ~us,** *m.,* the faculties of perception; any of the five senses.

    *** mors, mortis, *f.,* death.

    absum, abesse, afui, afuturus, (*w.* **a/ab** + *abl.*) to be absent, away (*from*).

    * sapiens, sapientis, wise, educated; (*as subst.*) a wise man.

374. *** pertineo, pertinere, pertinui,** to pertain, relate to.

    ** cogitatio, cogitationis, *f.,* the act of thinking, thought; reflection; acknowledgment; recognition.

    spes, spei, *f.,* hope.

375. **** delecto, ~are, ~avi, ~atus,** to charm, delight, please.

Optional Reading: On the *Peroratio* (Appendix III, p. 118)

subj + result clause

365 arbitremur? An statuas et imagines, non animorum
simulacra, sed corporum, studiose multi summi homines
reliquerunt; consiliorum relinquere ac virtutum nostrarum
effigiem nonne multo malle debemus summis ingeniis expressam et politam? Ego vero omnia quae gerebam iam
370 tum in gerendo spargere me ac disseminare arbitrabar
in orbis terrae memoriam sempiternam. Haec vero sive
a meo sensu *world* post mortem afutura est, sive, ut sapientis-
simi homines putaverunt, ad aliquam animi mei partem
pertinebit, nunc quidem certe cogitatione quadam speque
375 delector.

365–369. **An:** the second rhetorical question of the EXPOLITIO, made up of two independent clauses joined in ASYNDETON. **non animorum simulacra, sed corporum:**
(sc. *simulacra*) in APPOSITION to *statuas et imagines,* direct objects of *reliquerunt.*

consiliorum...politam?: "ought we not to prefer all the more to leave behind
a representation of our character and intelligence, carved and polished by most
outstanding talents?" **consiliorum:** the emphatic, first-position placement of the
genitive, which modifies *effigiem* and should be grouped with *virtutum nostrarum,*
indicates that the point of the antithesis looks back to the genitives *non animorum...*
sed corporum from the previous clause. **nonne:** the interrogative signals a question
(that expects an affirmative answer) and therefore should come first, but has been
postponed for emphasis. **relinquere:** complementary infinitive of *malle* (= *magis
velle*), which in turn serves as the complementary infinitive of *debemus.* **multo:** ablative of degree of difference with *malle.* **summis ingeniis:** ablative of means with the
passive participles *expressam et politam* modifying *effigiem.*

369–370. **Ego vero:** an emphatic shift from the first person plural of the previous two sentences to the first person singular, "I for my part..." **omnia:** neuter accusative plural, direct object of *spargere...ac disseminare,* infinitives in the indirect
statement dependent on *arbitrabar.* **me:** subject of *spargere* and *disseminare.* **iam tum:**
construe with *in gerendo,* "even at the very moment I was doing them" (note the
play with *gerebam*).

371–375. **Haec:** i.e., *memoria,* subject of *afutura est* and *pertinebit,* verbs of the two
sive...sive clauses. **vero:** repetition of the adverb signals closure of the CONFIRMATIO.
a meo sensu: ablative of separation with *afutura est.* **ut:** + indicative = "as." **sapien-
tissimi homines:** i.e., philosophers. **pertinebit:** sc. *post mortem* from the first *sive*
clause. **quidem:** a post-positive particle with adverbial force emphasizing the word
it follows, here *nunc,* "for the time being, at any rate," i.e., while still alive. **cogitatione quadam speque:** ablatives of cause with *delector* (B 219.1), "I take pleasure in
the hope and expectation, such as it is" (i.e., that *memoria* will be *sempiterna*).

PERORATIO
(376–397)

In the final few minutes of the speech, Cicero concludes his defense with an emotional appeal to the iudices *for the restoration of his client.*

376. **conservo, ~are, ~avi, ~atus,** to save, perserve, rescue.

    pudor, pudoris, *m.,* shame; modesty; honor.

377. **comprobo, ~are, ~avi, ~atus,** to approve, sanction, ratify.

    dignitas, dignitatis, *f.,* rank, status, professional or public standing or position.

378. * **vetustas, vetustatis,** *f.,* the people, customs, or institutions of the distant past; antiquity.

    convenio, convenire, conveni, conventus, to come together; (*impers.*) to be fitting, proper.

379. ** **existimo, ~are, ~avi, ~atus,** to judge, consider, hold an opinion.

    *** **expeto, expetere, expetivi (~ii), expetitus,** to seek after, desire; to try to obtain.

380. * **beneficium, ~i,** *n.,* favor, formal thanks; a reward.

381. *** **auctoritas, auctoritatis,** *f.,* the quality of leadership, authority; personal influence, prestige.

    ** **municipium, ~i,** *n.,* a community with the rights of Roman citizenship but without the right to vote (**civitas sine suffragio**).

    * **testimonium, ~i,** *n.,* evidence given by a witness in court.

31 Quare conservate, iudices, hominem pudore eo
quem amicorum videtis comprobari cum dignitate, tum
etiam vetustate, ingenio autem tanto quantum id convenit
existimari, quod summorum hominum iudiciis expetitum
380   esse videatis, causa vero eius modi quae beneficio legis,
auctoritate municipi, testimonio Luculli, tabulis Metelli

[handwritten margin notes: ablative of description; tricolon of description; abl. of means; relative clause of characteristic (introduce by quod)]

376–381. **Quare:** the adverb signals the end of the CONFIRMATIO and introduces
the PERORATIO. **pudore...ingenio...causa:** three ablatives of quality or description (*B*
224) modifying *hominem;* each ablative in turn is modified by a word or phrase that
serves to ANTICIPATE the relative clause that immediately follows, and modifies, it:

pudore *eo* ⇒ *quem***...comprobari:** "with a sense of decency which you see con-
firmed by both the stature of his friends and the duration of their friendship." **amicorum:** genitive plural, dependent on **dignitate...vetustate:** ablatives of means with
comprobari: present passive infinitive in indirect statement governed by *videtis.*
cum...tum: "both...and."

ingenio...*tanto* ⇒ *quantum***...existimari:** "with talent as great as it is appropriate
to be valued." **quod...videatis:** a relative clause of result or characteristic, modifying
id (antecedent = *ingenium*), B 284.2. **expetitum esse:** perfect passive infinitive in indirect statement governed by *videatis.* **iudiciis:** ablative of means with *expetitum esse.*

causa...*eius modi* ⇒ *quae***...comprobetur:** "with a case of the kind which is
sanctioned by the support of the law, the authority of a municipality, the evidence
of Lucullus, and the public records of Metellus." **beneficio... auctoritate...testimo-
nio:** ablatives of means with *comprobetur.* **beneficio legis:** i.e., the *Lex Plautia Papiria.*
auctoritate municipi: i.e., the declaration of the embassy from Heraclea confirming
Archias' citizenship. **testimonio Luculli:** apparently Lucullus appeared as a witness on Archias' behalf at the trial.

382. ** **peto, petere, petivi (~ii), petitus,** to seek; to aim for, attack.
383. ** **humanus, ~a, ~um,** human, of man or mankind, civilized.
384. **commendatio, commendationis,** *f.,* a recommendation; the act of entrusting or committing (*something, someone*) to the care of another.
386. ** **orno, ~are, ~avi, ~atus,** to adorn, decorate.

    recens, recentis, fresh, recent.
387. **domesticus, ~a, ~um,** internal, domestic, civil.

    ** **testimonium, ~i,** *n.,* evidence given by a witness in court.
388. ** **profiteor, profiteri, professus,** to state openly, declare publicly; (*w.* **apud praetorem**) to submit one's name, register.
389. ** **sanctus, ~a, ~um,** scrupulous, upright, virtuous.
390. ** **accipio, accipere, accepi, acceptus,** to take, receive.

    *** **fides, fidei,** *f.,* faith, confidence; a trust or agreement.

    *** **humanitas, humanitatis,** *f.,* civilization, formal society.

    levo, ~are, ~avi, ~atus, to relieve; (*w. abl.*) to free (*someone from something, etc*).
391. **acerbitas, acerbitatis,** *f.,* harshness, severity, cruelty; suffering, distress.

    * **violo, ~are, ~avi, ~atus,** to violate.

comprobetur. Quae cum ita sint, petimus a vobis, iudices,
si qua non modo humana verum etiam divina in tantis ingeniis commendatio debet esse, ut eum qui vos, qui

385   vestros imperatores, qui populi Romani res gestas semper ornavit, qui etiam his recentibus nostris vestrisque
domesticis periculis aeternum se testimonium laudis
daturum esse profitetur, quique est ex eo numero qui
semper apud omnis sancti sunt habiti itaque dicti, sic in

390   vestram accipiatis fidem ut humanitate vestra levatus potius
quam acerbitate violatus esse videatur.

382–391. Quae cum ita sint: see note on 200–203 above. **petimus...videatur:** a
long, complex sentence similar in style and structure to those of the EXORDIUM. The
basic framework runs as follows: *petimus a vobis...ut eum...sic...accipiatis...ut...levatus
potius quam violatus esse videatur.*

383–384. si...esse: the conditional clause is inserted between *petimus* and its indirect command (*ut eum...accipiatis*), because it can be understood as modifying either
petimus or *accipiatis*. **qua:** = *aliqua* (see note on 1 above); note how the HYPERBATON of
qua...commendatio BRACKETS *humana* and *divina*, modifying *commendatio* and symmet-
rically arranged by the correlatives *non modo...verum etiam.* **in tantis ingeniis:** "in
the presence of," or "when dealing with such great talent." **ut eum:** There are five
relative pronouns (nominative singular) that have *eum* (Archias) as the antecedent.
The first three are used as subjects of *ornavit* (used only once) with three separate
direct objects: (1) *qui vos*; (2) *qui vestros imperatores*; (3) *qui [populi Romani,* genitive] *res
gestas*; (4) *qui profitetur* (with Archias as subject), introducing an indirect statement;
(5) *qui est ex numero* (again Archias is the subject). The sixth *qui* (the antecedent is
numero, group of poets) introduces another relative clause with a plural verb, *sunt
habiti itaque dicti.* **qui vos:** sc. *semper ornavit.*

384–389. qui...imperatores: sc. *semper ornavit.* **res gestas:** "achievements." **his recentibus...periculis:** dative indirect object of **daturum esse:** future active infinitive
in indirect statement governed by *profitetur.* **aeternum...testimonium:** direct object
of *daturum esse.* **quique est ex eo numero qui...sunt...dicti:** although its antecedent
is singular (*numero*), the subject of the relative clause takes its plural number from
the meaning of its antecedent (*B* 250.4), "and who is from that profession" (i.e., of
poets). **omnis:** = *omnes* (see note on 62–63 above). **sancti sunt habiti itaque dicti:**
"are held (to be) sacred and are thus said (to be)."

392. ** **consuetudo, consuetudinis,** *f.,* practice, one's customary manner.
     breviter, (*adv.*) briefly.

393. **simpliciter,** (*adv.*) easily, simply.
     confido, confidere, confisus, (*semi-deponent*) to trust, be confident.
     * **probo, ~are, ~avi, ~atus,** to approve, commend.

394. **forum, ~i,** *n.,* a marketplace, public square; the **Forum Romanum**.
     * **alienus, ~a, ~um,** a stranger, non-citizen; of another race, etc.
     iudicialis, ~e, of or relating to the law courts or their administration; judicial, forensic.

395. **communiter,** (*adv.*) both or all alike, indiscriminantly; jointly, in common, together.
     * **loquor, loqui, locutus,** to speak, say.

396. * **spero, ~are, ~avi, ~atus,** to hope.
     pars, partis, *f.,* a part, portion.

397. ** **exerceo, exercere, exercui, exercitus,** to carry on, perform, execute.
     certo, (*adv.*) certainly, without a doubt (< **certus**); (*w.* **scire**) to know for certain.
     ** **scio, scire, scivi (~ii), scitus,** to know (*as fact*); to have certain knowledge of.

Optional Reading: On What Qualities and Practices Make a Good Teacher
     (Appendix III, p. 122)

32 Quae de causa pro mea consuetudine breviter simpliciterque dixi, iudices, ea confido probata esse omnibus; quae a foro aliena iudicialique consuetudine et
395 de hominis ingenio et communiter de ipso studio locutus sum, ea, iudices, a vobis spero esse in bonam partem accepta, ab eo qui iudicium exercet, certo scio.

392–394. **Quae:** neuter accusative plural, object of *dixi* and antecedent of *ea*, the subject of *probata esse* in the indirect statement dependent on *confido*. **omnibus:** (= *vobis*) either "by all of you," or "as far as all of you are concerned." Although the dative of agent often occurs with compound tenses in the passive voice, the verb *probare* idiomatically requires a dative of reference when used passively.

394–397. **quae...ea:** Cicero repeats the construction of the first part of the sentence, with *quae* serving as the object of *locutus sum* and ANTICIPATING *ea*, the subject of *esse...accepta*, the indirect statement dependent on both *spero* and *scio*. **ab eo qui... exercet:** i.e., Quintus Cicero, Marcus' brother and the PRAETOR presiding at the trial (see note on 24–25 above). **certo:** the adverb, construe with *scio*. Regarding the acceptance of his speech in good faith, Cicero contrasts his hope for the jury against his certainty of his brother, the praetor.

APPENDIX I
A BRIEF GLOSSARY OF PROPER NAMES AND PLACES

ACHILLES: the great tragic hero of Homer's *Iliad* (q.v.). Achilles was born in Phthia, a town in eastern Thessaly, to Peleus, a mortal, and Thetis, a goddess. His semi-divine birthright made him the mightiest of all the Greeks who fought in the Trojan War. Though the account of his death is not included in the *Iliad*, tradition maintains that Paris, one of the sons of Priam, killed Achilles with an arrow in the final year of the war, fulfilling Achilles' destiny to perish at Troy after killing Hector, the mightiest warrior of the Trojans.

AETOLIA: a region in central Greece, north of the Isthmus of Corinth. Because it had always been hostile to Macedonia, Aetolia became Rome's first ally in Greece until its cooperation with Antiochus III, a move in direct defiance of Rome's interests, at the end of the second century. As a result of this betrayal, Rome conquered the region in 189 B.C., and forced the Aetolians to accept a treaty which left them, in effect, the subjects of Rome.

AFRICANUS: see Scipio, P. Cornelius Africanus (Minor) Numantinus.

ALEXANDER III (the Great): born heir to the Macedonian kingdom in 356 B.C., as a youth he was tutored by Aristotle, and by the age of eighteen had already proven himself a brilliant military strategist and an inspiring leader. Following the murder of his father, Philip II (336 B.C.), he succeeded to the throne at the age of twenty despite rumors of his involvement in the assassination. Before his death, Philip was preparing to mount an invasion of the Persian empire, then under the rule of Darius III. Although Philip's untimely death cut short these plans, Alexander carried them out himself in 334 B.C. when he crossed the Hellespont, the narrow watercourse connecting the Aegean Sea to the Propontis, with an army composed of Macedonian soldiers and Greek mercenaries. While the pretense for the invasion was to free the Greek cities of Asia from Persian rule, Alexander's true motivation for crossing the Hellespont—the conquest of the entire Persian empire and the seizure of its capital cities (Persepolis, Susa, Ecbatana, and Babylon)—was revealed when he refused to negotiate an armistice after defeating Darius at the battle of Issus. Instead, Alexander pressed his Persian adversary all the way to Persepolis, where Darius was killed by his own men (330 B.C.). Alexander then pressed his army by forced marches into the heart of the Punjab, deep in the Indian interior, until they finally refused to go any further. Faced with turning back, Alexander died of illness at Babylon in 323 B.C.

Antiochia: Antioch of ancient Syria (the modern city Antakya in southern Turkey), originally founded by Antiochus, a general under Alexander the Great. It was the capital of ancient Syria, one of Rome's most important provinces.

Appius Claudius Pulcher: see Claudius, App. Pulcher.

Archias, A. Licinius: See Introduction, pp. xx–xxi.

Armenia: a mountainous region of Asia (q.v.). At first a satrapy of the Persian Empire, Armenia was forced by the hostility between Rome and Mithridates VI (q.v.) to seek protection from Rome. From about 100 B.C. on, it became an object of contention between Rome and its old rival Parthia.

Asia: part of modern Turkey with its capital at Pergamon, it was one of the largest and most important of the Roman provinces, rich in natural resources and agricultural exports. Its many fine harbors allowed a wealth of trade from the far east to flow into the heart of the Roman empire. Although Rome and the Pontic kingdom shared good relations under the rule of King Mithridates V (Euergetes), Rome's continuing expansion into the region inevitably led to conflict. Finally, under the command of Euergetes' successor, Mithridates VI (Eupator Dionysius,) "the Great" (q.v.), the Romans found themselves entangled in a drawn-out war in Asia for the next two decades (88–69 B.C.).

Athenae: the city of Athens, for centuries the literary, cultural, and political center of the Mediterranean world. Its brilliance began to dim, however, after the invasion of Philip II of Macedon in the fourth century B.C., then darkened when the Athenians threw their support behind Mithridates VI "the Great" (q.v.) against Rome. In retaliation,

Sulla (q.v.) besieged the city and sacked the Acropolis (87–86 B.C.). From that point on, Athens was reduced to little more than a university town where wealthy Romans sent their sons to be educated in rhetoric and philosophy.

BRUTUS, DECIMUS IUNIUS CALLAICUS: as consul in 138 B.C., and as proconsul in the following year, he carried out a successful military campaign against the Lusitani and Callaici (hence his *agnomen*), inhabitants of the region of western Iberia (modern Spain).

CAECILIUS, Q. METELLUS: See Metellus, Q. Caecilius.

CAESAR, L. IULIUS: as consul of 90 B.C., after spending that year commanding Roman forces in southern Italy during the Social War (91–87 B.C.), he returned to Rome where he carried the *Lex Iulia de Civitate Latinis et Sociis Danda*, which granted citizenship to all Latins and Italians who had remained loyal to Rome during the war.

CAPITO, P. GABINIUS: one of the praetors of 89 B.C., as propraetor of Achaea he would be convicted of extortion.

CARBO, C. PAPIRIUS: as tribune of 89 B.C. he co-authored the *Lex Plautia Papiria de Civitate Sociis Danda* with his colleague Marcus Plautius Silvanus (q.v.).

CATO, M. PORCIUS (1): "Cato the Elder," he was the great-grandfather of Cato Uticensis (q.v.), the contemporary of Cicero. Consul in 195 B.C., he was also known as "Cato the Censor," not simply because he held that office in 184 B.C., but for his austere manner, old-fashioned values, and strict opposition to foreign influences of any kind, which he felt would corrupt the *virtus Romana* of his ancestors. He wrote several treatises on a range of topics; however, substantial fragments survive from only two, the *De Re Rustica* and the *Origines* (on the early history of Rome and Italy).

CATO, M. PORCIUS (2): the grandson of Cato the elder (1) and father of Cicero's contemporary, Marcus Cato Uticensis (3).

CATO, M. PORCIUS UTICENSIS (3): great-grandson of the statesman "Cato the Elder" (1), later given the agnomen "Uticensis" because of his suicide in Utica in 46 B.C., after the battle of Thapsus.

CATULUS, Q. LUTATIUS (1): served his consulship in 102 B.C. with Marius (q.v.), and together in 101 they defeated the Cimbri (q.v.), a barbaric tribe from northern Germany. Catulus' role in the defeat of the Cimbri was eclipsed by Marius, who was quick to take credit for the victory, leading to Catulus' public disgrace and ultimate suicide.

CATULUS, Q. LUTATIUS (2): son of (1), he became an associate of Sulla (q.v.) and helped bring about the death of Marius in revenge for the suicide of his father. A leader of the Optimates, he was elected consul with Sulla's support in 78 B.C. He quarreled with his colleague, Marcus Aemilius Lepidus, who had revolutionary ambitions, and in the following year took up with Sertorius, another revolutionary. In the end, Lepidus attempted to march on Rome, but was defeated by Catulus. Catulus later opposed both laws granting Pompey extraordinary powers (*Lex Gabinia*, *Lex Manilia*) and subsequently lost the office of Pontifex Maximus to Julius Caesar in 63 B.C.

CHIOS: an island in the Aegean Sea (modern Khio).

CIMBRI: the German tribe that invaded Gaul and Italy at the end of the second century B.C. They were defeated by Marius (q.v.) and Catulus (q.v. [1]) on 30 July, 101 B.C.

CLAUDIUS, APP. PULCHER: father of Publius Clodius, the arch-enemy of Cicero. As praetor of 89 B.C. he enrolled as Roman citizens some newly enfranchised allies.

COLOPHON: a Greek city of Ionia, a region on the coast of western Asia Minor.

CORDUBA: (modern Cordoba) a town in ancient Hispania Baetica.

CRASSUS, L. LICINIUS: the outstanding orator whom Cicero extols in his treatises on oratory, the *Brutus* and the *De Oratore*. Consul in 95 B.C., he passed a law with his colleague, Quintus Mucius Scaevola, against illegal aliens in Rome.

CRASSUS, P. LICINIUS: consul in 97 B.C. As censor in 89, he enrolled as citizens the first Italians after the Social War.

CYZICENUS: an inhabitant of the city of Cyzicus in the Propontis. An important port for the commercial traffic in and out the Black Sea, Cyzicus was besieged by Mithridates (q.v.) and relieved by Lucullus (q.v.) in 73 B.C.

DRUSUS, M. LIVIUS: an adherent of Crassus and a somewhat radical reformer, his visionary, though ultimately unsuccessful, political agenda aimed to reconcile the social, political, and economic conflicts of the Populares and Optimates, thereby winning the popular support of several classes in Rome. Among his proposals as tribune (91 B.C.) was a failed attempt to grant citizenship to Italian allies. He was assassinated.

ENNIUS, Q.: (239–169 B.C.), the author of the *Annales*, one of the first epic poems written in Latin and composed in hexameter verse. Born in the town of Rudiae in the region of Calabria, the "heel" of the Italian boot, he came to Rome and flourished there under the patronage of M. Fulvius Nobilior (q.v.).

EPICUREAN SCHOOL: founded by Epicurus, an Athenian schoolmaster who advanced a philosophy whose principal doctrine was to lead a life free from the daily stress of human ambitions. It originated as a small group of men who lived with Epicurus on his property, having as little as possible to do with society in general. Embraced by many upper-class Romans, who saw it as a convenient way to justify their hedonistic lifestyles, Epicureanism became, though unjustly, the object of criticism.

FULVIUS, Q. FLACCUS: consul of 237, 224, 212, and 209 B.C. Very active in Campania during the Second Punic War (218–201 B.C.), Fulvius captured the Carthiginian camp at Beneventum, and then seized Capua, which had revolted against Rome and opened its gates to Hannibal in 216 B.C.

FULVIUS, M. NOBILIOR: the patron of the epic poet Quintus Ennius (q.v.), as consul in 189 B.C. he defeated the Aetolians (s.v. **AETOLIA**). He sent back to Rome a mass of plundered art, among which were statues of the nine Muses. After his triumph in Rome, he built a temple to Hercules Musarum and there installed the statues.

Furius, L. Philus: consul in 136 b.c., one of the leading orators of his day and a close associate of Scipio Aemilianus (q.v.). In his *De Re Publica* Cicero praises him for his excellent Latin prose style and education.

Graecia: see Magna Graecia.

Grattius: the prosecutor in the case against Archias. Nothing more is known about him than what Cicero says in this speech.

Heraclea: a city in Lucania (modern Policoro) originally settled by Tarentines (s.v. **Tarentini**) in 432 b.c. It was here that Pyrrhus won his first expensive victory over Rome (280 b.c.) when he came to the aid of Tarentum. By granting Heraclea a peace on especially favorable terms, Rome won the city away from the Tarentines.

Homer: according to popular tradition, the blind Greek poet from Chios (or Smyrna) and author of the epic poems the *Iliad* and the *Odyssey*.

Hortensius, Q. Hortalus: one of the leading orators of Rome and a contemporary rival of Cicero, whom Cicero defeated in his prosecution of Verres (70 b.c.), the corrupt governor of Sicily. Despite this defeat, Hortensius remained a prominent orator and held the consulship in 69 b.c. In later years he would appear as a fellow advocate of Cicero in the defense of several eminent Romans.

Iliad: the *Iliad* of Homer (q.v.), an epic poem of 24 books written in hexameter verse that describes events in the final year of the ten-year siege of Troy by the Greek forces under Agamemnon.

Laelius, C.: consul of 140 b.c., he was a close friend of Scipio Aemilianus (q.v.) and leading statesman of his day.

Latium: the territory of the Latin area of central Italy which included Rome and its environs.

Lentulus, L.: apparently one of the praetors of 89 b.c.; nothing more is known of him.

Locrenses: the citizens of Locri, one of the principle towns of Magna Graecia (q.v.).

Lucullus, L. Licinius (1): praetor urbanus in 104 B.C., he campaigned unsuccessfully as commander against a slave revolt in Sicily in the following year. When he returned to Rome in 101 B.C. he was convicted of extortion and exiled to Lucania.

Lucullus, L. Licinius (2): the son of (1) above, as consul of 74 B.C. he secured for himself a command against Mithridates (q.v.), which he later lost, much to his chagrin, to Pompey in 66 B.C. He returned to Rome where he withdrew from public life and lived in remote, but notorious luxury until his death in 57 B.C.

Lucullus, M. Licinius: the younger brother of (2) above, he was adopted by Varro, Cicero's brother-in-law. He enjoyed an active political career, culminating in the consulship of 73 B.C. As proconsul, he extended the Roman frontier in Thrace up to the Danube and eastward to the Black sea, for which he was awarded a triumph by the senate in 71 B.C. He died shortly after his brother, whom he supported politically.

Magna Graecia: the collective term for the Greek cities in southern Italy, among which were: Cumae (the earliest settlement), Tarentum (s.v. **Tarentini**), Locri (s.v. **Locrenses**), Rhegium (s.v. **Regini**), Neapolis (s.v. **Neapolitani**), and Heraclea (q.v.).

Marcellus, M. Claudius: consul in 222 B.C., as proconsul during the Second Punic War he laid siege to and ultimately captured Syracuse in 211 B.C.

Marius, C.: a fellow townsman of Arpinum, Cicero's birthplace, Marius rose from humble beginnings to become the leader of the popular party in Rome. He was consul in 107 B.C., and became again consul for the next five consecutive years, from 104 to 100 B.C.

Mars: the Roman god of War.

Maximus, Q. Fabius Verrucosus Cunctator: consul in 233, 228, 215, 214, and 209 B.C., he is best known for his policy of employing "delaying" guerrilla tactics in fighting Hannibal in Italy following the disasters at Trebia (218 B.C.), Lake Trasimene (217 B.C.), and Cannae (216 B.C.). Called the "shield of Rome," he is credited with Hannibal's ultimate defeat in Italy.

Metellus, Q. Caecilius: consul of 206 B.C., he fought against Hannibal in the southern Italian region of Bruttium during the Second Punic War (218–201 B.C.).

Mithridates VI ("the great"): king of Pontus on the Black Sea and enemy of Rome. He fought three wars against Rome and was finally defeated by Pompey. Shortly thereafter, in 63 B.C., he committed suicide.

Neapolitani: the inhabitants of Neapolis (modern Naples), one of the early Greek settlements (c. 600 B.C.) on the west coast of Italy in the region of Campania, and always one of the major cities of Magna Graecia (q.v.).

Numidicus, Q. Metellus: consul 109 B.C., was sent to fight Jugurtha with Marius as one of his legates. He was a most distinguished member of the *Metellus gens*. He earned the cognomen, *Numidicus*, from his service in North Africa in the war against Jugurtha before Marius became general in that conflict. In 100, as senator, he was exiled for refusing to swear an oath to observe an agrarian law.

Octavius, Cn.: elected consul with Cinna in 87 B.C., but a supporter of Sulla (q.v.), he managed to drive Cinna and his confederates from the city. Cinna, with the aid of Marius, Carbo, and Sertorius, marched on Rome and defeated Octavius, who was killed while wearing his consular robes.

Papius, C.: tribune of the plebs in 65 B.C., he passed the *Lex Papia de Peregrinis*, a law intended to check illegally gained Roman citizenship through the expulsion of all foreigners who did not meet certain residential criteria.

Plotius, L. Gallus, one of the first men to teach formal rhetoric at Rome at the turn of the first century B.C.

Pontus: see Mithridates VI.

Regini: the inhabitants of Rhegium, one of the early Greek colonies of Magna Graecia (q.v.), located in Bruttium, the "toe" of Italy, directly opposite Messina. It was awarded the status of *municipium* by Rome after 90 B.C.

Roma: the city Rome.

Roscius, Q. Gallus: the leading actor in Rome during Cicero's time, and a friend of both Catulus (q.v.) and the dictator Sulla (q.v.). Cicero defended Roscius' brother-in-law, Quinctius, in 81 B.C., in a civil suit that was also Cicero's first important case. Several years later (77 B.C.?) Cicero would defend Roscius himself in another suit.

Salamis: a city on the east coast of the island of Cyprus, off the southern coast of Asia Minor.

Scaurus, M. Aemilius: consul of 115 B.C.; in 112 he led a special embassy of senators to Jugurtha, heir to the throne of Numidia in North Africa, to persuade him (though ultimately unsuccessfully) from attempting to usurp the throne from his brother, Adherbal. As censor in 109 B.C. he built the Via Aemilia.

Scipio, P. Cornelius Aemilianus Africanus (Minor) Numantinus: (185–129 B.C.), a leading statesman of Rome. Consul in 147 B.C., in the following year he distinguished himself in the siege and ultimate destruction of Carthage, and so received the *agnomen* "Africanus," as his grandfather had before him. He was responsible for the utter destruction of the city and the organization of new provinces of Africa.

Sicilia: the island of Sicily.

Sigeum: a town in the Troad; in antiquity believed to be the site of the tomb of Achilles.

Silvanus, M. Plautius: as tribune in 89 B.C. he passed, along with his colleague C. Papirius Carbo (q.v.), the *Lex Plautia Papiria de Civitate Sociis Danda,* which granted Roman citizenship to all citizens of allied states who (1) maintained a residence in Rome at the time the law was passed and, (2) appeared before a praetor within sixty days of the passing of the law.

Smyrna: a major city on the coast of Ionia.

Stoicism: the Greek philosophical school, founded by Zeno of Citium around 300 B.C. Stoics strove for virtue based on knowledge, and a life in harmony with nature. Stoicism was taken up by the Roman nobility of Cicero's day and adapted it somewhat to the needs of statesmen and soldiers.

Sulla, L. Cornelius Felix: he served as quaestor under Marius (q.v.) in 107 B.C., and accompanied him to North Africa, where he secured the surrender of Jugurtha, heir to the throne of Numidia. The success of his subordinate caused bitter feelings in Marius, and the enmity and competition between the two men led to one of Rome's bloodiest civil wars. Sulla ultimately triumphed, and ruled Rome as dictator from 81 to 79 B.C., during which time he enacted legislative reforms designed to return power to the senate, whose ranks he increased in number from three hundred to six hundred. After stepping down from the dictatorship in 79 B.C., he retired to Campania in southern Italy, where he died shortly thereafter in 78 B.C.

Tarentini: the inhabitants of Tarentum (modern Taranto), a town in southern Italy.

Tenedos: an island in the Aegean Sea off the coast of the Troas in Asia Minor, within sight of Troy.

Themistocles: the famous fifth-century B.C. Athenian statesman who commanded the Athenian navy against the Persians at Salamis in 480 B.C.

Theophanes: a Greek historian from Mytilene, the capital city of Lesbos off the coast of Asia Minor. He met Pompey during the Third Mithridatic War (74–63 B.C.), and following his successful completion of the campaign (62 B.C.) accompanied him back to Rome where he was awarded citizenship. During the Civil War he fought on the republican side under Pompey. After being pardoned by Caesar in 48 B.C., he wrote a history of Pompey's military campaigns in Greek.

APPENDIX II
A BRIEF GLOSSARY OF TERMS

AEDILE — In the CURSUS HONORUM, the magistracy between QUAESTOR and PRAETOR. During the late republic the chief responsibilities of the aedile were the maintenance of public works (buildings, temples, streets, aqueducts, etc.), as well as the mounting of public games. Traditionally, the financial burden for producing these spectacles would be in large part assumed by the aediles responsible for putting them on. Even so, those with serious political ambitions spent lavishly, often going deeply into debt in the hope that a popular and successful aedileship would lead to election to higher office.

† **ALLITERATION** — The device of beginning several consecutive, or parallel, words or phrases with the same letter or sound. (EXAMPLE: *Martis manubias Musis* [336].)

† **ANAPHORA** — The repetition of a single word (with the same or different inflection) introducing a series of parallel clauses or phrases, thereby linking them as consecutive units. (EXAMPLE: ***nostra*** *sunt tropaea,* ***nostra*** *monumenta,* ***nostri*** *triumphi* [274–275].)

ANTICIPATION [ANTICIPATES, ETC.] — The use of certain words or phrases (pronouns, adverbs, etc.) to raise the audience's expectation of particular grammatical constructions, dependent clauses, etc. (EXAMPLE: *ab* **eis** ⇒ *artibus* ⇐ **quibus** *aetas puerilis ad humanitatem informari solet* [42–44]; *hominem pudore* **eo** ⇔ **quem**...*videtis* [376–377].)

ANTITHESIS — The juxtaposition of contrasting terms or grammatical units for rhetorical effect. (EXAMPLE: *cum esset cum M. Lucullo* **in Siciliam profectus** *et cum* **ex ea provincia** *cum eodem Lucullo* **decederet** [77–79].)

APPOSITION — A noun used to describe another noun, usually standing next to it and set off by commas, is said to be "in apposition." (EXAMPLE: *apud praetorem populi Romani,* **lectissimum virum** [24–25].)

---

† Terms preceded by a "dagger" indicate those required for the Advanced Placement Examination.

Apodosis [see also Bipartite Construction] — The conclusion, or main clause, of a conditional sentence; it usually follows the Protasis, but can precede it for emphasis.

† Asyndeton [asyndetically, in asyndeton, etc.] — The arrangement of two or more words, phrases, or clauses, without conjunctions or connectors (e.g., *et, atque, sed,* etc.), but typically punctuated by editors with a comma or semicolon. For example, a Tricolon of clauses in Asyndeton would be arranged one after the other in sequence, without anything to connect them. (Example: *Erat temporibus illis iucundus Q. Metello, audiebatur a M. Aemilio, vivebat cum Q. Catulo...*[69–71].)

Bipartite Construction — Simply, any construction consisting of two parts, ranging from words and phrases, to clauses and sentences. When one or more elements of the two members are arranged in parallel construction, Cicero may be using the device to underscore antithesis between them. (Example: *ille corporis motu tantum amorem sibi conciliarat a nobis omnibus; nos animorum incredibilis motus celeritatemque ingeniorum neglegemus?* [218–220].)

Bracketing [see also Hyperbaton] — The insertion of a word or phrase between two elements of a separate grammatical construction that syntactically should stand together. Usually, the two words forming the bracket are modified by the words or phrases enclosed by them, and so the entire construction represents a single idea. (Example: *ratio*⇒ *aliqua ab optimarum artium studiis ac disciplina* ⇐ *profecta* [4–5].)

† Chiasmus [chiastic, etc.] — The reversal of the order of words or phrases in corresponding pairs (a b :: b a), often used by Cicero to achieve Antithesis. (Example: *spatium* (A) *praeteriti temporis* (B) *et pueritiae* (B) *memoriam* (A) [8–9].)

Comparandum — A clause containing the second part, or resolution, of a comparison. (Example: *si quis minorem gloriae fructum putat ex Graecis versibus percipi quam ex Latinis* [288–289].)

Confirmatio — The part of a judicial speech where the orator presents his case.

CONNECTING RELATIVE PRONOUN — A relative pronoun that stands at the beginning of a new sentence and serves to connect it to the one preceding in which its antecedent lies. (EXAMPLE: *Archias...venit Heracleam.* **Quae** [= *et Heraclea*] *cum esset civitas...* [79–80].)

CONSUL — Originally strictly a military commission, over time it evolved into a civic magistracy, but it was always the office of supreme executive power in the government. Each year two consuls were elected from a field of candidates all of whom had held the lower prerequisite offices of the CURSUS HONORUM.

CURSUS HONORUM — The technical term for the succession of offices that all Romans with political ambitions traditionally had to follow. These were: QUAESTOR, AEDILE, PRAETOR, and CONSUL.

EXORDIUM — The introduction, or opening statement, of a judicial speech designed to win the *benevolentia* (good will) of the *iudices* (jury).

EXPOLITIO — The elaboration of a theme previously introduced (employed by Cicero at 351 ff.).

† HENDIADYS — An expression composed of two elements, generally nouns, joined by a conjunction, where the sense strictly demands a single modified noun: "law and order" = "the order of law," or, "rainy days and Mondays," = "rainy Mondays." (EXAMPLE: *in iudiciis periculisque* for *in iudiciorum periculis* [35–36].)

† HYPERBATON [SEE ALSO BRACKETING] — (1) The separation of a noun and its modifier, usually in order to BRACKET other words or constructions. (EXAMPLE: **Pontum**⇒ *et regiis quondam opibus et ipsa natura et regione* ⇐ **vallatum** [265–266]); (2) in a broader sense, the suspension of any word syntactically necessary to complete a clause or phrase (see PERIODICITY).

HYPOTAXIS [HYPOTACTIC, ETC.] — The opposite of PARATAXIS, it is the occurrence of often elaborate syntactic subordination (i.e., clauses within clauses) in a single sentence; typically, the resolution of one subordinate clause is interrupted by the insertion of another which must be resolved first. (EXAMPLE: *...tam parvi animi videamur esse omnes, qui in re publica...ut, cum usque ad extremum spatium nullum tranquillum... duxerimus, nobiscum simul moritura omnia arbitremur?* [361–365].)

† **HYSTERON PROTERON** — A reversing of the natural order of ideas, as "to fall and slip" where "to slip and fall" would be the natural sequence of events. (EXAMPLE: *praedicari de se ac nominari volunt* [331–332].)

† **LITOTES** — The affirmation of something by the denial of its opposite: "not a few," "not unlike." (EXAMPLE: *non neglegebantur* [55].)

NARRATIO — The part of a judicial speech where the orator presents the facts of the case, such as they are.

OCCUPATIO — The rhetorical device of anticipating an opponent's objection and then refuting it.

PARALLELISM — In effect the opposite of ANTITHESIS, it involves the symmetrical arrangement of a series of related words, phrases, or clauses. (EXAMPLE: *proximis censoribus hunc cum clarissimo imperatore L. Lucullo apud exercitum fuisse, superioribus* [*sc. censoribus*] *cum eodem quaestore fuisse in Asia, primis* [*sc. censoribus*] *Iulio et Crasso nullam populi partem esse censam* [132–135].)

PARATAXIS [PARATACTIC, ETC.] — The opposite of HYPOTAXIS, it is the arrangement of sentences into syntactically coordinate clauses without subordination. (EXAMPLE: *at haec studia adulescentiam acuunt, senectutem oblectant, secundas res ornant, adversis perfugium ac solacium praebent, delectant domi, non impediunt foris, pernoctant nobiscum, peregrinantur, rusticantur* [207–211].)

PERIODICITY [PERIODIC, A PERIOD, ETC.] — A trademark of Ciceronian rhetorical style, it involves the suspension until final position of a word that is syntactically necessary (e.g., the subject or main verb) to complete the sense of a sentence or clause.

PERORATIO — The last section of a speech, it was the orator's "closing argument," in which he would rally all of the themes raised during the course of the speech in a final appeal to the *iudices* (jury).

PRAETOR — The magistracy at Rome usually held immediately prior to the office of CONSUL. During the late republic there were eight praetors elected annually. Chief among their official duties was the responsibility of presiding over the law courts.

PROCONSUL — After serving their one-year term as consul, magistrates would then be eligible for a provincial governorship. The assignment, which usually lasted a year, sometimes longer, entitled the magistrate to *imperium*, or right to command an army, in one of the provinces under Roman control.

† PROLEPSIS — The use of a word in the clause preceding the one where it should naturally appear: "See the eagle, how high it flies," for "see how high the eagle flies." (EXAMPLE: *Si quid est in me ingeni, iudices, quod sentio quam sit exiguum* [1–2].)

PROTASIS [PROTASES] — The dependent, or "if" clause, of a conditional sentence that anticipates resolution in the APODOSIS, or main clause.

QUAESTOR — The lowest of the elective magistracies, it was the first office of the CURSUS HONORUM. A quaestor would be assigned by sortition to a higher-ranking magistrate under whom he served during his term. This often involved foreign service, as many quaestors were assigned to accompany pro-magistrates in their provinces.

REFUTATIO — The part of a judicial speech containing a rebuttal, or counter-argument, to the opposition's case.

SYNCOPATION [SYNCOPATED, ETC.] — The omission of a letter or syllable from the middle of a word. (EXAMPLE: *donarunt = donaverunt* [57].)

† SYNECDOCHE — The use of the name of a part for the whole. (EXAMPLE: *animus ex hoc forensi strepitu reficiatur et aures convicio defessae conquiescant* [145–147].)

TRIBUNE — The tribunate was not strictly part of the CURSUS HONORUM, since it was open only to men of plebeian birth. It was in the early days of the republic strictly a military commission, but as time went on there appeared three very different figures: (1) the *tribunus militum*, who preserved the military essence of the office; (2) the *tribunus aerarius*, about whom our knowledge is sketchy, but who seems to have been in charge of the collection of war tax and the distribution of pay to the soldiers; and, 3) the *tribunus plebis*. This tribunate of the *plebs* had become, by the end of the republic, one of the most powerful political offices, as it carried with it the *tribunicia potestas*, which

entitled whoever occupied the office not only to submit his own leg-
islation, which was of itself significant, but also to veto that of others. This veto power was one of the features of the office that was
routinely abused by demagogues whose sole aim was to obstruct the
government in order to advance their own revolutionary agenda.

† **Tricolon** — The arrangement, or grouping, of three words, phrases,
or clauses, often coupled with **Anaphora**. (Example: *hoc concursu hominum litteratissimorum, hac vestra humanitate, hoc denique praetore exercente iudicium* [31–33].)

Tripartite Construction — Simply, any construction consisting of
three parts, ranging from words and phrases, to clauses and sentences. One of Cicero's favorite rhetorical devices, it is one of the most
readily appreciable stylistic features of his oratory. (Example: *hoc concursu hominum litteratissimorum, hac vestra humanitate, hoc denique praetore exercente iudicium* [31–33].)

Variatio — Any deviation from verbal or structural expectation for
the sake of avoiding predictable symmetry or repetition. (Example:
*famam ingeni exspectatio hominis, exspectationem ipsius adventus admira-
tioque superaret* [49–51].)

† **Zeugma** — A rhetorical device through which a single verb governs
two or more objects in different ways: "he held his breath and the
door for his wife." (Example: *studium atque auris adhibere posset* [63].)

APPENDIX III
QUINTILIAN TEXT, VOCABULARY, AND NOTES

I ON THE *EXORDIUM*
(To be read after line 41)

As Quintilian explains (and Cicero knew and practiced), winning the benevolentia *(good will) of the presiding magistrate or* iudex *(usually a praetor) was one of the most important purposes of the* exordium, *and to this end the proper presentation of the* persona *of the orator was most important. (4.1.6.11–7.16)*

1   **benevolentia, ~ae,** *f.,* a feeling of good will (*toward someone*); (*leg.*) the term for winning the hearts and minds of the jury in a court of law.

      persona, ~ae, *f.,* a role, part, or position (*assumed or adopted*); (*leg.*) the character or personality of a person involved in a case or playing a role (*as prosecutor, defendant, or judge*).

      duco, ducere, duxi, ductus, to lead or take away into one's possession.

2   **plerusque, ~aque, ~umque,** the greater part or number of; (*as subst.*) most people, the majority.

3   **triplex, triplicis,** having three parts; tripartite.

      ratio, rationis, *f.,* (*w. defining gen.*) the explanation (*for something*); the result of reasoning; a conception or concept; a way of thinking about something, a reckoning; an idea as the central concept of a thing.

      litigator, ligatoris, *m.,* a litigant; (*leg.*) any party, on either side, engaged in or bringing a legal suit.

      adversarius, ~i, *m.,* any opposing party; (*leg.*) one's rival in court.

4   **exordium, ~i,** *n.,* the opening statement of a formal speech or oration.

      numquam, (*adv.*) never, at no time; (*emphatic*) by no means.

      actor, actoris, *m.,* (*w.* **causae**) any pleader before the court, for either side.

      soleo, solere, solui, solitus, (*w. complementary inf.*) to be accustomed to.

5   **quamquam,** (*conj.*) although.

      paucus, ~a, ~um, a few, not many.

      dico, dicere, dixi, dictus, to speak, pronounce (*judgment*); say, tell (*w. acc. + inf.*); (*political*) to appoint, designate.

      parcius, (*comp. adv.*) sparingly, thriftily.

6   **plurimus, ~a, ~um,** the greatest number, the most; (*n. sing. as subst.*) the greatest amount.

      momentum, ~i, *n.,* (*leg.*) something of weight, importance; an important and influencing factor.

      pono, ponere, posui, positus, to put, place, position.

Benevolentiam aut a personis ducimus aut a causis accepimus. Sed personarum non est, ut plerique crediderunt, triplex ratio: ex litigatore, et adversario, et iudice. Nam exordium duci non numquam etiam ab actore causae solet.

5   Quamquam enim pauciora de se ipso dicit et parcius, plurimum tamen ad omnia momenti est in hoc positum, si vir bonus creditur.

1–2. benevolentiam: note the emphatic placement of the noun, underscoring the idea that winning the good will of his audience was the orator's first and foremost priority in the *exordium*. **aut...aut:** "either...or..." The correlative construction balances *ducimus* and *accepimus* as well as the two prepositional phrases *a personis...a causis* (both sharing the semantic feature of "source" or "origin"). **ducimus...accepimus:** semantically, in this context both verbs are very close in meaning: "we take or receive..." This sort of semantically redundant coupling of verbs is very Ciceronian. **a personis...a causis:** the two sources on which a lawyer can base his case: either on the character of those involved (*personae*) or on the facts of the case (*causa*), or both.

2–3. personarum: gen. pl. (picking up on *a personis*), construe with *ratio*. **non est...triplex ratio:** "But the guiding principle behind the issue of 'character' is not, as many have believed, threefold in nature." See note following on who the "three *personae*" of the case are, and whose is the most important. **ut...crediderunt:** an adverbial aside: "as many have believed..." **ex litigatore, et adversario, et iudice:** "from the (personality) of the plaintiff, his adversary (the defendant), and the judge" (i.e., the *triplex ratio personarum*).

3–4. duci: the passive infinitive, complementary with *solet*: "is accustomed to be derived..." **non numquam:** an example of LITOTES, "not never" = "sometimes," or "often." **etiam:** construe closely with *ab actore*. **ab actore:** the lawyer himself (i.e., the man representing either the plaintiff or the defendant), construe with *duci*. **causae:** gen. sing., construe with *actore*. Although many of Cicero's famous cases were prosecutions, he preferred, as most attorneys do today, to be a defendant's lawyer.

5–7. pauciora: acc. pl. n., object of *dicit*; the use of the comparative adjective as SUBSTANTIVE without a COMPARANDUM: "relatively few things..." **de se ipso:** the ANTECEDENT is *actore*. **parcius:** the comparative adverb. **dicit:** the subject is an understood *actor*. **plurimum:** nom. sing. n. **pauciora...et parcius, plurimum...est...positum:** note how the ALLITERATION underscores the contrast between these words as Quintilian concludes this definition of the EXORDIUM. **ad omnia momenti:** "as pertains to everything of importance." **in hoc:** ANTECEDENT is *actore...de se ipso* (note how the prepositional phrase is BRACKETED between *est* and *positum*). **si vir bonus creditur:** sc. *esse*.

II ON THE *NARRATIO*
(To be read after line 89)

The narratio *is that part of the speech in which the orator presents the facts of the case and as such it helps either one side or the other, or a combination thereof* (aut tota pro nobis aut tota pro adverariis aut mixta); *therefore, in Quintilian's eyes, the facts of the case, such as they are, are ultimately inconclusive on their own. Quintilian succinctly defines the role of the* narratio *specifically as a vehicle by which the orator can portray the facts as he wants them to impact the* iudex, *and then only in three specific ways* (intellegat, meminerit, credit). *(4.2.33.6–9)*

1   **narratio, narrationis,** *f.*, that part of a forensic speech in which the orator presents the facts of the case, such as they are, and any history leading up to them.

     totus, ~a, ~um, entirely, wholly, completely.

     adversarius, ~i, *m.*, any opposing party; (*leg.*) one's rival in court on either side.

2   **mixtus, ~a, ~um,** mixed, of two or more parts.

     uterque, utraque, utrumque, (*pron.*); (*sing.*) each one, each other; (*plur. of two parties*) each side, both, both at once.

     contentus, ~a, ~um, content, satisfied (*w. dat.*).

3   **tres, tria,** three.

     efficio, efficere, effeci, effectus, to work out, bring about, effect, cause.

     quo, (= *ut eo*); *abl. sing. of rel. pron. used as conj. w. a comp. adj. or adv. expressing degree of difference*) whereby (*the more*), whereby (*the less*).

     facilius, (*comp. adv.* > **facilis, ~e**) easy, ready to hand.

4   **intellego, intellegere, intellexi, intellectus,** to know, understand; to think, apply rational thought (*to an issue, problem, etc.*).

     memini, meminisse, (*defective verb*) to remember, hold in one's memory.

Narratio est aut tota pro nobis aut tota pro adversariis aut mixta ex utrisque. Si erit tota pro nobis, contenti sumus his tribus partibus, per quas efficitur quo facilius iudex intellegat, meminerit, credat.

1–2. aut...aut...aut: "either...or...or." Note how the repetition of the conjunction creates a TRICOLON in which the first two members are grammatically completely PARALLEL (*aut tota pro nobis* :: *aut tota pro adversariis*) while in the third member Quintilian employs VARIATIO (*aut mixta ex utrisque*) substituting *mixta* for *tota* and the prepositional phrase *ex utrisque* for the contrasting *pro nobis* :: *pro adversariis*. VARIATIO in the third member of a TRICOLON is stylistically a traditional Ciceronian trademark. **tota:** "entirely."

2–3. si erit...contenti sumus: a mixed condition where the PROTASIS is stated in the future and the APODOSIS is stated in the present tense; the effect is rhetorical in order to represent the conclusion as a foregone conclusion. **erit:** sc. *narratio* as subject. **his tribus partibus:** dative plural, construe with *contenti sumus*. **his:** note how the use of the demonstrative indicates that *tribus partibus* refers to the TRIPARTITE definition of the *narratio* Quintilian offers in the first sentence. **per quas:** "through which"; the prepositional phrase modifies *efficitur* and expresses the semantic feature "means." **quas:** the antecedent is *partibus*. **efficitur:** the impersonal passive, "it is brought about," "it happens." **quo:** (= *ut eo*) abl. sing. of the relative pronoun used as a conjunction to show degree of difference with the comparative adverb *facilius*, "whereby the judge might more easily understand, remember, believe." **intellegat, meminerit, credat:** subjunctives in the final clause governed by *quo + facilius*.

III ON EVIDENCE AND WITNESSES
(To be read after line 106)

On the question of the credibility of written records versus the word of a witness, Quintilian makes a distinction between those witnesses who merely give their testimony by proxy through a written statement (tabulae), *and those who are actually willing to show up in person* (praesentes) *and subject themselves to examination by the court. Obviously, a good advocate wants to subject a live witness to a rigorous cross-examination and character assault. But if he is faced with just a statement, he can always call into question the character of the guarantors* (signatores) *of the signed statement.* (5.7.1.16–21)

1   **patronus, ~i,** *m.,* the advocate, lawyer.

    circa, *(prep. w. acc.)* about, concerning.

    testimonium, ~i, *n.,* testimony, evidence given in court.

    sudor, sudoris, *m.,* sweat; the sweat of exertion or toil; *(figuratively)* work, exertion, worry, trouble.

2   **praesens, praesentis,** present, in person.

    simplicior, *(comp. adj. >* **simplex**) more simple, less complicated, easier.

    contra, *(prep. w. acc.)* before, against, in front of, facing.

3   **pugna, ~ae,** *f.,* a fight, battle; *(leg.)* a court fight.

    obsto, obstare, obstiti, to be an obstacle.

    video, videre, vidi, visus, to see, watch, notice, discern, perceive; *(in the passive in formal decisions)* to seem right, be decided, be adjudged.

4   **paucus, ~a, ~um,** a few, not many.

    signator, signatoris, *m.,* the guarantor of a signature; the witness to a written document submitted as evidence in court; a notary public.

    diffidentia, ~ae, *f.,* a lack of confidence.

    premo, premere, pressi, pressus, to push, press, urge, attack; *(pass. w.* **pro** + *abl.)* to lay emphasis *(on).*

    absentia, ~ae, *f.,* an absence where presence is normally required; *(leg.)* an absence of appearance in court.

5   **reprehensio, reprehensionis,** *f.,* blame, censure, reprehension.

    capio, capere, cepi, captus, to take; *(figuratively)* to incur, suffer, endure *(an injury, insult, etc.).*

    persona, ~ae, *f., (in court)* the character of a participant in a legal proceeding on either side.

    infamo, ~are, ~avi, ~atus, to disgrace, dishonor, defame.

6   **licet, licere, licui, licitum est,** *(impersonal verb)* it is lawful, permitted *(usu. w. subj. inf. clause).*

Maximus tamen patronis circa testimonia sudor est. Ea dicuntur aut per tabulas aut a praesentibus. Simplicior contra tabulas pugna: nam et minus obstitisse videtur pudor inter paucos signatores et pro diffidentia premitur absentia. Si
5   reprehensionem non capit ipsa persona, infamare signatores licet.

1–2. maximus...sudor est: the PERIODIC structure of the sentence creates a HYPERBATON between subject (*sudor*) and the adjective (*maximus*) that BRACKETS both the dative (*patronis*) and the prepositional phrase (*circa testimonia*) modifying the three words. PERIODIC sentences of this type that make use of HYPERBATON and BRACKETING to help guide the reader through the syntax of the sentence is another trademark of Ciceronian rhetorical style. **patronis:** dat. of possession with *sudor est*. **testimonia:** acc. pl. n., object of the preposition *circa*. **est:** the "existential" use of the verb, not linking: "the greatest worry is..." **ea:** n. nom. pl., subject of *dicuntur*, the ANTECEDENT is *testimonia*. **dicuntur:** "are entered into evidence..."

2–3. aut...aut: "either...or..." **per tabulas:** the prepositional phrase has the semantic feature "means," "through written records." **a praesentibus:** the prepositional phrase expresses the semantic feature "agency," "through witnesses." Quintilian is making a distinction between those witnesses who merely give their testimony by proxy through a written statement or the presentation of documents and records (*tabulae*), and those who actually show up in person (*praesentes*) to subject themselves to the court's full examination. **simplicior...pugna:** sc. *est*; note how the BOOKEND word order echoes that of the first sentence, BRACKETING the prepositional phrase *contra tabulas*. **contra tabulas:** i.e., against the person who has supplied the written evidence. **nam:** the word signals that a clarification of the previous statement is coming.

3–4. et...et: "both...and..." **minus obstitisse videtur pudor inter paucos signatores:** "for the guilt (of the person providing testimony through written records) seems both to have presented less of an obstacle (for him when testifying) before only a few witnesses of his signature..." i.e., as opposed to the many people he would have had to answer to if he had actually come to court and testified in person. **pro diffidentia premitur absentia:** "and his absence (from court) can be attacked for showing lack of confidence." The clear insinuation Quintilian is making is that witnesses who submit their testimony *per tabulas* have something to hide which, if made known to the court, would discredit their testimony and be for them a source of guilt (*pudor*).

4–5. si...persona: the PROTASIS of a simple condition. **ipsa persona:** i.e., the character of the person presenting evidence *per tabulas*. **infamare signatores:** the infinitive clause functions as the subject of the impersonal verb *licet* in the APODOSIS of the condition.

IV ON THE FOUR TYPES OF LOGICAL PROOF
(To be read after line 143)

Quintilian quantifies the four different ways an advocate can argue the facts of his case as logical "proofs" that puts one in mind of a Platonic dialogue, or the philosophical dialogues of Cicero or Seneca. (5.8.7.26–3)

1   **adhuc,** *(adv.)* up to this point, as yet, by now, already.

       probatio, probationis, *f.,* legal proof, evidence.

       quadruplex, quadruplicis, of or consisting of four parts; four-part.

       ratio, rationis, *f.,* *(w. qualifying gen.)* the guiding principle *(behind something)*, a concept, a way of thinking about something, a reckoning; an idea as the central concept of a thing.

       vel, *(conj.)* or; **vel...vel,** either...or; *(adv.)* even.

2   **quia,** *(conj.)* because.

       aliquis, aliquid, *(indefinite pron.)* someone, anyone; *(n.)* something, anything; **aliquid...aliquid,** something...something else.

       alius, ~a, ~ud, another, other, else; **alius...alius,** one...another *(etc.).*

       dies, diei, *m. & f.,* day.

3   **sol, solis,** *m.,* the sun.

       super, *(prep. w. acc. & abl.)* above, on top of, over, upon.

       terra, ~ae, *f.,* the earth, ground, land, dirt.

4   **nox, noctis,** *f.,* night, nightfall.

       rationalis, ~e, rational, of or concerning rational thought or reasoning.

5   **homo, hominis,** *m. & f.,* a human being, man, person.

Et adhuc omnium probationum quadruplex ratio est, ut vel
quia est aliquid, aliud non sit: ut "dies est, nox non est"; vel
quia est aliquid, et aliud sit: "sol est super terram, dies est"; vel
quia aliquid non est, aliud sit: "non est nox, dies est"; vel quia
5   aliquid non est, nec aliud sit: "non est rationalis, nec homo est."

1–2. omnium probationum: genitive plurals, clarifying *ratio*. **ut...ut:** the first *ut*
stands in APPOSITION to the statement of the main clause (*quadruplex ratio est*), and
serves to introduce the entire passage, which contains four hypotheses introduced
by the ANAPHORA of *vel quia...vel quia*, and is best translated "namely that..."; the second *ut* introduces an example in quotation marks that illustrates, or expands upon,
that hypothesis, and is best translated "for example." The second *ut* is then to be
understood as repeated before the next three statements that appear in quotation
marks.

1–2. The First Hypothesis: vel quia...non sit: "namely that because something
is, something else is not." **est...sit:** both are examples of the "existential" use of *esse*,
where there is no predicate nominative; the difference between the indicative and
the subjunctive may be felt as the difference between the existence of one thing
and the consequent potential existence for something else. Quintilian repeats this
construction in the following three hypotheses. **ut "dies est, nox non est":** "for example: 'it is day, (therefore) it is not night.' "

2–3. The Second Hypothesis: vel quia est...sit: "or because something is, something else also is."

3–4. The Third Hypothesis: vel quia...non est...sit: "or because something is
not, something else is."

4–5. The Fourth Hypothesis: vel quia...non est, nec...sit: "or because something
is not, nor is something else." **rationalis:** sc. *homo*: "he is not a rational human being,
(therefore) he is not a human being."

V ON THE BENEFITS OF READING POETRY
(To be read after line 157)

Quintilian recounts how the Greek philosopher Theophrastus praised the benefits of reading poetry, and actually makes reference to Cicero's praising of poetry in the Pro Archia. *Note how closely Quintilian's language echoes the very words of Cicero in his oration. (10.1.27.24–5)*

1   **plurimum,** (*adv.*) to the greatest extent, most of all, above all things.

    orator, oratoris, *m.,* a public speaker; one who speaks on another's behalf.

    Theophrastus, ~i, *m.,* (370–288 B.C.) a Greek scientist and philosopher, a pupil and protégé of Aristotle.

    lectio, lectionis, *f.,* a reading, a selection of something to be read.

2   **sequor, sequi, secutus,** to follow (*esp. in the process of time or sequence of events*).

3   **immerito,** (*adv.*) undeservedly, without merit, without justification.

    in, (*prep. w. abl.*) in terms (*of*); in regard (*to*).

4   **sublimitas, ~tatis,** *f.,* loftiness of style, sublimity of language; (*gen.*) grandeur.

    adfectus, ~us, *m.,* affect, disposition, mood, emotion.

    motus, ~us, *m.,* the ability or power to stir (*a person*) to action; the stirring of the emotions (*of someone*).

    persona, ~ae, *f.,* (*in court*) the character of a participant in a legal proceeding on either side.

    decor, decoris, *m.,* decorum, appropriateness, correctness.

5   **peto, petere, petivi (~ii), petitus,** to seek, aim for; (*pass.*) to obtain, receive.

    praecipue, (*adv.*) especially, to a greater extent.

    velut, (*adv.*) as it were.

    attritus, ~a, ~um, worn down, worn away.

    actus, ~us, *m.,* a recital, the delivery of a speech or oration.

6   **talis, ~e,** such, of such a kind or quality.

    libertas, libertatis, *f.,* (*w. gen.*) the freedom or release, a source of refuge (*from a burden or obligation*).

    reparo, ~are, ~avi, ~atus, to recover, restore, repair.

    ideo, (*adv.*) for that reason, on that account, therefore.

7   **Cicero, Ciceronis,** *m.,* (106–43 B.C.) a statesman of Rome's republic and her most celebrated orator, Consul 63 B.C.

    requiesco, requiescere, requievi, requietus, to rest, relax.

Plurimum dicit oratori conferre Theophrastus lectionem poetarum, multique eius iudicium sequuntur neque immerito. Namque ab his in rebus spiritus et in verbis sublimitas et in adfectibus motus omnis et in personis decor
5   petitur, praecipueque velut attrita cotidiano actu forensi ingenia optime rerum talium libertate reparantur. Ideoque in hac lectione Cicero requiescendum putat.

1–3. plurimum: the adverb, "above all things," construe with *conferre* (see note below). **poetarum:** gen. pl. modifying *lectionem*, "the reading of poets," i.e., "reading poetry." **oratori:** dative, construe with *conferre*. **conferre...lectionem:** the indirect statement governed by *dicit*. **lectionem:** the acc. subject of *conferre*. **multique:** (sc. *oratores*) although the ANTECEDENT is obviously *oratori* Quintilian shifts from the singular to the plural and here the adjective is being used SUBSTANTIVELY as the subject of *sequuntur*: "and many follow..." **eius:** gen. sing. m., modifying *iudicium* (the ANTECEDENT is *Theophrastus*). **neque immerito:** "and not without merit," an example of LITOTES.

3–5. In this sentence Quintilian describes how poets and poetry serve orators in four specific areas of public advocacy: in handling the actual facts of the case (*in rebus*); in handling the words they choose (*in verbis*); in handling the exhibition of emotions (*in adfectibus*); and in the persona that they project (*in personis*). **ab his:** agency, construe with *petitur*; the ANTECEDENT of *his* is *poetarum*. **in rebus...decor:** note the strict PARALLELISM of the word order (*in* + abl. pl. + nom. sing.), with the same pattern repeated four times, the only VARIATIO being the addition of *omnis* in the third member, a dramatic example of PARATAXIS that gives structure to this compound subject of *petitur* (see note below). **in rebus spiritus...petitur:** "in handling the actual facts of the case inspiration is supplied by poets." Follow this pattern when translating each of the four clauses introduced by the ANAPHORA of the preposition *in*. **in verbis:** "in the choice of words." **in adfectibus motus omnis:** "in the exhibition of emotions every kind of power to excite them." **in personis:** "in the exposition of the personae of the case." **petitur:** "is supplied." Note the singular verb with the compound subject (*spiritus...sublimitas...motus...decor*), a construction often employed by Cicero. **praecipueque velut attrita...ingenia:** "and especially intellects worn down, as it were..." **velut:** apply its force to the passive participle *attrita* and the ablatives that modify it (see note following). **cotidiano actu forensi:** abl. sing. (means) construe with *attrita* (note how *attrita...ingenia* BRACKETS the ablative of means). **optime:** construe w. *reparantur*. **rerum talium:** gen. pl. (partitive, or separation), construe w. *libertate*. **libertate:** ablative (means), modifying the passive verb *reparantur*: "by offering a refuge from such things."

6–7. ideoque: "and on this account." **in hac lectione:** note the force of the demonstrative pronoun: "by the very act of reading." **requiescendum:** sc. *esse*, the future passive periphrastic infinitive in indirect statement, governed by *putat* (the reader should not fail to take into account that the future passive periphrastic generally carries with it the semantic feature of strong obligation). **putat:** the present tense because Quintilian is referring to Cicero's writings, specifically echoing his very words concerning the value of poets and poetry at *Pro Archia* 12.145–150.

VI ON THE BENEFITS OF READING AND CULTIVATING A READING LIFESTYLE

(To be read after line 211)

Like Cicero, Quintilian has much to say on the subject of the many benefits that reading repays the reader. In this passage he discusses how students might "digest" what they read. (10.1.19.6–12)

1   **lectio, lectionis,** *f.,* the act of reading; that which is read, reading matter, a passage in a book, a selection of text, a text.

liber, libera, liberum, free, of one's own choice.

actio, actionis, *f., (of orators)* declamation, giving speeches, public speaking.

impetus, ~us, *m.,* rapid movement, speed, drive.

transcurro, transcurrere, transcurri (~cucurri), transcursus, to hurry past, overlook or treat in a cursory manner.

2   **licet, licere, licui, licitum est,** *(impersonal verb)* it is lawful, permitted *(usu. w. acc. + inf. as subj.).*

dubito, ~are, ~avi, ~atus, to doubt, hesitate *(w. inf.).*

penitus, *(adv.)* deeply, far within.

adfigo, adfigere, adfixi, adfixus, to fix in position, put or place *(w. dat.).*

3   **retracto, ~are, ~avi, ~atus,** to reconsider, treat or deal with again; to rehash.

cibus, ~i, *m.,* food.

maneo, manere, mansi, mansus, to remain; *(pass.)* to be held *(as food in the mouth).*

4   **liquefacio, liquefacere, liquefactus,** to reduce something to liquid state, liquefy.

demitto, demittere, demisi, demissus, *(with food, medicine, etc.)* to swallow.

quo, *(conj.)* (= *et eo*) the ablative of the relative pronoun used as a conjunction in final clauses containing a comparative adverb and a verb in the subjunctive.

digero, digere, digessi, digrestus, to separate, divide, distribute.

5   **crudus, ~a, ~um,** *(of food)* undigested.

iteratio, iterationis, *f.,* the act of re-reading, going back over again and again.

mollio, mollire, mollivi, mollitus, to soften, make soft.

velut, *(adv.)* even as, just as, like.

6   **conficio, conficere, confeci, confectus,** *(of food)* to break down into small pieces, to masticate.

imitatio, imitationis, *f.,* the act of making a copy.

trado, tradere, tradidi, traditus, to give up, hand over.

Lectio libera est nec actionis impetu transcurrit, sed repetere saepius licet, sive dubites sive memoriae penitus adfigere velis. Repetamus autem et retractemus, et ut cibos mansos ac prope liquefactos demittimus quo facilius digerantur, 5 ita lectio non cruda, sed multa iteratione mollita et velut confecta memoriae imitationique tradatur.

1–2. lectio: "reading," subject of both *est* and *transcurrit*. **libera:** nom. sing. f., translate predicatively as subject complement of *lectio*. **actionis:** gen. sing., modifying *impetu*. **impetu:** abl. sing. (means), construe with *transcurrit*. **repetere:** i.e., "to re-read"; sc. *te* as acc. subject of *repetere*; taken together the phrase *te repetere* is a non-finite noun clause that functions as the subject of *licet*. **saepius:** (*comp. adv.*) construe with *repetere*, "to re-read again and again," or "over and over." **sive dubites... sive...adfigere velis:** "whether you have doubts (about what you have read)...or if you wish to fix it deeply into your memory." The two pres. impf. subjunctives, introduced by the ANAPHORA of *sive...sive*, serve to form the PROTASIS of a potential condition without a stated APODOSIS, or with the APODODIS implied by statements made in the preceding main clause. **dubites...velis:** note the shift to the "generalizing" second person sing., not nearly as common in Latin as it is in English. **dubites:** i.e., should you have any doubt about what you have just read. **adfigere:** complementary infinitive with *velis*. **memoriae:** dat. sing., construe with *adfigere*. **penitus:** construe the adverb with *memoriae...adfigere* (note how the noun and the infinitive BRACKET the adverb).

3–6. repetamus...et retractemus: (sc. *lectionem*) independent potential subjunctives; note the shift from second person sing. to first person pl. verbs, and how they continue the generalizing effect: "we may re-read, moreover, and reconsider (what we have read)." Quintilian introduces through a SIMILE the notion that because we can re-read and rehash written material, the way our minds process a written text (*lectio*) is similar to the way our bodies process food (*cibus*) after we put it in our mouths. **et ut...ita:** "and just as...so also..." **cibos mansos:** i.e., food that remains in our mouths before we swallow it. **ac prope:** "and nearly." **liquefactos:** sc. *cibos*: i.e., food in a state of liquefaction (from having remained in our mouths). **quo:** the CONNECTING RELATIVE PRONOUN (= *et eo*); the ablative of the relative pronoun is used as a conjunction in final clauses such as this one that contains a comparative adverb (*facilius*) and a verb in the subjunctive (*digerantur*). **quo facilius digerantur:** "whereby the more easily the food (*cibos*) may be digested." **lectio:** i.e., what we have read. **non cruda, sed...mollita et velut confecta:** both the adjective and two passive participles are nom. sing. fem., and agree with *lectio*, but should be translated predicatively after *tradatur*. **multa iteratione:** here "re-reading." ablative (means), construe with *tradatur*. **memoriae imitationique:** dat. sing., indirect object with *tradatur*: "handed over to memory and (future) imitation." Quintilian's coupling of *memoria* and *imitatio* is interesting as well as instructive, as it indicates that in Cicero's and Quintilian's day, it was common practice for the orator to strive to process what they read correctly and completely, so that they are not only able to recall it, but to imitate it as well (either in their own writings or in the things they say).

VII ON THE *PERORATIO*
(To be read after line 375)

According to Quintilian, the orator should direct his peroratio, *or closing statement, so that it targets either the facts of the case or the emotions of the* iudices, *and that in any case, an appeal to the emotions of the* iudices *is to be employed by both sides though in different ways and to different ends. (6.1.1.13–15; 6.1.8.28–4)*

1   **peroratio, perorationis,** *f.,* the summation, or closing statement of a formal speech or oration.

    sequor, sequi, secutus, to follow (*esp. in the process of time or sequence of events*).

    cumulus, ~i, *m.,* (*of a speech*) the capstone, conclusion, summation.

    conclusio, conclusionis, *f.,* a conclusion (*of a speech or discourse*); the *peroratio*.

2   **voco, vocare, vocavi, vocatus,** to call, name.

    duplex (duplicis), of two kinds, that takes two forms.

    ratio, rationis, *f.,* (*w. qualifying gen.*) the guiding principle (*behind something*).

    pono, ponere, posui, positus, to put, place, set; (*pass. of arguments*) to be grounded (*in, among, etc.*).

3   **adfectus, ~us,** *m.,* emotion.

    pars, partis, *f.,* a part; (*figuratively*) an aspect, angle.

    accusator, accusatoris, *m.,* the prosecutor in a public trial; one who brings a formal accusation before a judge or jury.

    patronus, ~i, *m.,* the advocate for the defense (*as opposed to the* **accusator**).

4   **aequus, ~a, ~um,** equal.

    communis, ~e, common, held in common.

    quoque, (*adv.*) also, even.

    isdem, eadem, idem, (*intensive pron. & adj. usu. referring to a person or thing previously mentioned*) this or that same (*man, woman, thing, etc.*).

    fere, (*adv.*) in most cases, generally, as a rule.

5   **utor, uti, usus,** (*w. abl.*) to use, make use of, employ, exploit.

6   **concito, ~are, ~avi, ~atus,** to rouse, urge to action.

    flecto, flectere, flexi, flectus, to soften, mollify, win over (*to one's side*), prevail upon.

    convenio, convenire, conveni, conventus, (*impers. w. dat. + inf.*) to be suited (*for someone to do something*).

Peroratio sequebatur, quam cumulum quidam, conclusionem alii vocant. Eius duplex ratio est, posita aut in rebus aut in adfectibus. Haec pars perorationis accusatori patronoque ex aequo communis est. Adfectibus quoque isdem fere
5   utuntur, sed aliis hic, aliis ille saepius ac magis: nam huic concitare iudices, illi flectere convenit.

1–2. peroratio sequebatur: "the peroration was the next topic (I wanted to discuss)." Quintilian uses the past imperfective tense because he is speaking on various topics of rhetoric in a certain sequence from which the above quotation was taken out of context. **quam:** acc. sing. f. of the relative pronoun, the ANTECEDENT is *peroratio*. **quidam...alii:** "some...others..." Both are nom. pl. m. in PARALLEL construction, serving as the subjects of two FACTITIVE clauses joined by ASYNDETON that share a common verb (*vocant*) and direct object (*quam*). **quam cumulum quidam:** sc. *vocant*, the first of the two FACTITIVE clauses, with *quam* as direct object and *cumulum* as the object complement. **conclusionem alii vocant:** sc. *quam*. **eius:** gen. sing. f., modifying *ratio* (the ANTECEDENT is *peroratio*). **eius duplex ratio est:** "the guiding principle (*ratio*) of the (*eius*) *peroratio* takes two forms (*duplex*)." **aut...aut:** "either... or..." the two correlative conjunctions juxtapose the prepositional phrases *in rebus* and *in adfectibus*. **posita:** nom. sing. fem. pass. participle, "grounded..."

3–4. haec pars perorationis: "this latter part of the peroration..." i.e., the importance of exploiting the emotions of the case, something that Quintilian will go on to explain in some detail. **accusatori patronoque:** datives with the adjective *communis*. **ex aequo:** "equally," construe with *communis est*.

4–6. adfectibus...isdem: abl. pl., direct object of *utuntur*. Note how the demonstrative pronoun *isdem* ANTICIPATES the two ablatives (*aliis...aliis*) of the following clause introduced by *sed*. **hic...ille:** i.e., the *accusator* and the *patronus*, respectively, named in the previous sentence; note how the two singular pronouns form the compound subject of the third person plural verb *utuntur*. **aliis...aliis:** the ANTECEDENT of both adjectives is *adfectibus*; the point Quintilian is making is that the prosecutor (*hic*) exploits (*utuntur*) some emotions (*aliis*) and the advocate for the defense (*patronus*) exploits others (*aliis*). **saepius ac magis:** "more often and with greater scope." The comparative adverbs apply only to the second *aliis* clause. **nam:** the particle alerts the reader to an explanation of the foregoing statement. **huic...illi:** dat. sing. m.; the ANTECEDENTS of these two demonstrative pronouns are, respectively, the preceding *hic* (the *accusator*) and *ille* (the *patronus*). **concitare iudices...flectere:** sc. *iudices*; the two infinitive clauses function as the subjects of *convenit*: "for it is suitable for the one side (*huic*) to rouse the jury, and for the other side (*illi*) to mollify them."

7   **verum,** (*conj. assenting to what has just been said, but adding qualification*) and yet, but still.

     accusator, accusatoris, *m.,* the prosecutor in a public trial; one who brings a formal accusation before a judge or jury.

     habeo, habere, habui, habitus, to have, hold, possess; (*figuratively with nouns of feelings or emotions*), to display, show, etc.; (*w.* **lacrimas**) to shed tears.

     interim, (*adv.*) sometimes, at times, from time to time.

     lacrima, ~ae, *f.,* a tear; (*pl. w.* **habere**) to shed tears.

     miseratio, miserationis, *f.,* pity, compassion, empathy.

     reus, ~i, *m.,* an accused party; the defendant (*or plaintiff*) involved in a lawsuit or any legal dispute; one charged with a crime.

8   **ulciscor, ulcisci, ultus,** to avenge, seek justice from (*in court*).

     indignitas, indignitatis, *f.,* indignity, humiliation, unworthy treatment.

     calumnia, ~ae, *f.,* calumny; a false statement or accusation; a deliberate misrepresentation of the facts.

9   **conspiratio, conspirationis,** *f.,* a conspiracy.

     vehementius, (*comp. adv. >* **vehemens**) more vehemently; more aggressively, violently.

     queror, queri, questus, to complain, express grief, lament, bewail.

Verum et accusator habet interim lacrimas ex miseratione eius rei quem ulciscitur, et reus de indignitate calumniae conspirationis vehementius interim queritur.

7–9. verum: the conjunction signals the reader that Quintilian is going to qualify the preceding statement. **et accusator...et reus:** note the PARALLEL word order, "both accuser...and defendant..." **habet interim...ex miseratione eius rei** :: **de indignatione calumniae conspirationis...interim queritur:** note the CHIASMUS (verb [A₁] adverb [B₁] prepositional phrase + genitive + genitive [C₁] :: prepositional phrase + genitive + genitive [C₂] adverb [B₂] verb [A₂]). **habet...lacrimas:** "sheds tears." **eius:** objective genitives, construe with *ex miseratione*: "out of pity for the defendant..." **rei:** gen. sing. m. (> *reus*). **quem:** the ANTECEDENT is *rei*. **eius rei quem:** note how the demonstrative pronoun *eius* ANTICIPATES the relative pronoun *quem*. **calumniae:** objective gentive, construe with *de indignitate*. **conspirationis:** a second objective genitive, modifying *calumniae*.

VIII ON WHAT QUALITIES AND PRACTICES MAKE A GOOD TEACHER

(To be read upon completion of the oration)

Quintilian gives his definition of a good praeceptor *(or* magister*) and what qualities, customs, and attributes he should and should not possess. (2.2.4.27–2.2.8.14; 2.2.13.33–1; 2.3.12.9–11)*

1   **parens, parentis,** *m. & f.,* a parent (*father, mother*).

       erga, (*prep. w. acc.*) toward, in relation to, in respect of.

       discipulus, ~i, *m.,* a student, pupil.

2   **succedo, succedere, successi, successus,** to follow (*in the place of*); to succeed.

       locus, ~i, *m.,* a place, location; (*figuratively*) an opportunity.

3   **liberi, liberorum,** *m.,* children, sons or daughters.

       trado, tradere, tradidi, traditus, to give up, hand over.

       existimo, ~are, ~avi, ~atus, to think, consider, hold (*as an opinion*), regard (*w. acc. + inf. ind. stat.*).

       vitium, ~i, *n.,* fault, defect, blemish, imperfection, vice.

       fero, ferre, tuli, latus, to tolerate, put up with.

4   **austeritas, austeritatis,** *f.,* austerity, strictness, sternness.

       tristis, ~e, gloomy.

       dissolutus, ~a, ~um, lax, remiss, negligent, irresponsible.

       comitas, comitatis, *f.,* comity, gentleness, courtesy, affability, congeniality.

5   **odium, ~i,** *n.,* hatred.

       hinc, (*adv.*) from this place, from here; (*of arguments, topics, etc.*) from this point, following on this; **inde...hinc,** (*distinguishing between two alternatives*), from the former...from the latter; from the one...from the other.

       contemptus, ~a, ~um, despised, despicable, vile.

       orior, oriri, ortus, to rise, rise up, become visible, appear.

Sumat igitur ante omnia parentis erga discipulos suos
animum, ac succedere se in eorum locum a quibus sibi
liberi tradantur existimet. Ipse nec habeat vitia nec ferat.
Non austeritas eius tristis, non dissoluta sit comitas, ne inde
5   odium, hinc contemptus oriatur.

1–2. sumat: hortatory subjunctive (sc. *praeceptor*): "let the teacher adopt..." **parentis:** gen. sing., construe with *animum,* direct object of *sumat:* "the attitude of a parent..." **omnia:** acc. pl. n., object of the preposition *ante.* **erga discipulos suos:** construe closely with *parentis...animum* (note how the genitive and the noun it modifies BRACKET the prepositional phrase). **ac:** connects *sumat* with *existimet,* a second hortatory subjunctive (note the BOOKEND word order of the two main verbs of the sentence, one in first and one in last position).

2–3. succedere se: an indirect statement governed by *existimet.* **se:** i.e., the *praeceptor.* **in...locum:** construe with *succedere.* **eorum:** gen. pl., i.e., the parents, but the pronoun does not find its ANTECEDENT in the singular genitive *parentis,* but rather ANTICIPATES the following relative clause. **a quibus...tradantur:** "by whom the children are placed in his charge." The ANTECEDENT of the relative clause is *eorum.* The prepositional phrase introduces the relative clause, but also expresses agency, and so modifies *tradantur,* the verb of its clause. **sibi:** dat. sing. m., the ANTECEDENT is *se* (i.e., the *praeceptor*). **liberi:** nom. pl., subject of *tradantur.*

3. ipse: i.e., the *praeceptor.* **habeat...ferat:** another pair of independent, hortatory subjunctives. **vitia:** acc. pl. n., direct object of both *habeat* and *ferat.*

4–5. non austeritas...tristis: sc. *sit.* **eius:** gen. sing. (> *is, ea, id*), the ANTECEDENT is *ipse* (i.e., the *praeceptor*): "his austerity should not be gloomy..." **non dissoluta sit comitas:** a second, PARALLEL independent clause joined by ASYNDETON, an example of PARATAXIS; note how Quintilian reverses the word order from the first clause to the second, creating CHIASMUS: *austeritas* (A₁) *tristis* (B₁) :: *dissoluta* (B₂) *comitas* (A₂). **ne:** introduces a negative result caluse: "so that...not" or "lest." **inde...hinc:** "from the former (i.e., *austeritas*)...from the latter (i.e., *comitas*)..." **inde odium:** sc. *oriatur.*

6   **plurimus, ~a, ~um,** (*superl. adj.* > **multus**) most, the greatest amount (*of*).

sermo, sermonis, *m.,* language (*in the classroom*), discussion (*with his students*).

7   **moneo, monere, monui, monitus,** to admonish.

rarius, (*comp. adv.*) less often, more rarely.

castigo, ~are, ~avi, ~atus, to punish, correct.

iracundus, ~a, ~um, prone to anger or angry outbursts.

8   **emendo, ~are, ~avi, ~atus,** to emend, correct, revise.

dissimulator, dissimulatoris, *m.,* one who deliberately overlooks something, who looks the other way.

9   **simplex (simplicis),** simple, free from affectation.

doceo, docere, docui, doctus, to teach, instruct.

patiens (patientis), (*of persons w. gen.*) able or willing to undergo something.

adsiduus, ~a, ~um, assiduous, painstaking in detail, ever present (*toward his class*).

10   **immodicus, ~a, ~um,** immoderate, excessive, not showing restraint.

interrogo, ~are, ~avi, ~atus, to ask, inquire.

11   **percontor, percontari, percontatus,** to pose questions.

ultro, (*adv.*) conversely, in turn.

Plurimus ei de honesto ac bono sermo sit: nam quo saepius monuerit, hoc rarius castigabit; minime iracundus, nec tamen eorum quae emendanda erunt dissimulator, simplex in docendo, patiens laboris, adsiduus potius quam
10   immodicus. Interrogantibus libenter respondeat, non interrogantes percontetur ultro.

6–7. plurimus ei...sermo sit: "let his (classroom) discussion be especially about the honorable and the good." **plurimus:** used here quasi-adverbially. **ei:** (i.e., the *praeceptor*) dat. of possession with *sit*. **de honesto ac bono:** adverbial with *sit*. **nam:** signals an explanation of what just preceded. **quo saepius...hoc rarius:** with comparative adjectives and adverbs (as here) the ablative is used to denote degree of difference. **monuerit...castigabit:** note the shift from the future perfect in the *quo* clause, to the future imperfect in the subsequent *hoc* clause: "the more often he will have admonished (his students), the less often he will punish (them)."

7–10. The following five clauses are arranged PARATACTICALLY, connected by ASYNDETON, the verb *sit* to be supplied in each.

7–8. minime iracundus, nec tamen...dissimulator: sc. *praeceptor sit.* **eorum:** gen. pl. n. (> *is, ea, id*), construe with *dissimulator* (note how the demonstrative pronoun ANTICIPATES the following relative clause): "he should not be prone to anger, and yet not be an overlooker of those things which..." **quae emendanda erunt:** the future passive periphrastic, expressing strong obligation (i.e., things which the teacher must be sure to correct).

9. simplex: sc. *praeceptor sit.* **in docendo:** *in* + the abl. of the gerund. **patiens laboris:** (sc. *sit*) the adjective patterns idiomatically with the gen. case: "let him be receptive of hard work." **potius quam:** "rather than."

10–11. interrogantibus...respondeat: the first of two PARATACTICALLY assembled clauses, joined in ASYNDETON. **interrogantibus:** dat. pl., the active participle is acting as a SUBSTANTIVE (construe with *respondeat*); translate: "to those (students with) questions..." **respondeat:** (sc. *praeceptor*) instead of as another in the series of hortatory subjunctives that has so far characterized the style of this passage, translate *respondeat* and *percontentur* (see note below) as potential subjunctives. **libenter:** note how the adverb is BRACKETED by the dative and the verb: "let him respond freely to those (students with) questions..." **non interrogantes percontetur ultro:** the second PARATACTIC clause, joined by ASYNDETON. **non interrogantes:** "those not asking questions..." i.e., those students who normally sit silent in class; note the SUBSTANTIVE use of the active participle, here as introducing the clause as its subject: **percontetur ultro:** "they should feel free to ask questions in turn."

12 **dictio, dictionis,** *f.,* the act of speaking; *(rhet.)* a recitation or declaration, the act of delivering a speech or formal statement.

malignus, ~a, ~um, *(adj.)* grudging, wretched.

13 **effusus, ~a, ~um,** *(of speaking)* effusive, overgenerous.

taedium, ~i, *n.,* *(w. gen.)* the state of being tired or weary *(of something).*

securitas, securitatis, *f.,* a sense of security, complacency, self-satisfaction.

14 **pario, parere, peperi, partus,** to bring forth, produce; give birth to.

corrigo, corrigere, correxi, correctus, to correct.

acerbus, ~a, ~um, sarcastic, caustic.

15 **contumeliosus, ~a, ~um,** full of reproach, abusive, insulting.

16 **propositio, propositionis,** *f.,* an idea or notion.

studeo, studere, studui, *(w. inf.)* to be eager.

fugo, ~are, ~avi, ~atus, to put to flight, scare away, frighten off.

quod, *(adv. and conj.);* *(adv.)* in respect of which, as to the fact that, wherein; *(conj.)* since, because.

sic, *(adv.)* in such a way; **sic...quasi,** in such a way...as if.

obiurgo, ~are, ~avi, ~atus, to find fault with, rebuke.

quasi, *(adv.)* as if; **sic...quasi,** in such a way...as if.

18 **auditor, ~oris,** *m.,* *(in a classroom)* one's students, pupils.

refero, referre, retuli, relatus, to carry back, bring back.

In laudandis discipulorum dictionibus nec malignus nec
effusus, quia res altera taedium laboris, altera securitatem
parit. In emendando quae corrigenda erunt non acerbus
15 minimeque contumeliosus; nam id quidem multos a
propositio studendi fugat, quod quidam sic obiurgant quasi
oderint. Ipse aliquid—immo multa—cotidie dicat quae
secum auditores referant.

12–13. in laudandis...dictionibus: the gerundive construction. **discipulorum:**
gen. pl., construe with *dictionibus* (note how the gerundive and the object of the
preposition BRACKET the noun). **nec malignus nec effusus:** sc. *sit.*

13–14. res: nom. sing., subject of the *quia* clause, standing in APPOSITION to the
preceding main clause. **res altera...altera:** the compound subject of *parit:* "the former scenario..." (i.e., if the *praeceptor* is *malignus*), "the latter scenario..." (i.e., if the
praeceptor is *effusus*). **taedium:** direct object of the first *altera* clause. **laboris:** objective genitive, construe with *taedium.* **securitatem:** direct object of the second *altera*
clause.

14–15. in emendando: the abl. of the gerund as object of the preposition. **quae
corrigenda erunt:** the relative clause serves as the object of *emendando.* **non acerbus
minimeque contumeliosus:** sc. *praeceptor sit.*

15–16. nam: signals that the following clause is explanatory. **id:** nom. sing. (>
is, ea, id), the pronoun is the subject of *fugat*, and it ANTICIPATES the following *quod*
clause, its own ANTECEDENT (see note below). **multos:** (sc. *discipulos*) the adjective is
functioning SUBSTANTIVELY as the direct object of *fugat*. **a propositio:** construe the
prepositional phrase with *fugat.* **studendi:** gen. of the gerund. **fugat:** note that this
verb is transitive.

16–17. quod...oderint: the clause stands either in APPOSITION to or as the ANTE-
CEDENT of the preceding clause introduced by *id.* **quod:** "namely that..." **quidam:**
nom. pl. m., subject of both *obiurgant* and *oderint* (sc. *praeceptores*); note how Quintilian switches to the plural as he now talks about "teachers" in general. **sic obiurgant
quasi oderint:** "they find fault (with their students) in such a manner (that makes it
seem) as if they hate them."

17–18. ipse: i.e., the *praeceptor*, subject of *dicat.* **aliquid:** acc. sing. n., direct object of *dicat.* **aliquid...cotidie dicat:** "he should practice declaration on a daily basis
himself..." **immo multa:** the particle introduces a PARENTHESIS, a correction of the
preceding *aliquid* that strongly substitutes *multa* as the direct object of *dicat:* "even
better, on many things." **dicat:** a return to the hortatory subjunctive. **quae:** acc. pl.
n., direct object of *referant*; the ANTECEDENT of the relative pronoun is the PARENTHETI-
CAL *multa.* **secum:** = *cum se.* **se:** acc. pl., the reference is to *auditores.* **auditores:** i.e., the
students. **referant:** i.e., take back home with them.

19   **licet,** (*impers. verb*); (*as a conj., w. subjunctive*) although.

     imitor, imitari, imitatus, to imitate, copy.

     lectio, lectionis, *f.,* a reading, a selection of things to read; a student's reading list, assignments or curriculum.

20   **suppedito, ~are, ~avi, ~atus,** to supply, make available.

     alo, alere, alui, altus, to nourish, feed, support.

21   **praecipue,** (*adv.*) especially, to a greater extent; in a manner peculiar to the specific case mentioned, peculiarly.

     praeceptor, praeceptoris, *m.,* a teacher, instructor.

     modo, (*adv.*) only; **si modo,** if only, provided that; **quomodo,** in what manner.

22   **amo, ~are, ~avi, ~atus,** to find satisfying (*intellectually*), to look on constructively, fondly, with affection.

     vereor, vereri, veritus, to revere, stand in awe of; to fear.

     vix, (*adv.*) with difficulty; hardly, scarcely, barely.

     autem, (*conj.*) furthermore, moreover.

23   **quanto,** (*adv.*) by how much, by as much as.

     faveo, favere, favi, fautus, (*w. dat.*) to show favor to.

Licet enim satis exemplorum ad imitandum ex lectione
20   suppeditet, tamen viva illa, ut dicitur, vox alit plenius,
praecipueque eius praeceptoris quem discipuli, si modo
recte sunt instituti, et amant et verentur. Vix autem dici
potest quanto libentius imitemur eos quibus favemus.

19–20. licet...suppeditet: the usually impersonal verb *licet* can pattern with the subjunctive and serve nearly as an adversative conjunction, in effect subordinating the clause it introduces: "although he may supply..." **satis:** the indecl. adv., here used SUBSTANTIVELY as a n. noun as the object of *suppeditet*. **exemplorum:** gen. pl., construe with *satis*. **ad imitandum:** *ad* + the gerund expresses the semantic notion of purpose. **ex lectione:** construe with *exemplorum*; note how the genitive and the prepositional phrase BRACKET *ad imitandum*.

20–22. tamen: introduces the main clause. **viva illa...vox:** note the emphasis placed on the noun. **ut dicitur:** sc. *vox*, an idiomatic, PARENTHETICAL aside that is neutral in tone: "it is that living voice, as it is called, that..." Quintilian's point: nothing replaces the one-on-one contact between teacher and student. **alit:** note the metaphor behind the verb: a teacher's words have a physical, nourishing effect. **praecipueque eius praeceptoris:** the genitive modifies an understood *vox* (note how Quintilian uses the ALLITERATION of the adverb and the noun to bracket *eius*). **quem:** the ANTECEDENT of the relative pronoun is *praeceptoris*. **eius...quem:** note also note how the relative clause was anticipated by the demonstrative pronoun *eius*, one of the primary uses of this particular demonstrative pronoun. **si modo... instituti:** a PARENTHETICAL clause stating the condition under which the following statement may become true: "provided that..." **et amant et verentur:** the subject of both verbs is *discipuli*.

22–23. dici: present pass. inf. (> *dicere*), complementary with *potest*. **vix autem dici potest:** the subject is the following *quanto* clause: "moreover, it is scarcely possible to be expressed in words how much more freely..." **quanto:** the relative adverb, construe with *libentius* (the ablative of degree of difference from *quantus, ~a, ~um* with the comparative adverb *libentius*). **imitemur:** (sc. *nos*) the potential subjunctive (note the generalizing effect of the shift to the first person plural). **eos quibus:** note how the demonstrative pronoun ANTICIPATES the following relative clause. **quibus:** dat. pl., the ANTECEDENT is *eos* (construe with *favemus*) "those for whom we show favor."

24   **intente,** *(adv.)* intently, with concentrated interest.

     modeste, *(adv.)* with respect; in a restrained manner.

25   **magister, magistri,** *m.,* schoolteacher, teacher, instructor.

26   **ergo,** *(particle)* accordingly, therefore, then *(intransitive, a resultant event, state of affairs, a logical consequence).*

     eloquentia, ~ae, *f.,* eloquence, the art or practice of speaking publicly in a professional or forensic capacity.

     mos, moris, *m.,* custom; *(pl.)* personal actions, professional conduct, habits, ways.

27   **praestans (praestantis),** outstanding, excellent, preeminent.

     Phoenix, Phoenicis, *m.,* the tutor of Achilles, who accompanied the hero to Troy and makes an appearance in Homer's *Iliad* (9.168ff.).

     Homericus, ~a, ~um, of or pertaining to Homer or his poems; Homeric.

Sed se quoque praeceptores intente ac modeste audiri velint:
25   non enim iudicio discipulorum dicere debet magister, sed
discipulus magistri. Sit ergo tam eloquentia quam moribus
praestantissimus, qui ad Phoenicis Homerici exemplum
dicere ac facere doceat.

---

24. se: acc. pl. of the third person reflexive pronoun, subject of *audiri* (see note below); the ANTECEDENT is *praeceptores*. **intente ac modeste:** construe the adverbs with *audiri*. **audiri:** the passive infinitive (> *audire*), construe with *se* as the predicate clause of *velint* (sc. *a discipulis*, expressing agency with the passive infinitive). **velint:** an example of the jussive subjunctive: "teachers also wish for themselves to be listened to with interest and with respect."

25–26. enim: the particle explains the adverbs *intente ac modeste* from the previous clause: when addressing his class, the teacher is not seeking the approval of his students; therefore he expects their undivided attention no matter what the subject. **iudicio:** abl. sing. (attendant circumstance), construe with *dicere*. **discipulorum:** gen. pl., modifying *iudicio*. **dicere:** complementary infinitive with *debet*: "for the teacher ought not to speak based on the judgment of his students..." **magistri:** gen. sing. **discipulus magistri:** sc. *dicere debet*. **discipulorum...magister...discipulus magistri:** note the CHIASMUS: gen. [A_1] nom. [B_1] :: nom. [B_2] gen. [A_2].

26–28. tam eloquentia quam moribus: i.e., not only what he says but also how he acts; the correlatives balance two ablatives of cause; construe with *praestantissimus* (sc. *magister*). **qui...doceat:** a relative clause of characteristic: literally "the kind of teacher who teaches"; or can be rendered as a purpose clause: "so that he may teach..." **ad...exemplum:** "after the example of..." **Phoenicis:** construe the genitive with *exemplum*. **Homerici:** construe the genitive with *Phoenicis*. Note how the preposition and its object BRACKET the two genitives. **dicere ac facere:** (sc. *discipulos* as acc. subject of the two infinitives) "so that he may teach his students, after the example of Homer's Phoenix, how to speak and act." The two infinitives pick up on the idea of *eloquentia...moribus* (see note above). For the Phoenix in Homer's *Iliad* cf. 9.168ff.

GENERAL VOCABULARY

The guiding principle in compiling this lexicon was clarity and ease of use. For this reason, abbreviations are used only for those nouns, adjectives, and verbs whose paradigms present no possibility for ambiguity or confusion. Generally, all words included in this vocabulary are given in the standard dictionary format, with the following exceptions:

1) VERBS: for regular verbs of the first conjugation, the last three principal parts appear in standard abbreviated form (e.g., **amo, ~are, ~avi, ~atus**); for verbs of the second, third, and fourth conjugations, and all irregular verbs, principal parts are given in full (e.g., **teneo, tenere, tenui, tentus**).

2) NOUNS: for regular nouns of the first, second, and fourth declensions, the genitive is supplied in abbreviated form (e.g., **adulescentia, ~ae; ingenium, ~i,** etc.); genitives of third and fifth declension nouns, on the other hand, appear in full, unabbreviated form (e.g., **facultas, facultatis; effigies, effigiei,** etc.).

3) ADJECTIVES: two- and three-termination adjectives appear in abbreviated form to reflect the morphology of the three genders (e.g., **carus, ~a, ~um; fortis, ~e**); for single-termination adjectives, the nominative and genitive are given in full, unabbreviated form (e.g., **excellens, excellentis**).

A

a, ab, (*prep. w. abl.*) from, away from; (*of time*) from, after, since; (*expressing agency with passive verbs*) by.

abdo, abdere, abdidi, abditus, to put away; to bury; (*reflex.*) to devote oneself completely (*to someone, something, etc.*).

abhorreo, abhorrere, abhorrui, to avoid, be adverse to.

absens, absentis, not present, absent; *esp.* despite being absent (*i.e., without benefit of meeting the other party*).

abstraho, abstrahere, abstraxi, abstractus, to distract, divert.

absum, abesse, afui, afuturus, (*w. a/ ab + abl.*) to be absent, away (*from*).

ac, (*conj.*) and.

accedo, accedere, accessi, accessus, to draw near, approach; to be added (*to something, a group, etc.*).

accipio, accipere, accepi, acceptus, to take, receive; (*w. acc. + inf.*) to understand, learn, hear, be told.

accommodo, ~are, ~avi, ~atus, to suit, accommodate, be appropriate (*to someone, something, etc.*).

acerbitas, acerbitatis, *f.,* harshness, severity, cruelty; suffering, distress.

acer, acris, acre, sharp, harsh, keen.

acroama, acroamatis, *n.,* an act; any form of entertainment.

accurate, (*adv.*) with attention to detail; meticulously, carefully.

acuo, acuere, acui, acutus, to stir up, arouse, incite; (*of the senses*) to sharpen, make keen.

ad, (*prep. w. acc.*) to, toward; at, near; among, by.

adaequo, ~are, ~avi, ~atus, to equate, make (*someone, something*) equal (*to someone, something else*).

adeo, adire, adii, aditus, to enter, come into; accept the duties or responsibilities (*of a certain position*).

adfero, adferre, attuli, adlatus, to bring (*as a contribution, etc.*).

adficio, adficere, adfeci, adfectus, to affect, influence; (*pass.*) to be treated (*by others*).

adfluo, adfluere, adfluxi, adfluctus, (*w. abl.*) to be rich. **adhibeo, adhibere, adhibui, adhibitus,** to offer, furnish, provide.

aditus, ~us, *m.,* a means of approach, access; an entry-way.

adiungo, adiungere, adiunxi, adiunctus, to add, attribute; to mention in addition.

adiuvo, ~are, ~avi, ~atus, to help, aid; (*w. dat.*) to give aid (*to someone, something, etc.*); (*w.* **ad** *or* **in** *+ acc.*) to facilitate progress toward, contribute to (*a goal, end, cause, etc.*).

administro, ~are, ~avi, ~atus, to manage, perform the duties of, administer.

admiratio, admirationis, *f.,* admiration, veneration.

admiror, ~ari, ~atus, to admire, hold in high esteem or regard.

admoneo, admonere, admonui, admonitus, to warn, caution, admonish (*w. acc. of person, abl. or gen. of thing*); to remind (*w. acc. + inf.*).

adorno, ~are, ~avi, ~atus, to decorate, adorn, praise.

adservo, ~are, ~avi, ~atus, to keep safe, guard, protect.

adsum, adesse, afui, afuturus, to be present, at hand.

adulescens, adulescentis, young, youthful.

adulescentia, ~ae, *f.,* youth, young manhood; adolescence.

adventus, ~us, *m.,* an arrival, visit, appearance.

adversus, ~a, ~um, adverse, unfavorable, hostile.

aequus, ~a, ~um, (*of actions, laws, etc.*) fair, just, reasonable.

aerarium, ~i, *n.,* the treasury.

aetas, aetatis, *f.,* one's life or lifetime; the span of a life.

aeternus, ~a, ~um, eternal, lasting through all time; timeless.

ago, agere, egi, actus, to do, act; to be actively engaged (*in something*); to be involved, take part (*in an action or activity, etc.*).

agrestis, ~e, boorish, coarse, unrefined, unsophisticated.

aiunt, (< **aio,** to say) they say (a *defective verb. It has an incomplete set of forms, the most common being third person singular or plural, and usually occurs with an indefinite subject*).

alienus, ~a, ~um, of or belonging to another; foreign, of another country.

aliquando, (*adv.*) from time to time, occasionally.

aliquis, aliquid, (*indef. pron., adj.*) someone, anyone; some, any; **aliquo,** (*adv.*) to somewhere; somewhere.

alius, ~a, ~ud, another, other, else; **alius...alius,** one...another; **alii... alii,** some...others.

alter, ~tera, ~terum, one of two; the other; another; **alter... alter,** the one...the other.

alternus, ~a, ~um, occuring in alternation with something else; (*of poetry, w.* **versus,** *etc.*) a reference to the alternating metrics of elegaic verse.

alveolus, ~i, *m.,* a gaming board.

amicissimus, ~a, ~um, (*superl. adj* . < **amicus**) most friendly, well-disposed.

amicus, ~i, *m.,* a friend.

amor, amoris, *m.,* love, affection; the object of love or desire.

amplius, (*comp. adv.* < **amplus**) more, further; in addition; besides.

amplissimus, ~a, ~um, (*superl. adj.* < **amplus**) largest, most magnificent, distinguished, etc.

amplus, ~a, ~um, (*of things*) large, spacious, extensive; (*of persons, status, etc.*) magnificent, distinguished, great.

an (*interrog. conj. introducing the second member of an alternate question or a single rhetorical question*).

ango, angere, anxi, anctus, to cause mental pain or distress; to vex, irk, afflict; (*pass.*) to be distressed, feel anxious.

animus, ~i, *m.,* the mind.

annus, ~i, *m.,* year.

ante, (*prep. w. acc.*) before, previous to.

antecello, antecellere, (*w. dat.*) to excel, surpass.

aperio, aperire, aperui, apertus, to open up (*a territory*); to make available, place at one's disposal.

appello, ~are, ~avi, ~atus, to name, call; (*w. spec. titles, epithets, etc.*) to address, recognize (*as*).

approbo, ~are, ~avi, ~atus, to approve, express approval.

apud, (*prep. w. acc. denoting position or relationship*) at (*the house of*); in (*the army of*); before, in the presence of (*a magistrate, etc.*).

arbitror, ~ari, ~atus, to think, suppose.

argumentum, ~i, *n.,* evidence; the basis for a charge.

armatus, ~a, ~um, armed; (*as subst.*) an armed man, a soldier.

ars, artis, *f.,* cultural pursuits, liberal studies.

artifex, artificis, *m.,* an artisan; (*w.* **scaenicus**) an actor.

ascisco, asciscere, ascivi, ascitus, to admit (*someone*) to the citizenship.

ascribo, ascribere, ascripsi, ascriptus, to enroll as a citizen.

aspectus, ~us, *m.,* the range of vision, sight, view.

asto, astare, astiti, (*w.* **ad** + *acc.*) to stand at or on (*a place, etc.*).

at, (*conj.*) but; yet; at least.

atque, (*conj.*) and; even.

attendo, attendere, attendi, attentus, (*w. acc.*) to listen to, pay attention to.

attingo, attingere, attigi, attactus, to touch, make physical contact with; to touch upon, treat, address (*a subject, issue, etc.*).

auctoritas, auctoritatis, *f.,* the quality of leadership, authority; personal influence; prestige.

audio, audire, audivi, auditus, to hear, listen to.

auris, auris, *f.,* the ear.

aut, *(conj.)* or; **aut...aut,** either...or.

autem, *(conj.)* but, however; on the other hand.

aversus, ~a, ~um, *(w.* **a/ab** + *abl.)* estranged *(from),* averse *(to),* at variance *(with).*

avoco, ~are, ~avi, ~atus, to call away one's attention, distract, divert.

B

barbaria, ~ae, *f.,* lack of civilization, brutality, barbarism.

bello, ~are, ~avi, ~atus, to wage war, take part in battle.

bellum, ~i, *n.,* war.

beneficium, ~i, *n.,* favor, formal thanks; a reward.

benignitas, benignitatis, *f.,* kindness, indulgence.

bestia, ~ae, *f.,* a beast, animal, creature *(distinct from man).*

bonus, ~a, ~um, good, kind, kindhearted.

brevis, ~e, brief, short.

breviter, *(adv.)* briefly.

C

caelum, ~i, *n.,* sky; heaven.

calamitas, calamitatis, *f.,* misfortune, disaster, ruin, calamity.

cantus, ~us, *m.,* singing, a song.

carmen, carminis, *n.,* a song or poem.

carus, ~a, ~um, dear, valued, beloved *(w. dat.).*

causa, ~ae, *f.,* cause, reason, pretext; *(leg.)* a case, trial; *(abl. w. gen.)* for the sake of.

celebro, ~are, ~avi, ~atus, to throng, attend in large numbers, honor with ceremonies; to praise, extol, celebrate *(in speech, song, poetry, etc.).*

celeber, ~bris, ~bre, busy, frequented, populous.

celebritas, celebritatis, *f.,* renown, notoriety.

celeritas, celeritatis, *f.,* swiftness, speed.

celeriter, *(adv.)* swiftly.

censeo, censere, censui, census, to think, assess; to express an opinion, recommend; *(spec.)* to register or enroll at a census.

censor, censoris, *m.,* one of two magistrates whose duties included the taking of the **census** *(i.e., registering citizens according to their property).*

census, ~us, *m.,* the registration of Roman citizens and their property *(usu. every five years);* the written records of the census; the census roll; census returns.

certe, *(adv.* < **certus)** certainly, surely; at least, at any rate.

certus, ~a, ~um, fixed, definite, certain; *(of individuals)* resolute, trusty, faithful.

ceterus, ~a, ~um, other, the rest or remaining.

circumscribo, ~scribere, ~scripsi, ~scriptus, to define, mark the bounds of, delimit.

civis, civis, *m. or f.,* citizen, fellow countryman.

civitas, civitatis, *f.,* citizenship.

clamor, clamoris, *m.,* shout, outcry; protest; applause.

clarissimus, ~a, ~um, *(superl. adj. <* **clarus)** most distinguished (*an honorific expression used espec. to designate men of senatorial rank*).

classis, ~is, *f.,* a naval force, fleet.

coepi, coepisse, coeptus, *(w. inf.)* to begin.

cogitate, *(adv.)* with thought; carefully.

cogitatio, cogitationis, *f.,* the act of thinking, thought; reflection; acknowledgement; recognition.

cognatio, cognationis, *f.,* a blood relationship, kinship.

cognitio, cognitionis, *f.,* recognition.

colo, colere, colui, cultus, to cultivate, develop, foster.

comes, comitis, *m.,* a friend, companion, comrade.

commemoratio, commemorationis, *f.,* a recollection, memory.

commendo, ~are, ~avi, ~atus, to give, entrust for safekeeping; to recommend (*someone for something, etc.*).

commendatio, commendationis, *f.,* a recommendation; the act of entrusting or committing (*something, someone*) to the care of another.

commodum, ~i, *n.,* advantage, interest.

commoveo, commovere, commovi, commotus, to stir the emotions of; to disturb, trouble, make anxious.

communis, ~e, common, shared jointly by two parties.

communiter, *(adv.)* both or all alike, indiscriminantly; jointly, in common, together.

commuto, ~are, ~avi, ~atus, to change, exchange one for another.

comprobo, ~are, ~avi, ~atus, to approve, sanction, ratify.

concedo, concedere, concessi, concessus, to concede, grant.

concilio, ~are, ~avi, ~atus, to procure, get; to win over, obtain.

concito, ~are, ~avi, ~atus, to excite, stir up; to rouse, incite.

concursus, ~us, *m.,* a crowd, assembly.

condicio, condicionis, *f.,* a condition, term, stipulation.

confero, conferre, contuli, collatus, to devote, bestow, apply; to bring together; (*refl. w.* **se**) to betake oneself, go.

confido, confidere, confisus, (*semideponent*) to trust, be confident.

confirmo, ~are, ~avi, ~atus, to establish, confirm; to assure, reassure.

confiteor, confiteri, confessus, to confess, admit.

conformo, ~are, ~avi, ~atus, to train, shape, mold; (*w.* **animus, mens,** *etc.*) to educate oneself.

conformatio, conformationis, *f.,* training through formal instruction; education.

conlegium, ~i, *n.,* a board or body of magistrates.

conloco, ~are, ~avi, ~atus, to settle, establish, set up.

conquiesco, conquiescere, conquievi, to rest, take repose; to relax, take a break.

consecro, ~are, ~avi, ~atus, to vow, consecrate, devote (*i.e., as an offering to a god, etc.*).

conservo, ~are, ~avi, ~atus, to save, perserve, rescue.

consilium, ~i, *n.,* deliberation; counsel; advice; an advisory body.

consisto, consistere, constiti, to come to a stop, stand still.

constituo, constituere, constitui, constitutus, (*of people*) to set up, place, establish (*in a position, etc.*); (*of objects, statues, etc.*) to erect.

consto, ~are, ~avi, ~atus, (*w.* **e/ex** + *abl.*) to consist (*of*).

consuetudo, consuetudinis, *f.,* the practice, or customary manner (*of doing something*); a custom or convention of society; friendship.

consul, consulis, *m.,* consul, the highest magistrate in the Roman republican government.

consulatus, ~us, *m.,* consulship, the office of consul.

contego, contegere, contexi, contectus, to cover; to entomb, bury.

contemno, contemnere, contempsi, contemptus, to treat with contempt, regard of little value.

contendo, contendere, contendi, contentus, to assert, allege, maintain; to argue (*a point, an issue, etc.*); to take issue (*over something*).

contentio, contentionis, *f.,* conflict, contention; a disagreement, quarrel.

contentus, ~a, ~um, content, satisfied.

continentissimus, ~a, ~um, (*superl. adj.* < **continens**) most temperate, etc.

continens, continentis, self-restrained, temperate.

contineo, continere, continui, contentus, to hold together (*e.g., by bonds of relationship or common interest*); to contain, hold, keep.

contio, contionis, *f.,* a public assembly, rally.

convenio, convenire, conveni, conventus, to come together; (*impers.*) to be fitting, proper.

conventus, ~us, *m.,* an assembly, a court of law.

convicium, ~i, *n.,* noise, clamor, shouts (*usu. angry*).

convivium, ~i, *n.,* a dinner party, banquet, feast.

copia, ~ae, *f.,* (*sing.*) abundance, plenty; (*pl.*) troops, forces.

copiosus, ~a, ~um, rich, well-supplied.

corpus, corporis, *n.,* the body.

corrumpo, corrumpere, corrupi, corruptus, to tamper with, corrupt.

cotidianus, ~a, ~um, daily, every day.

cotidie, (*adv.*) every day, daily, day by day.

credo, credere, credidi, creditus, (*w. acc. and inf.*) to believe, suppose; (*often used sarcastically as an aside*).

cresco, crescere, crevi, cretus, to grow; (*w.* **ab** *or* **de**), to arise from.

criminor, ~ari, ~atus, to accuse, make an allegation.

cruciatus, ~us, *m.,* pain, anguish, agony; the act of physical torture.

cum, (*prep. w. abl.*) with, together with; (*conj.*) [*temporal*] when, while; [*causative*] since, because; [*adversative*] though, although; (*correl.*) **cum...tum,** not only...as well as; on the one hand...on the other hand; both...and.

cunctus, ~a, ~um, whole, entire, all together; the whole of, all.

cupio, cupere, cupivi (~ii), cupitus, (*w. inf.*) to desire, want.

cur, (*interrog. adv.*) why.

cura, ~ae, *f.,* care, anxiety, distress, trouble (*usu. daytime*).

curriculum, ~i, *n.,* a course, track, race; (*w.* vitae) the course or race of life.

D

damnatio, damnationis, *f.,* condemnation in a court of law.

de, (*prep. w. abl.*) from, about, concerning.

debeo, debere, debui, debitus, (*w. inf.*) to be under obligation to do something.

decedo, decedere, decessi, decessus, to go away, depart, leave.

decoro, ~are, ~avi, ~atus, to decorate (*with honors, etc.*), embellish, praise, extoll.

dedo, dedere, dedidi, deditum, to devote oneself to.

dedico, ~are, ~avi, ~atus, to dedicate.

defendo, defendere, defensi, defensus, to defend (*in court*).

defero, deferre, detuli, delatus, to confer, recommend (*for an award, etc.*).

defetiscor, defetisci, defessus, to be worn out, suffer exhaustion.

definio, definire, definivi (~ii), definitus, to define the limits, bound; to define.

delectatio, delectationis, *f.,* the gaining of pleasure or delight; a source of enjoyment.

delecto, ~are, ~avi, ~atus, to delight, charm; (*pass. w. abl.*) to take pleasure (*in*), be delighted (*by someone, something*).

delubrum, ~i, *n.,* a shrine, temple.

denique, (*adv.*) finally, at length, at last.

depravo, ~are, ~avi, ~atus, to corrupt, deprave.

deprimo, deprimere, depressi, depressus, to press or force down; (*of ships*) to sink.

desidero, ~are, ~avi, ~atus, to desire, want.

despicio, despicere, despexi, despectus, to despise, look down on, view with contempt.

desum, deesse, defui, (*w. dat. of person, situation, etc.*) to fail (*in respect of*), be neglectful in one's duty (*to*) or support (*of someone, something*); to be lacking, not forthcoming.

detraho, detrahere, detraxi, detractus, to take away, remove, deprive; to cause the loss (*of something*).

deus, ~i, *m.,* god, deity.

devincio, devincere, devinxi, devinctus, to hold, bind (*under obligation*).

dico, dicere, dixi, dictus, to say, speak; to speak of, tell; to speak publicly, make a speech.

dies, diei, *m.* or *f.,* day; the appointed time.

difficilis, ~e, not easy, difficult; hard, painful; dangerous.

dignitas, dignitatis, *f.,* rank, status, professional or public standing or position.

dignus, ~a, ~um, (*w. abl.*) worthy or deserving (*of*).

diligo, diligere, dilexi, dilectus, to love, cherish; (*perf. pass. part.*) beloved.

diligenter, (*adv.*) diligently, with care.

diligentia, ~ae, *f.,* carefulness, attentiveness, diligence.

dimicatio, dimicationis, *f.,* struggle.

dimico, ~are, ~avi, ~atus, to struggle, contend, fight.

dimitto, dimittere, dimisi, dimissus, to give up, let go; to pass away (*into obscurity, etc.*).

disciplina, ~ae, *f.,* formal instruction, training.

dissemino, ~are, ~avi, ~atus, to scatter, disseminate; to broadcast.

dissimulo, ~are, ~avi, ~atus, to hide, conceal.

diu, (*adv.*) long, for a long time

divinus, ~a, ~um, divine, sacred, god-like.

do, dare, dedi, datus, to give, grant, endow.

doctissimus, ~a, ~um,
(*superl. adj.* < **doctus**) highly-educated, most educated, etc.

doctus, ~a, ~um, educated, learned.

doctrina, ~ae, *f.,* formal teaching, instruction; a branch or area of learning.

domesticus, ~a, ~um, internal, domestic, civil.

domicilium, ~i, *n.,* a permanent residence, domicile.

domus, ~us, *f.,* house, home; household.

dono, ~are, ~avi, ~atus, to award, endow (*w. abl. of thing given*).

donum, ~i, *n.,* a gift, award.

dubito, ~are, ~avi, ~atus,
(*w. acc.*) to doubt, question; (*w.* **de**) to be in doubt about.

duco, ducere, duxi, ductus, to lead, guide; to consider, believe.

dulcedo, dulcedinis, *f.,* pleasantness (*to the mind, etc.*); an object causing agreeable sensations or emotions.

durior (*comp. adj.* < **durus**).

durus, ~a, ~um, (*of people*) dull, slow, obtuse; insensitive, unresponsive.

dux, ducis, *m.,* a military leader, commander; a guide.

E

effero, efferre, extuli, elatus, to lift up, raise; to carry off, remove.

effigies, effigiei, *f.,* an image, representation, likeness.

ego, mei, (*pers. pron.*) I, me, etc.

eicio, eicere, eieci, eiectus, to throw out, drive away, banish.

enim, (*conj.*) for; indeed; in truth.

epigramma, epigrammatis, *n.,* a short poem, epigram.

eripio, eripere, eripui, ereptus, to snatch away.

ergo, (*adv.*) therefore, accordingly.

erro, ~are, ~avi, ~atus, to err, be wrong, make a mistake.

erudio, erudire, erudivi (~ii), eruditus, to instruct, train, educate.

eruditus, ~a, ~um, (< **erudio**) learned, educated; accomplished.

et, (*conj.*) and; **et...et,** both...and; (*adv.*) also, too.

etenim, (*conj.*) for, and indeed, the fact is.

etiam, (*adv.*) also, even, too.

ex, e, (*prep. w. abl.*) out of, from; after; according to.

excellens, excellentis, outstanding, excellent.

excedo, excedere, excessi, excessus, to grow out of.

excito, ~are, ~avi, ~atus, to rouse, stir (*the senses*), to stimulate (*the spirit*), to inspire.

excolo, excolere, excolui, excultus, to improve, develop; to cultivate.

exemplum, ~i, *n.,* example; (*leg.*) a precedent.

exerceo, exercere, exercui, exercitus, to carry on, perform, execute; (*w.* **iudicium**) to preside (*over a trial*).

exercitatio, exercitationis, *f.,* practice, experience.

exercitus, ~us, *m.,* a military force, an army.

exiguus, ~a, ~um, small, scanty, slight, insignificant

eximius, ~a, ~um, special, remarkable, outstanding, exceptional.

eximie, (*adv.*) especially, exceptionally, outstandingly.

existimo, ~are, ~avi, ~atus, to judge, consider, hold an opinion.

exorno, ~are, ~avi, ~atus, (*of things*) to adorn, decorate, beautify; (*of people*) to enhance, embellish, decorate (*i.e., w. honors, offices, etc.*).

exspectatio, exspectationis, *f.,* expectation.

expeto, expetere, expetivi (~ii), expetitus, to seek after, desire; to try to obtain.

exprimo, exprimere, expressi, expressus, to make, produce; to express, portray (*in painting, sculpture, etc.*).

exsilium, ~i, *n.,* the condition of banishment, exile.

exsisto, exsistere, exstiti, to come into being, emerge, arise.

exspectatio, expectationis, *f.,* expectation, anticipation.

exsto, exstare, exstiti, to emerge, stand out, exist (*in a given manner or capacity*).

extremus, ~a, ~um, occurring at the end, last, final.

F

facilis, ~e, easy; ready at hand.

facio, facere, feci, factus, to make, do, execute, offer.

facultas, facultatis, *f.,* ability, skill.

fama, ~ae, *f.,* reputation, public opinion.

familiaris, ~e, intimate, close, closely associated (*by bonds of kinship or friendship*); (*w. dat.*) congenial, welcome, intimate, familiar (*to someone, something, etc.*).

familiarissimus, ~a, ~um, (*superl. adj.* < **familiaris**) very close, extremely familiar, most intimate, etc.

fateor, fateri, fassus, to confess, acknowledge; to admit, declare.

fauces, faucium, *f.,* (*usu. pl.*) throat, jaws; (*of a house*) the entryway; (*of a mountain, etc.*) a pass, an approach.

faveo, favere, favi, fautus, (*w. dat.*) to show favor, give support.

fere, (*adv.*) nearly, almost, virtually.

fero, ferre, tuli, latus, to carry, bear, convey, bestow; to endure; (*esp. in pass.*) to mention, spread abroad, cite; to speak of, refer to (*someone, something*) as (*someone, something else*).

festus, ~a, ~um, festal, taking place on a holiday.

fides, fidei, *f.,* faith, confidence; a trust or agreement; honesty.

filius, ~i, *m.,* a son.

finis, finis, *m.,* end, limit; (*of countries, territories, etc.*) the boundary, border.

flagito, ~are, ~avi, ~atus, to ask for, demand.

flecto, flectere, flexi, flectus, to bend, turn, prevail upon, influence.

foederatus, ~a, ~um, federated, bound by treaty to Rome.

foedus, foederis, *n.,* a formal agreement between states, peoples, or cities; a treaty.

fons, fontis, *m.,* the source (*usu. of a river*); origin.

forensis, ~e, of, or connected to, the law courts.

foris, (*adv.*) abroad; outside; away from home.

fortasse, (*adv.*) perhaps.

forte, (*adv.*) perhaps, by chance.

fortis, ~e, brave, fearless.

fortuna, ~ae, *f.,* fortune, chance, fate, luck (*either good or bad*). (*pl.*) wealth, property.

fortunatus, ~a, ~um, fortunate, lucky, successful.

forum, ~i, *n.,* a marketplace, public square; the **Forum Romanum.**

frango, frangere, fregi, fractus, to break, crush, destroy.

frequentia, ~ae, *f.,* a crowd, large attendance.

fructus, ~us, *m.,* advantage, gain, profit; enjoyment, gratification, pleasure.

fundo, fundere, fudi, fusus, to pour out, scatter; to rout, put to flight, defeat utterly.

G

genus, generis, *n.,* type, style.

gens, gentis, *f.,* family, race, clan.

gero, gerere, gessi, gestus, to carry on, perform (**res gestae:** deeds, exploits, achievements).

gloria, ~ae, *f.,* fame, renown, glory, pride.

gratia, ~ae, *f.,* popularity, esteem or the influence derived thereof.

gratuito, (*adv.* < **gratuitus**) without payment, for nothing.

gravis, ~e, heavy, ponderous; (*of people*) venerable, serious, severe, distinguished.

gusto, ~are, ~avi, ~atus, to taste.

H

habeo, habere, habui, habitus, to have, hold, possess; regard, consider, treat.

habitus, ~us, *m.,* quality, character.

haurio, haurire, hausi, haustus, to draw (*usu. water*); to take in; to derive.

hereditas, hereditatis, *f.,* inheritance, hereditary possession.

hic, haec, hoc, this, this one; **hic... hic,** this...that, the one... the other; **hic,** (*adv.*) here, in this place, at this point.

homo, hominis, *m. or f.,* man, mankind, human being.

honestas, honestatis, *f.,* moral rectitude, decency; honor or honorableness.

honos, honoris, *m.,* respect, esteem.

hortatus, ~us, *m.,* encour-agement.

hospitium, ~i, *n.,* a formal relationship existing between host and guest.

hostis, hostis, *m. or f.,* enemy, foe.

humanus, ~a, ~um, human, of man or mankind.

humanissimus, ~a, ~um, (*superl. adj.* < **humanus**) most human, entirely civilized, etc.

humanitas, humanitatis, *f.,* civilization, culture.

humilis, ~e, suitable to humble persons or situation, lowly, insignificant.

I

iaceo, iacere, iacui, iaciturus, to lie, lie dead; be situated.

iam, *(adv.)* now, at length; *(to denote the completion of an action or state of affairs prior to the time indicated)* by this time, by now, already.

ibi, *(adv.)* in that place, there.

idem, eadem, idem, *(pron. and adj. usu. referring to a person or thing previously mentioned)* the same man *(woman, thing).*

igitur, *(conj.)* therefore, then.

ille, ~a, ~ud, he, she, it; that one; *(with proper names)* the famous, that well-known *(man, woman, thing, etc.).*

imago, imaginis, *f.,* the death-masks of their ancestors that Romans displayed in the **atria** of their houses and carried in funeral processions.

imitor, ~ari, ~atus, to copy the conduct of, imitate.

immanis, ~e, huge, vast; monstrous, dreadful.

immo, *(adv. particle implying complete denial of the preceding statement)* on the contrary.

imperator, imperatoris, *m.,* commander, general.

impedio, impedire, impedivi (~ii), impeditus, to obstruct, impede.

imperium, ~i, *n.,* dominion, the power of government; military command.

impero, ~are, ~avi, ~atus, to order, command; to lead an army.

impertio, impertire, impertivi (~ii), impertitus, to present, offer.

impetro, ~are, ~avi, ~atus, to obtain by request or application *(w.* **a** *or* **ab** + *the person or source).*

impetus, ~us, *m.,* attack, assault; violence or violent behavior.

in, *(prep.)* 1) [*w. acc.*]: into, to; upon; on; against, toward; for, among; 2) [*w. abl.*]: in, on, upon; among; in case of.

incendio, incendere, incensi, incensus, to burn.

incoho (inchoo), ~are, ~avi, ~atus, to start, begin work on *(a task, topic, etc.).*

incitamentum, ~i, *n.,* that which urges or incites; a stimulus, incentive.

incolumis, ~e, safe, unharmed, intact.

incredibilis, ~e, incredible, beyond belief.

inde, *(adv.)* from that time or place; thence; then, next

indico, ~are, ~avi, ~atus, to make known, show, point out, indicate.

infirmo, ~are, ~avi, ~atus, to weaken, invalidate; void, annul.

infitior, infitiari, infitiatus, to deny.

inflo, ~are, ~avi, ~atus, to blow into, fill with breath; to inspire.

informo, ~are, ~avi, ~atus, to mold, shape.

ingenium, ~i, *n.,* natural ability or talent.

ingredior, ingredi, ingressus, to begin, embark.

inlustro, ~are, ~avi, ~atus, to give glory to, embellish, make famous.

inlustris, ~e, illustrious, famous, distinguished.

innumerabilis, ~e, countless, endless.

inquam, inquis, inquit, to say (a *defective verb, cf.* **aiunt.**).

inrepo, inrepere, inrepsi, to slip in; to insinuate oneself (*into a position, etc.*).

inscribo, inscribere, inscripsi, inscriptus, to write, inscribe (*a name, title, etc., on something*).

insideo, insidere, insedi, insessus, (*w.* **in** + *abl.*) to be present (*in a situation, with an individual*).

instituo, instituere, institui, institutus, to form, set in order; to instruct, teach.

integer, integra, integrum, (*of places*) in an undiminished state, not affected by war.

integerrimus, ~a, ~um, (*superl. adj.* < **integer**) completely untouched, entirely pure, etc.

inter, (*prep. w. acc.*) between, among, amid.

interficio, interficere, interfeci, interfectus, to kill, murder.

interim, (*adv.*) meanwhile.

intereo, interire, interii, interitum, (*of things*) to be destroyed; (*of persons*) to die, perish.

intersum, interesse, interfui, interfuturus, to be among, attend; be present (*as an onlooker*).

intervallum, ~i, *n.,* an intervening period of time, an interval.

intueor, intueri, intuitus, to watch, gaze at; to examine, consider, reflect upon (*as an example*).

inusitatus, ~a, ~um, unusual, unfamiliar.

invenio, invenire, inveni, inventus, to come upon, find, discover.

ipse, ~a, ~um, himself, herself, itself; (*pl.*) themselves.

is, ea, id, that, this; he, she, it.

ita, (*adv.*) so, thus, in this way; as follows.

Italia, ~ae, *f.,* Italy.

Italicus, ~a, ~um, Italian; (*as substantive*) an inhabitant of Italy.

itaque, (*adv.*) accordingly.

item, (*adv.*) in addition, as well; in the same manner, likewise.

iubeo, iubere, iussi, iussus, to order, command.

iucundus, ~a, ~um, (*w. dat.*) congenial, agreeable.

iudex, iudicis, *m.,* one appointed to decide a case, a juror.

iudicialis, ~e, of or relating to the law courts or their administration; judicial, forensic.

iudicium, ~i, *n.,* a legal proceeding, a trial.

iudico, ~are, ~avi, ~atus, to judge, appraise.

iure, (*adv.* < **ius**) according to the law; with good reason, rightly.

iuro, ~are, ~avi, ~atus, to take an oath, swear.

ius, iuris, *n.,* that which is sanctioned, law; (*of cities, communities*) privileges of citizenship; (*of individuals*) one's right, what one is entitled to; (*w. defining gen.*) a legal code, system, or its branches.

L

labor, laboris, *m.,* labor, task; effort, struggle; trial, hardship.

largior, largiri, largitus, to bestow, confer, grant.

Latina, ~ae, *f.,* the Latin language.

laudo, ~are, ~avi, ~atus, to praise, commend, extol.

laus, laudis, *f.,* praise, glory, renown, distinction.

lectus, ~a, ~um, excellent, special, worthy of choice.

lectissimus, ~a, ~um, *(superl. adj. <* **lectus)** most choice, choicest.

legatus, ~i, *m.,* an ambassador, envoy, delegate.

legitimus, ~a, ~um, of or concerned with the law.

lego, legere, legi, lectus, to read.

levior *(comp. adj. <* **levis).**

levis, ~e, unimportant, of little consequence; insignificant; trivial; slight.

levitas, levitatis, *f.,* unreliability, frivolity.

levo, ~are, ~avi, ~atus, to relieve; *(w. abl.)* to free *(someone from something, etc).*

lex, legis, *f.,* law; legal reasoning or argument.

libellum, ~i, *n.,* book; *(spec.)* a small book, pamphlet.

libentissime, *(superl. adv. <* **libenter)** most gladly, graciously, etc.

libenter, *(adv.)* gladly, willingly, of one's own free will.

libentius, *(comp. adv. <* **libenter)** more freely, rather willingly.

liber, libri, *m.,* book; a written account.

liberalis, liberale, gentlemanly, decent; characteristic of a liberal arts education; *(w.* **studium)** the liberal arts.

liberalissimus, ~a, ~um, *(superl. adj. <* **liberalis)** most liberal, etc.

libere, *(adv.)* freely, at will.

liberius *(comp. adv. <* **libere),** more freely.

littera, ~ae, *f., (usu. pl.)* what is learned from books or formal education, erudition or culture.

litteratus, ~a, ~um, well-read, cultured.

litteratissimus, ~a, ~um, *(superl. adj. <* **litteratus)** most educated, very well-read, etc.

litura, ~ae, *f.,* a rubbing out; an erasure, correction.

locus, ~i, *m.,* place, spot, region; site, position; situation.

longe, *(adv.)* far, by far, a far way off.

longissime, *(superl. adv. <* **longe)** very long, far, etc.

longiusculus, ~a, ~um, a little longer *(in length, duration, extent, etc.).*

longus, ~a, ~um, long, prolonged, lengthy.

loquor, loqui, locutus, to speak, say.

lux, lucis, *f.,* light, daylight; *(of individuals)* glory, brilliance.

ludus, ~i, *m., (pl.)* public games, festivals, holidays.

lumen, luminis, *n.,* brilliance, excellence.

M

magis, *(adv.)* more *(w.* **quam** *or abl. of comparison);* rather.

magnus, ~a, ~um, big, large, great.

maior, maioris, *(comp. adj. <* **magnus)** greater, larger; *(pl. as subst.)* **maiores,** one's ancestors.

malo, malle, malui, to prefer.

malus, ~a,~um, bad, evil.

mandatum, ~i, *n.,* a commission, charge; a directive; official orders *(usu. conveyed by* **legati).**

mando, ~are, ~avi, ~atus, to hand over, entrust; to order, command.

manus, ~us, *f.,* a military force, an army.

manubiae, ~arum, *f., (pl.)* booty, spoils.

mare, maris, *n.,* the sea.

marmor, marmoris, *n.,* marble; something made of marble, a statue.

maximus, ~a, ~um, *(superl. adj. <* **magnus)** greatest, largest; outstanding.

maxime, *(superl. adv. <* **magis)** most, very much, especially.

meus, ~a, ~um, my, mine.

mediocris, ~e, ordinary, average, common, undistinguished.

mediocriter, *(adv.)* somewhat, to a moderate extent, moderately.

memoria, ~ae, *f.,* memory.

mens, mentis, *f.,* the mind, intellect.

merces, mercedis, *f.,* reward, prize; fee.

-met, *(encl. particle)* attached for emphasis to pronouns.

miles, militis, *m., (sing.)* a soldier; *(pl.)* soldiers, the army.

minime, *(adv.)* hardly, not really, not at all.

minor, minus, *(comp. <* **parvus)** smaller *(in size, qualtiy, value, etc.);* less, less important; *(of people)* younger.

miror, mirari, miratus, to wonder.

mirus, ~a, ~um, extraordinary, remarkable, strange.

moderatissimus, ~a, ~um, *(superl. adj. <* **moderatus)** most moderate, etc.

moderatus, ~a, ~um, temperate, restrained, moderate.

modestus, ~a, ~um, restrained, temperate, mild.

modus, ~i, *m.,* a manner, mode, way; a kind, form, type.

modo, *(adv.)* but; just now; only, merely; **non modo,** not only.

molestus, ~a, ~um, annoying, tiresome.

monumentum, ~i, *n.,* memento, monument; a remembrance, token.

morior, mori, mortuus, to die, be killed.

mors, mortis, *f.,* death.

motus, ~us, *m.,* motion, movement.

moveo, movere, movi, motus, to move, remove; arouse, excite; *(pass.)* to be moved, affected *(esp. emotionally).*

multus, ~a, ~um, many.

munus, muneris, *n.,* duty; gift, tribute, offering; prize, reward.

municipium, ~i, *n.,* a self-governing community or township of Italy awarded the rights of Roman citizenship without the right to vote **(civitas sine suffragio).**

Musae, ~arum, *f., (pl.)* the Muses.

N

nam, *(explanatory particle)* for.

nanciscor, nancisci, nactus, to obtain; establish a relationship or connection with someone *(i.e., as an ally or supporter).*

nascor, nati, natus, to be born.

natura, ~ae, *f.,* inborn abilities; natural endowments.

navalis, ~e, of or pertaining to ships or the sea, naval.

ne, *(adv.)* not.

ne, *(conj.)* that...not; in order that... not; lest.

ne...quidem, not even.

nec (*see* **neque**).

neglegentius, (*comp. adv.* < **neglegens**) somewhat carelessly, without due caution.

neglego, neglegere, neglexi, neglectus, to neglect, fail to observe or respect.

nego, ~are, ~avi, ~atus, to deny.

neque or **nec,** (*conj.*) nor, and... not; **neque** (**nec**)...**neque** (**nec**), neither...nor.

nescio, nescire, nescivi (~ii), nescitus, to not know, be ignorant.

neqscioquid, indecl., *n.,* something or other (< **nescio, nescire, nescivi (~ii), nescitus** [to not know, be ignorant] + **quid** [something] (*often used to describe something ineffable or inscrutable*).

nihil (**nil**), *n.,* (*indecl.*) nothing; (*as adverb*) not, not at all.

nimis, (*adv.*) very much, too much, exceedingly.

nisi, (*conj.*) if not, unless.

nobilis, ~e, noble; well-mannered; high-born, well-known, famous.

nobilissimus, ~a, ~um, (*superl. adj.* < **nobilis**) most noble, well-known, etc.

nobilitas, nobilitatis, *f.,* renown, celebrity.

nolo, nolle, nolui, (*w. inf.*) to be unwilling, not to want.

nomen, nominis, *n.,* name; reputation.

nomino, ~are, ~avi, ~atus, to name, call by name.

non, (*adv.*) not, no.

nonne, (*interrog. particle introducing a question that expects a positive answer*) Is it not that case that...?

noster, nostra, nostrum, our, our own, of us.

notus, ~a, ~um, well-known, noted.

novus, ~a, ~um, new, strange.

nox, noctis, *f.,* night; darkness.

nullus, ~a, ~um, none, not any.

numerus, ~i, *m.,* number; **in numero,** in the company (*of*).

numquam, (*adv.*) never.

nunc, (*adv.*) now.

nuper, (*adv.*) recently, lately; (*as adj.*) recent.

O

obeo, obire, obivi (~ii), obitus, to take on, deal with, carry out.

obicio, obicere, obieci, obiectus, to throw, hurl, cast; (*refl.*) to offer, expose oneself.

oblecto, ~are, ~avi, ~atus, to delight, amuse, entertain.

obruo, obruere, obrui, obrutus, to bury, hide, conceal (*i.e., in obscurity*).

obscuro, ~are, ~avi, ~atus, to cover up, conceal; to obscure, make unclear.

obscurus, ~a, ~um, not clear, uncertain, doubtful; not widely known, obscure.

obtineo, obtinere, obtinui, obtentus, to have, possess.

olim, (*adv.*) for a long time past, since long ago, formerly.

omnis, ~e, (*sing.*) each, every; (*pl.*) all.

omnino, (*adv.*) altogether, wholly, entirely.

opinor, ~ari, ~atus, to hold as an opinion; to suppose, believe.

opitulor, opitulari, opitulatus, (*w. dat.*) to give help (*to*).

oppidum, ~i, *n.,* a town.

ops, opis, *f.,* power, resource; (*usu. pl.*) wealth.

optimus, ~a, ~um, (*superl. adj.* < **bonus**) best; (*of persons*) most excellent, virtuous; (*of ideas*) highest, most noble-minded; (*of studies*) most liberal.

optime, (*superl. adv.* < **bene**) competently, most satisfactorily.

opus, operis, *n.,* work, task, labor; **opus est** (*w. abl.*), there is need of.

oratio, orationis, *f.,* a speech, oration.

orbis, orbis, *m.,* circle, circuit, course; **orbis terrarum** (*or* **terrae**), the world.

os, oris, *n.,* mouth, lips; face; (*pl.*) expression.

orno, ~are, ~avi, ~atus, to adorn, decorate.

ostendo, ostendere, ostendi, ostentus, to show, reveal; (*pass.*) be evident.

otiosus, ~a, ~um, at leisure, idle.

otium, ~i, *n.,* leisure (*esp. as devoted to cultural pursuits*).

P

pars, partis, *f.,* a part, portion.

particeps, participis, *m.,* a participant, member (*of a group, office, etc.*).

parvus, ~a, ~um, small in size, amount, quantity; of little worth; insignificant, of no consequence.

patior, pati, passus, to allow (*w. inf.*).

pater, patris, *m.,* father.

paulo, (*adv.*) by a little, somewhat.

paulus, ~a, ~um, small, little.

penetro, ~are, ~avi, ~atus, to work a way, make one's way (*to or into a place, etc.*); to reach, enter, penetrate.

penitus, (*adv.*) completely, thoroughly.

per, (*prep. w. acc.*) through; over; among; throughout; during.

percipio, percipere, percepi, perceptus, to perceive, take in or grasp with the mind; to take possession of, acquire, derive.

peregrinor, ~ari, ~atus, to go or travel abroad.

peregrinus, ~a, ~um, foreign, alien.

perficio, perficere, perfeci, perfectus, to effect, bring about; to finish, bring to completion, complete.

perfugium, ~i, *n.,* a place of refuge, shelter; a means of safety; a sanctuary.

periculum, ~i, *n.,* danger, hazard; (*usu. pl.*) legal liability; the risks or hazards of litigation.

permultus, ~a, ~um, a great many, very many.

pernocto, ~are, ~avi, ~atus, to spend the night.

persequor, persequi, persecutus, to seek to obtain; to strive to accomplish.

persona, ~ae, *f.,* a role, part, or position (*assumed or adopted*).

pertineo, pertinere, pertinui, to pertain, relate to.

pervenio, pervenire, perveni, perventus, to arrive (*at a place, situation, station, etc.*); to attain (*a position*).

peto, petere, petivi (~ii), petitus, to seek; to aim for, attack.

philosophus, ~i, *m.,* a philosopher.

pila, ~ae, *f.,* a ball (*for play or exercise, etc.*).

pinguis, ~e, slow-witted, dull, obtuse; (*of literary works, style, etc.*) clumsy, unrefined, coarse.

plenus, ~a, ~um, (*w. gen.*) full, stocked.

poeta, ~ae, *m.,* poet.

politus, ~a, ~um, refined, elegant.

populus, ~i, *m.,* the Roman people.

possum, posse, potui, to be able (*w. inf.*).

post, (*prep. w. acc.*) after; behind; (*adv.*) afterward.

postea, (*adv.*) later on, thereafter, afterward.

posteritas, posteritatis, *f.,* the future; future generations.

posterus, ~a, ~um, next, following; (*of time*) in the future, posterity.

potius, (*adv.*) preferably, rather; **potius...quam,** rather...than.

prae, (*prep. w. abl.*) before, in front of.

praebeo, praebere, praebui, praebitus, to offer, supply, present.

praeceptum, ~i, *n.,* instruction, precept.

praeclarus, ~a, ~um, illustrious, glorious, distinguished.

praeco, praeconis, *m.,* one who makes public announcements; an auctioneer.

praeconium, ~i, *n.,* the action of announcing or proclaiming in public, a declaration.

praedico, ~are, ~avi, ~atus, to announce, proclaim, declare publicly.

praedicatio, praedicationis, *f.,* an announcement, public address.

praeditus, ~a, ~um, (*w. abl.*) endowed (*with*).

praemium, ~i, *n.,* reward, prize, legal benefit.

praesentio, praesentire, praesensi, praesensus, to apprehend beforehand; to predict, have a presentiment of.

praesertim, (*adv. emphasizes single words or subordinate clauses*) especially; (*w.* **cum**) especially since; (*w.* **si**) especially if.

praeter, (*prep. w. acc.*) by; beyond; before.

praeterea, (*adv.*) moreover; besides; after that.

praeteritus, ~a, ~um, past, bygone, former.

praetextatus, ~a, ~um, wearing the **toga praetexta** (*worn by boys up to the official age of manhood, about 16 or 17*).

praetor, praetoris, *m.,* the Roman magistrate, second only to the consul; often presided over a public court.

primus, ~a, ~um, (*superl. adj. < prior*) first; (*w. gen.*) the first part (*of something*); **in primis,** especially; first and foremost.

princeps, principis, first in time, earliest.

pro, (*prep. w. abl.*) for; in return for; before; on account of; in place of; instead of.

proavus, ~i, *m.,* a great-grandfather; any distant ancestor.

probo, ~are, ~avi, ~atus, to approve, commend.

prodo, prodere, prodidi, proditus, to hand down, transmit.

proficiscor, proficisci, profectus, to start a journey, set out, depart; (*of things*) to derive (*from*).

profecto, (*adv.*) surely, certainly; without doubt.

**profero, proferre, protuli, prola-
tus,** to produce, bring before the
public.

professio, professionis, *f.,* a formal
declaration before a magistrate.

profiteor, profiteri, professus, to
state openly, declare publicly;
(apud praetorem) to submit one's
name, register, enroll.

profligatus, ~a, ~um, ruined; des-
perate.

prope, *(adv.)* almost, nearly, all but.

**propono, proponere, proposui, pro-
positus,** *(refl. w. dat.)* to hold up to
oneself *(as a model).*

propter, *(prep. w. acc.)* because of, on
account of.

propterea, *(adv.)* for this reason,
because of this, therefore.

provincia, ~ae, *f.,* a province; the
provincial assignment of a pro-
magistrate.

proximus, ~a, ~um, *(of place)* nearest,
next; *(of periods of time)* immediately preceding, last.

publicus, ~a, ~um, public, official
before the **populus Romanus.**

pudeo, pudere, pudui, *(usu. impers.)* to fill with shame, make
ashamed, shame.

pudor, pudoris, *m.,* shame; modesty;
honor.

puerilis, ~e, of a boy or boyhood;
youthful.

puer, ~i, *m.,* boy.

pueritia, ~ae, *f.,* boyhood, childhood.

pugna, ~ae, *f.,* a fight, battle.

pugno, ~are, ~avi, ~atus, to fight,
contend.

puto, ~are, ~avi, ~atus, to think, suppose, consider.

Q

**quaero, quaerere, quaesivi (~ii),
quaesitus,** to search for, hunt,
seek; to try to obtain; to ask for.

quaestio, quaestionis, *f.,* a judicial
investigation, trial.

quaestor, quaestoris, *m.,* the lowest-ranking elected magistrate
in the Roman government, often
assigned as a deputy to a higher
magistrate.

quam, *(conj. w. adj. and adv.)* how;
*(w. comp. adj. or adv. introducing a
comparison)* than; *(w. superl. adj. or
adv.)* as...as possible.

**quantuscumque, ~acumque, ~um-
cumque,** *(rel. adj.)* of whatever
size; however great *(or small).*

quantum, *(interrog. and rel. adv.)*
to what extent, to the extent to
which.

quare *(interrog. and rel. adv.)* for what
reason, wherefore.

quasi, *(adv.)* as it were, in a manner
of speaking.

quemadmodum, (= **ad quem modum**; *interrog. and rel. adv.)* as, in
the manner in which.

qui, quae, quod, *(rel. pron. and adj.)*
who, which, what; that *(man,
woman, thing, etc.).*

quia, *(conj.)* because.

quis, quid, *(interrog. pron.)* who,
what; **quid,** *(adv.)* why.

**quidam, quaedam, quoddam (quid-
dam),** *(indef. pron. and adj.)* some
or a certain *(man, woman, thing).*

quidem, *(particle)* indeed, certainly,
to be sure *(usu. emphasizes the
word it immediately follows);* **ne...
quidem,** not even *(always brackets
the word or phrase it emphasizes).*

**quispiam, quaepiam, quippiam
(quidpiam)** an unspecified
person or thing; someone, something; anyone, anything.

quisquam, quicquam, *(indef. pron.)*
anyone, anything.

quisque, quidque, *(pron. and adj.)*
each, every.

quo, *(interrog. and rel. adv.)* to what
place, where; *(abl. sing. of rel. pron.
used as conj.)* whereby, in order
that.

quoad, *(interrog. and rel. adv.)* as far as.

quondam, *(adv.)* formerly, once upon
a time.

quoniam, *(conj.)* since, because.

quoque, *(adv. emphasizes the word it
follows)* also, even, too.

quotiens, *(interrog. and rel. adv.)* how
many times? how often? *(rel.)* as
often as; whenever.

R

ratio, rationis, *f., (w. gen.)* a methodology, strategy, or system; a
professional ethic directing one's
actions.

recens, recentis, fresh, recent.

recipio, recipere, recepi, receptus,
to receive, admit.

recolo, recolere, recolui, recultus, to
resume a practice, pursuit, etc.

recordor, recordari, recordatus, to
call to mind, recall.

reficio, reficere, refeci, refectus, to
restore, refresh, revive.

regius, ~a, ~um, kingly, characteristic
of a king; royal, on a regal scale.

regio, regionis, *f.,* the geographical
position or situation of a territory; a region.

reicio, reicere, reieci, reiectus, to
refuse to admit, reject; to exclude.

relaxo, ~are, ~avi, ~atus, to relieve
the tension *(of someone, something,
etc.)*; to relax, unbend.

religio, religionis, *f.,* reverence for
what is divine; the quality of
evoking awe or respect.

**relinquo, relinquere, reliqui, relic-
tus,** to leave, leave behind.

remissio, remissionis, *f.,* the act of
relaxing; *(w.* **animi**) the relaxation of the mind.

**repeto, repetere, repetivi (~ii),
repetitus,** to seek in return, to
trace, search for.

**reprehendo, reprehendere, rep-
rehensi, reprehensus,** to find
fault with, rebuke; to mark with
disapproval.

repudio, ~are, ~avi, ~atus, to refuse,
reject; to disregard as false or
invalid.

requies, requietis, *f.,* rest, repose,
relaxation.

**requiro, requirere, requisivi (~ii),
requisitus,** to ask for, inquire
about; to try to obtain; to demand.

res, rei, *f.,* thing, affair, occurrence,
incident, event, matter, issue; *(leg.)*
a case, trial; any point of law or
legal issue; *(pl.)* achievements *(cf.*
res gestae) exploits.

resigno, ~are, ~avi, ~atus, *(w.* **fidem**)
to break an agreement.

**respicio, respicere, respexi, respec-
tus,** to look back on.

**respondeo, respondere, respondi,
responsus,** to answer, respond.

retardo, ~are, ~avi, ~atus, to hold
back, inhibit, discourage.

reus, ~i, *m.,* the accused, a defendant.

revinco, revincere, revici, revictus, to convict of a falsehood; to rebut a charge.

revoco, ~are, ~avi, ~atus, to call back, recall (*esp. for an encore*).

ridiculus, ~a, ~um, absurd, ridiculus.

Romanus, ~a, ~um, Roman, of Rome.

Rudinus, ~a, ~um, of or belonging to Rudiae, the birthplace of Ennius (see Appendix I).

rusticor, ~ari, ~atus, to live or stay in the country.

rusticus, ~a, ~um, of or belonging to the country; rustic, uncultured, unrefined.

S

saepe, (*adv.*) often, continuously.

saepius, (*comp. adv.* < **saepe**) more often.

salus, salutis, *f.,* a means of (*judicial*) deliverance, security.

sanctus, ~a, ~um, holy, blessed, inviolate; scrupulous, upright, virtuous; secured by religious sanctions.

sane, (*adv.*) certainly, truly, absolutely.

sapiens, sapientis, wise, learned, educated; (*as subst.*) a wise man.

satis, (*adv.*) sufficiently.

saxum, ~i, *n.,* stone, rock, boulder.

scaenicus, ~a, ~um, of or connected with the stage; (*of persons*) of actors, stage perfomers.

scilicet, (*exclamatory particle affirming an obvious fact*) to be sure! obviously! (*often w. sarcastic overtone*) of course! certainly!

scio, scire, scivi (~ii), scitus, to know (*as fact*); to have certain knowledge of.

scribo, scribere, scripsi, scriptus, to write.

scriptor, scriptoris, *m.,* writer, author.

se, sui, sibi, (*reflex. pron.*) himself, herself, itself; (*pl.*) themselves.

secundus, ~a, ~um, favorable, advantageous.

sed, (*conj.*) but, on the other hand; (*conj. introducing a qualification of a previous idea*) but at the same time; (*with concessive force*) albeit, although.

sedes, sedis, *f.,* where an individual lives, a dwelling place, home.

sedulitas, sedulitatis, *f.,* assiduity, attention to detail.

segrego, ~are, ~avi, ~atus, to separate, exclude.

semper, (*adv.*) always.

sempiternus, ~a, ~um, lasting forever, perpetual, eternal.

senectus, senectutis, *f.,* the period of old age.

senex, senis, *m.,* an old man (*a term of distinction usu. applied to historical figures with allusion to their venerability*).

sensus, ~us, *m.,* the faculties of perception; any of the five senses.

sententia, ~ae, *f.,* thought, opinion; (*leg.*) a vote, ballot.

sentio, sentire, sensi, sensus, to realize, perceive; to feel (*with the senses*).

sepulcrum, ~i, *n.,* tomb.

sermo, sermonis, *m.,* a way or style of speaking.

servo, ~are, ~avi, ~atus, to defend (*e.g., in court*); to save, keep safe.

severus, ~a, ~um, strict, old-fashioned.

severissimus, ~a, ~um, (*superl. adj. <* **severus**) most (*i.e., extremely, etc.*) strict, severe, old-fashioned.

sexaginta, (*indecl. adj.*) sixty.

si, (*conj.*) if.

sibi, see **se.**

sic, (*adv.*) so, to such an extent.

simpliciter, (*adv.*) easily, simply.

simul, (*adv.*) at the same time, at once; **simul atque,** (*conj.*) as soon as.

simulacrum, ~i, *n.,* an image, statue, representation.

simulo, ~are, ~avi, ~atus, (*w. inf.*) to pretend.

sine, (*prep. w. abl.*) without.

singularis, ~e, singular, remarkable, unusual.

situs, ~a, ~um, placed or lying in one's control or power.

sive, (*conj.*) or if (*usu. following a conditional clause and introducing an alternate condition*); **sive...sive,** whether...or (*introducing each of two or more conditions*).

solacium, ~i, *n.,* relief in sorrow, solace; consolation or compensation (*spiritual, emotional, etc.*) for a loss.

soleo, solere, solui, solitus, (*w. inf.*) to be accustomed.

solitudo, solitudinis, *f.,* the state of being alone, solitude; (*of places*) a deserted place, uninhabited country.

solus, ~a, ~um, alone, only.

somnus, ~i, *m.,* sleep.

sono, ~are, ~avi, ~atus, to give out a sound, utterance (*usu. of a particular nature or quality*).

spargo, spargere, sparsi, sparsus, to scatter, sprinkle.

spatium, ~i, *n.,* a period, interval.

spes, spei, *f.,* hope.

spero, ~are, ~avi, ~atus, to hope.

spiritus, ~us, *m.,* divine inspiration.

statim, (*adv.*) immediately, at once.

statua, ~ae, *f.,* a statue.

stimulus, ~i, *m.,* something that rouses to fury, passion, or action; a spur, goad.

strepitus, ~us, *m.,* excessive sound; noise, noisy talking; clamour, uproar (*of a crowd, etc.*); the din, turmoil (*of business, etc.*).

studeo, studere, studui, (*w. inf.*) to devote oneself, be eager.

studium, ~i, *n.,* (*w. gen.*) the study (*of*).

studiose, (*adv.*) earnestly, assiduously; with serious application.

suadeo, suadere, suasi, suasus, (*w. dat. of person*) to persuade, give advice (*to*); to advise; to urge.

subicio, subicere, subieci, subiectus, (*w. acc. object, dat. of person*) to furnish, supply (*something to someone*).

summus, ~a, ~um, (*superl. adj. <* **superior**) the highest, greatest, supreme.

sumo, sumere, sumpsi, sumptus, to undertake (*an activity, etc.*); to take on, assume (*a duty, responsibility, etc.*).

superior, superioris, (*comp. adj. <* **superus**) preceding in time, earlier, previous; (*w. proper names*) the elder.

supero, ~are, ~avi, ~atus, to excell, surpass, outdo.

suppedito, are, ~avi, ~atus, to supply, make available.

suppeto, suppetere, suppetivi (~ii), (*of people*) to be available; (*of something*) to present itself when needed or required.

suscenseo, suscensere, suscensui, to be angry (*with*).

suscipio, suscipere, suscepi, susceptus, to undertake; (*w. inf.*) to attempt.

suus, ~a, ~um, (*reflex. adj.*) his own, her own, its own; (*pl.*) their own.

T

tabula, ~ae, f., a written document; (*pl.*) public records.

tabularium, ~i, n., the record-office; public registry.

taceo, tacere, tacui, tacitus, to keep silent; be quiet.

tam, (*adv.*) so, so much; **tam...quam,** (*correl. conj.*) so much...as.

tamen, (*adv.*) still, nevertheless.

tandem, (*adv.*) at length, at last.

tantus, ~a, ~um, so great, such great; **tantum,** (*adv.*) only.

telum, ~i, n., a weapon (*usu. defined in context, e.g., a dagger, knife, spear, etc.*).

tempestivus, ~a, ~um, timely, occurring at the right time; (*w.* **convivium**), a dinner party starting at an early hour (*i.e., an elaborate banquet*).

templum, ~i, n., a temple; the inaugurated site of a temple; any inaugurated location.

tempus, temporis, n., time, a moment or period, etc. (*spec.*) conditions or circumstances surrounding or affecting a particular person, group, etc.

tenebrae, ~arum, f., (*usu. pl.*) darkness, shadows; obscurity.

teneo, tenere, tenui, tentus, to hold, maintain, keep.

termino, ~are, ~avi, ~atus, to set the limits of; to define; to mark the boundaries.

terra, ~ae, f., land, the earth; a country.

testamentum, ~i, n., a will.

testimonium, ~i, n., evidence given by a witness in a court of law.

togatus, ~a, ~um, wearing a toga; living as a citizen (*i.e., Roman*).

tollo, tollere, sustuli, sublatum, to remove, take away; to raise, lift up; to elevate to a position of superiority.

tot, (*indecl. adj.*) so many.

totus, ~a, ~um, (*usu. w. defining gen.*) the whole of, all; whole, complete.

totiens, (*adv.*) so many times.

tracto, ~are, ~avi, ~atus, to have to do, be experienced (*w. something*).

traho, trahere, traxi, tractus, to drag, draw, pull.

tranquillitas, tranquillitatis, f., a peaceful condition.

tranquillus, ~a, ~um, calm, undisturbed, tranquil.

tribuo, tribuere, tribui, tributus, to grant, bestow.

triumphus, ~i, m., the triumphal procession, the highest award granted by the senate to a victorious general; the victory itself.

tropaeum, ~i, n., a trophy commemorating a military victory; victory itself.

tu, tui, you, yours, etc.

tum, (*adv.*) then, at that time (*in the past*).

tumulus, ~i, m., a burial- mound, grave, tomb.

tuus, ~a, ~um, yours, of you.

U

ubi, (*interrog. adv.*) where? (*rel. adv.*) where, when, as soon as.

ultimus, ~a, ~um, remotest in time, earliest.

umquam, (*adv.*) at any time, ever.

unus, ~a, ~um, one; only; alone.

universus, ~a, ~um, whole, altogether.

urbs, urbis, *f.,* city.

usque, (*adv.*) as far as; ever; continually.

ut (uti), (*conj. w. ind.*) as, when; (*w. subj.*) in order that, so that, that.

utor, uti, usus, (*w. abl.*) to use, employ, exploit.

V

valeo, valere, valui, valiturus, to be strong; to have power, influence.

vallo, ~are, ~avi, ~atus, to surround (*i.e., to deny access*), hem in; to fortify (*w. a rampart, palisade, etc.*).

varietas, varietatis, *f.,* a variety; the quality of being many different things, (*i.e., forms, aspects, natures, etc.*).

vehementer, (*adv.*) aggressively, vehemently; seriously, gravely.

vehementius, comp. adv. < **vehementer.**

vel, (*conj.*) or; **vel...vel,** either...or; (*adv.*) even.

vendo, vendere, vendidi, venditus, to sell, offer for sale.

venio, venire, veni, venturus, to come.

venia, ~ae, *f.,* indulgence, favor.

venustas, venustatis, *f.,* the quality of being charming, delightful.

verbum, ~i, *n.,* word, utterance; **verbum facere,** to say something, make a statement.

vere, (*adv.*) truly, in truth.

vero, (*adv. particle, with adversative force*), however, on the other hand (*often w.* **immo**).

verso, ~are, ~avi, ~atus, to turn; (*pass.*) to be engaged in.

versus, ~us, *m.,* a line of verse, poetry.

verum, (*conj.*) but, but yet.

verus, ~a, ~um, true, real, genuine; (*as noun*) **verum, ~i,** *n.,* truth.

vester, vestra, vestrum, your, of yours.

vetus, veteris, long-standing, well-established; veteran.

vetustas, vetustatis, *f.,* the people, customs, or institutions of the distant past; antiquity.

video, videre, vidi, visus, to see; (*pass.*) to appear, seem (*w. inf.*).

vigilia, ~ae, *f.,* (*usu. pl.*) the action or fact of keeping watch; watchful attention; vigilance.

vinculum, ~i, *n.,* bond.

vindico, ~are, ~avi, ~atus, to lay claim, assert one's title (*to something*).

violo, ~are, ~avi, ~atus, to violate.

vir, ~i, *m.,* man; hero; husband.

virtus, virtutis, *f.,* moral excellence, character.

vis, vis, *f.,* (*sing.*) force, power, violence; (*pl.*) physical strength, resources; (*of intellect, w.* **animus, mens,** *etc.*) capabilities, the ability or faculty (*of*).

vita, ~ae, *f.,* life.

vivo, vivere, vixi, victus, to live, be alive.

vivus, ~a, ~um, alive, living.

vox, vocis, *f.,* voice.

volo, velle, volui, to want, wish, desire (*w. inf.*).

voluntas, voluntatis, *f.,* free will, choice; personal inclination.

voluptas, voluptatis, *f.,* pleasure; organized formal entertainment.